CARPENTER FROM CONWAY

CARPENTER FROM CONWAY

George Washington Donaghey

as

Governor of Arkansas

1909–1913

CALVIN R. LEDBETTER, JR.

This book was designed by John Coghlan using the typeface Garamond.

The paper used in this publication meets the minimum requirements of the American National Standard for Permanence of Paper for Printed Library Materials
Z39.48-1984.   ∞

LIBRARY OF CONGRESS CATALOGING-IN-PUBLICATION DATA

Ledbetter, Cal.
    Carpenter from Conway: George Washington Donaghey as governor of Arkansas, 1909–1913 / Calvin R. Ledbetter, Jr.
        p.   cm.
    Includes bibliographical references and index.
    ISBN 1-55728-281-1
    1. Donaghey, George Washington 2. Governors—Arkansas—Biography.
3. Arkansas—Politics and government—To 1950.
I. Title.
F411.D66L43   1993
976.7'051'092—dc20
[B]   92-29038
                                                        CIP

Contents

Preface

On the afternoon of July 3, 1933, some 700[1] or possibly 1,500[2] people, depending upon whose newspaper article is believed, attended a ceremony to dedicate the Donaghey State Park. The ceremony was held in Union County, Arkansas, about one mile south of the town of Strong. It was to commemorate the one hundredth anniversary of the survey establishing the boundary between Arkansas and Louisiana and was also to celebrate the achievements of George Washington Donaghey, the twenty-second governor of the state of Arkansas.

Donaghey had been born in Louisiana about one mile south of the Arkansas boundary. The park included his family homestead, which was in both states, and forty acres donated by a lumber company, twenty of which were in Arkansas, and twenty in Louisiana. In the center of the park, on the line dividing Arkansas from Louisiana was placed a massive concrete monument, half of which rests in each state. On the base of the monument are messages from Huey Long, the governor of Louisiana at the time (1931); Harvey Parnell, the governor of Arkansas; and ex-Governor Donaghey.

The dedication was festive and quite optimistic. Charles H. Brough, former governor, gave the dedicatory address praising Donaghey's accomplishments both as governor and as a private citizen. Commissioners from the two states accepted the land donated to their states for use as a park, and Donaghey, who was seventy-seven at the time, graciously acknowledged the praise bestowed upon him. Success of the Donaghey State Park seemed assured because it was not only the first state park in south Arkansas,[3] but it also embodied the innovative approach of being shared and maintained by two separate states. In addition, there were rumors that a fund of $7,300,[4] partly federal, was available to develop the park.

These expectations were not realized. Although the Donaghey State Park is still carried on the rolls, it has virtually disappeared. My recent visit to the park required hours of riding up and down the Arkansas-Louisiana border on dirt roads and asking directions of people living in the area. Finally, one person seemed to remember something about a monument, and after following a logging road for some distance, the monument did materialize. It might have been better had it remained hidden since it is now scarred by someone's target practice and disfigured by graffiti. It is ironic that the state's memorial to George Donaghey is an inaccessible state park which no one has visited in years.

This lost park symbolizes the scholarly and popular neglect of George Donaghey who was certainly one of the state's best governors. The lack of scholarly attention may be due in part to the fact that Donaghey was a contemporary of both Jeff Davis and Charles Brough, two of the state's most colorful and most written about governors. Donaghey's personality may have suffered by comparison with these two influential chief executives. Donaghey may also be too much identified with just one issue, the building of the state capitol, and thus of limited interest to researchers. Whatever the cause, he remains relatively unknown in Arkansas.

In reality, Donaghey's career was not only interesting but was full of dramatic incidents, including but not limited to occasional fist fights. He spent about three years in Texas as a cowboy and about the same amount of time in Oklahoma as a railroad contractor when the Indian Territory in Oklahoma was first opened for settlement. He secured a contract in 1897[5] to build the courthouse at Longview, Texas, in competition with twelve[6] Texans and still got out of that state unscathed. As governor, he pardoned 360 convicts (37 percent of the state prison population)[7] in one day to destroy the convict lease system, called a special session in 1911 thirty minutes after the regular session of the legislature had adjourned, persuaded William Jennings Bryan to come to Arkansas for five days to campaign for the initiative and referendum amendment to the state constitution, and appointed the editor of the *Arkansas Gazette* to the U. S. Senate. He later donated his fortune to Little Rock Junior College.

Donaghey is worthy of historical study for a variety of reasons. One of the most important is that he was not a lawyer, not a planter, not a professional politician, but a businessman. As the first businessman governor in Arkansas, he is an interesting case study in what assets and liabilities businessmen, as contrasted with other occupations, bring to elected office. Even though he may not be typical of businessmen in general, it is interesting to note his preference for problem solving over rhetoric, his emphasis on the importance of nonpolitical appointments to state boards, and his leading the Progressive movement in Arkansas away from "its preoccupation with curbing the power of trusts and corporations, especially those based out of state,"[8] and stressing instead "the service role of the state, particularly in education, and in improving the level of efficiency in state government and taxation."[9] Since he was a business Progressive, Donaghey's political career illustrated the main themes of the Progressive movement in Arkansas.

Another important Donaghey accomplishment that sometimes is overlooked is the staggering defeat administered to Jeff Davis and his political machine in the Democratic primary in 1908 when Donaghey won against a candidate endorsed and supported by Davis. This Davis defeat signaled the transfer of leadership in the Progressive movement in Arkansas from Jeff Davis to George Donaghey. It meant an administration that emphasized an active state government and an end to the cultural and political isolation of the Davis period.

The building of the state capitol is the project with which Donaghey is most closely associated. It was his constant political companion for eighteen years. Donaghey was very proud of his role in constructing the capitol, but to look on this as his major accomplishment and to remember him only for this does a disservice to him and his administration. He was, above all, concerned with education. During his four years as governor, the four institutions which eventually became Arkansas State University in Jonesboro, Arkansas Tech University in Russellville, the University of Arkansas at Monticello, and Southern Arkansas University in Magnolia were established. While living in Conway, he was chiefly responsible in 1907 for bringing what is now the University of Central Arkansas to that city, and while living in Little Rock, he and his wife endowed a foundation for the support of what is now the University of Arkansas at Little Rock. Of the nine state-supported, four-year institutions of higher education in Arkansas, Donaghey was the founding father of six.

Donaghey was also supportive of private colleges. He played a significant role in bringing both Hendrix College and Central Baptist College to Conway, and he served as board member and chair of the board for both Hendrix and Philander Smith College in Little Rock.[10] Donaghey's interest in the public schools was no less vigorous, and in 1911, during his second term the State Board of Education was created. A State High School Board was also begun with a fifty-thousand-dollar appropriation, and the state began financing high schools for the first time.

Donaghey brought his problem-solving skills and public attention to other areas of neglect. Public health was one statewide concern that Donaghey experienced firsthand when two of his sisters died of typhoid fever at the ages of twenty and twenty-two because they drank contaminated water on a trip from Union County to Faulkner County. Another sister died of tuberculosis at age thirty-one. During his administration, bills were passed setting up a tuberculosis sanitarium at Booneville and a greatly strengthened State Board of Health with the power to regulate sanitation. The health board received state money to operate for the first time and was able to serve as a coordinating agency for the program to eradicate hookworm in cooperation with the Rockefeller Sanitary Commission.

Other problems that Donaghey chose to attack were convict leasing, tax assessments, and public accountability. He abolished convict leasing, tried but failed to reform tax assessments, and led the campaign to adopt an initiative and referendum amendment to the state constitution—the first in a southern state.

There are many problems involved in writing a biography, not the least of which in my case is inexperience. Generally, there is the problem of balance and perspective. Biographies no longer follow the tradition of the nineteenth century when the "notion prevailed that a biography should be like an extended obituary notice, full of extravagant praise and free from criticism."[11] Biographers should avoid the extremes of unrelenting hostility toward the subject on the one hand and inflexible adoration on the other. I began with a mildly favorable impression of Donaghey, which seems to be a fairly good starting place.

Donaghey lived at three important locations during his life. The first was Lapile Township in Union County, a small farming community where Donaghey spent his boyhood. The second was Conway, a small town of one thousand people when Donaghey moved there in 1880 and a place he regarded as his home for almost thirty years. Donaghey spent his young manhood in Conway and was a successful businessman when he left Conway in 1908 to move to Little Rock. The remaining thirty years of his life were spent in Little Rock, a big city by the standards of the day, where he was governor, an even more successful businessman and builder, and a leader in civic and community affairs.

One important purpose of a biography is to transmit personality, which is never an easy task. The special problem I had as Donaghey's biographer was that the people in each community where he lived seemed to have a somewhat different outlook on his personality. In Lapile, he was considered a restless boy dissatisfied with the hard life on his father's farm. In Conway, where he had many relatives, he was looked upon as kindly, friendly, given to small talk and storytelling, and above all, helpful. He was "Cousin George." In Little Rock, his image, at least in some cases, was more restrained. He was looked upon as businesslike, even aloof, a person before whom you state your business and leave. To some people in Little Rock, he was "The Governor," although some inclined toward the Conway personality profile, which interpretation I prefer, but Donaghey's personality is still elusive.

Another difficulty inherent in writing a biography is the scarcity of materials. In Arkansas in the 1890s and 1900s, record keeping often did not match the rich history of the state. Donaghey was elected town marshal of Conway in 1884 and apparently ran for mayor on a prohibitionist ticket in 1885,[12] but there were no courthouse records to verify this. The local newspaper files were destroyed by a fire, and consequently, Donaghey's first entry into politics remains mostly a mystery.

This gloomy picture of available historical sources is brightened considerably by three books written by Donaghey in his later years. One was his autobiography, which has already been cited, another deals with the building of the state capitol,[13] and the third is a collection of his articles written for the *Donaghey News* (a publication for the tenants of three buildings in Little Rock owned by Donaghey) from about 1927 to 1937.[14] These are rich sources of material and reflect Donaghey's strong personal desire to leave something permanent behind whether it be buildings, his record as governor, his endowment of Little Rock Junior College (later the University of Arkansas at Little Rock), or these three helpful books that present events as he saw them.

All biographies are time bound, probably contain factual and interpretive mistakes, and often miss the essence of the individual portrayed because "there can never be a definitive biography, merely a version, an attempt, an essay which in time reveals how completely all such attempts bear the impress of the age in which it was written."[15] Nevertheless, because the subject and his historical times are so interesting, a biographer perseveres, even knowing that "works of biography and history are imperfect. One can never get all the evidence, and if one tries to do so, one would never finish the book."[16]

Acknowledgments

When an individual writes a book, he or she is always in debt to a wide variety of people and institutions for furnishing materials, accommodations, research sources and suggestions, and incredible amounts of information. A network of obligations is created that an author can never satisfy by merely mentioning people who have been helpful in the long process of producing a book. An additional problem is the embarrassment that comes from the certainty that someone who has made a significant contribution will be overlooked. Still, there is no alternative but to try, and so I will.

Since work on this book required travel to many cities in Arkansas and Texas, I will try to express my thanks by listing individuals under the cities in which they lived or the institutions in those cities for which they worked.

Austin, Texas

My thanks to Donaley E. Brice, a reference specialist at the Texas State Library, for his efforts to track down Frank McMahan, the outlaw with whom Donaghey spent several months on the Chisholm Trail and in Bastrop, Texas.

Bastrop, Texas

Carolyn Crysup, the librarian at the Bastrop Public Library, found a letter from E. B. Burleson, the man with whom Donaghey stayed for eighteen months working as a farm laborer, describing conditions on his farm in 1877. She researched the *Bastrop Advertiser* for details about J. W. Fitzwilliam, who had a farm at Bastrop, and who also employed

Donaghey. I owe her my gratitude and then some. I would also like to acknowledge the assistance of the Reverend Ken Kesselus, rector of the Calvary Episcopal Church in Bastrop, who shared with me his detailed knowledge of local history and gave me a copy of his book, *Bastrop County before Statehood,* which was very useful.

Longview, Texas

Pauline Cox, the local history librarian at the Longview Public Library, was kind enough to locate for me the original building contract for a courthouse in Longview for $27,450, which Donaghey signed with the County Commissioners Court of Gregg County, Texas, in May of 1897.

Arkadelphia, Arkansas

Pamela Dennis, the archivist at Ouachita Baptist University, discussed with me the details of how Central Baptist College was founded and sent me relevant excerpts from the proceedings of the Arkansas State Baptist Conventions in 1891 and 1892.

Conway, Arkansas

Bob Meriwether, professor of education, political science, and American history at Hendrix College, and Guy Murphy, executive vice president of the Conway Chamber of Commerce, spent much time and energy briefing me on the local history of Conway about which they both have encyclopedic knowledge. Tom Dillard, director of the University of Central Arkansas Archives and Special Collections, guided me to material about Donaghey's role in founding UCA and also discovered the insanity pleading that Donaghey filed against his father. Likewise, Frank Robins III, editor of the *Log Cabin Democrat,* kept me abreast of little-known aspects of Donaghey's life in Conway, as did Edith Hammond, whom I put through two interviews. Mrs. Corinne Robinson furnished me a list of citations from various sources as well as a list of people to interview. Foy Lisenby and Waddy Moore, both professors of history at UCA, helped me with their thorough knowledge about the Progressive period in Arkansas.

El Dorado, Arkansas

Annie Laurie Spencer introduced me to the history of El Dorado and even loaned me her camera to take pictures of the Donaghey monuments at Donaghey State Park and Strong. Vicky Bussey checked some family history for me in El Dorado and kept in touch with the whereabouts in Strong of the Donaghey monument, which was moved in 1989 from Highway 82 to the city park.

Fayetteville, Arkansas

I am deeply grateful for the extraordinary cooperation provided by the Special Collections Department, University of Arkansas Library, Fayetteville, Arkansas. I want to thank Michael J. Dabrishus, head of the department; Andrea Cantrell, head of the Public Service Department; and Leon C. Miller, research assistant, for all their valuable assistance. The Donaghey papers at Fayetteville were microfilmed and sent to me; details about Donaghey's student life at the Arkansas Industrial University in 1882–1883 were hunted down, as well as records of the buildings Donaghey had constructed on the Fayetteville campus in 1905 and what they cost. In addition, other collections (Joe T. Robinson, Charles H. Brough, Hal Norwood, Harmon Remmel) available at the Special Collections Department were researched for material pertinent to Donaghey.

Little Rock, Arkansas
University of Arkansas at Little Rock:

I spent much of the last three years in the University of Arkansas at Little Rock Archives and Special Collections, and no one could ask for better treatment. I was furnished temporary office space, research assistance, expert guidance, and strong moral support. This book of mine is, in a sense, a joint product with the archives, and they deserve much of the credit but none of the blame. I want to recognize especially Linda Pine, head of the Archives, Jeff Lewellen, Joy Geisler, Paula Kyzer, Orethia Whitley, Chuck Rowe, Tracy Thomas, and Harry Williams.

The Media Center in the library made it very easy for me to go through twenty years (1900–1920) of newspaper articles, mostly unindexed, which formed the core of the biography. My deep appreciation to Dennice Alexander, Mary Massery, Fatiha "Jowa" Islam, and Vandell Bland. My thanks also to the people in the director's office—Don Sweet, director, Bill Traylor, Kathy Sanders, and Annette Turner—and to those working in circulation and reference—Linda Stipsky, Tony Rose, Maureen James-Barnes, Shelley Wold, and Nancy Gray. There are many others whom I have probably overlooked, and I apologize in advance.

My work was greatly assisted by an off-campus duty assignment in 1988–1989, approved by the UALR administration and the University of Arkansas Board of Trustees. The style, content, and readability of my book was scrutinized by the eagle eye of T. Harri Baker and necessary corrections were made. My colleagues in political science, history, and criminal justice were quite supportive and offered many useful ideas. I am also under a lifetime obligation to my chief manuscript preparer, Mary Anne Miller, and to Cheryl Patterson and Nan Bell for their work on the book. My obligation extends not only for manuscript preparation but also for creative suggestions concerning the manuscript itself.

Central Arkansas Library System:

In Little Rock itself, I did considerable research at the Main Library of the Central Arkansas Library System, and everyone there went out of his or her way to offer assistance in solving research puzzles and providing a nice place to work. I want to mention Linda Bly, Margaret Coakley, Alysanne Crymes, and Sarah Ziegenbein, who created such a pleasant environment. I also want to extend my appreciation to Bobby Roberts, who is now director of the Central Arkansas Library System, but was head of UALR Archives and Special Collections when I began this project. He was of great service to me in both capacities.

Arkansas History Commission:

I spent many hours in the Arkansas History Commission in Little Rock. John Ferguson, state historian, Russell Baker, and Lynn Eubank were absolutely essential in locating material on Donaghey and furnishing insights about his life and times.

General:

I want to express my gratitude to all people whom I interviewed, especially Bruce Bullion who was interviewed twice, and with whom I had much correspondence and many telephone calls; Judge William Smith and Mrs. Elizabeth Smith Palmer for alerting me to the close relationship between Raymond Donaghey and his uncle; my family for their support and useful comments; P.L. for his constant enthusiasm about my project; and many people whom I have failed to acknowledge but who aided me in my search for the real George Donaghey by discovering photographs, letters, building locations, family grave sites, pamphlets, speeches, furniture built by Donaghey, and other memorabilia of his life and times.

ONE

The Progressive Movement and the Political Environment of Arkansas

George Washington Donaghey, governor of Arkansas from 1909 to 1913, lived in a nation that was being radically altered by such developments as industrialism, urbanization, immigration, and the rise of big business. These changes helped to shape Donaghey's political philosophy, his professional career, and his outlook on the world.

During the late nineteenth century, the period of Donaghey's childhood and young manhood, big business and its philosophy dominated the United States. Many benefits came from these large corporations and their activities. Railroads linked the country together; industrial production was standardized and increased; wealth was created; the standard of living rose; and the quality of life was improved by such innovations as the telephone, household appliances, and electric lights.

These gains came at a price. Many areas of the American economy were completely controlled by what were called "trusts," giant corporations that tried to limit competition by absorbing competitors or forcing them out of business or, in some cases, by acting together with their competitors to fix prices or control output. So much economic power in so few hands worried many, especially when accompanied by impressive political power exercised by the trusts at both the national and state levels. Often there were alliances between big business and big-city machines to serve the interests of both. Working conditions in factories were abominable, and women and children who labored on the assembly lines were exploited unmercifully. Farmers also suffered since they had to compete in the world market where competition lowered prices they received for their crops while at the same time they often had to purchase goods and supplies from monopolies that could artificially raise prices.

The social and political philosophy that supported the status quo was called laissez faire but with American adaptations. It was a blend of industrialism, competition, an unregulated marketplace, and a limited role for government. This laissez faire ideology was reinforced by Social Darwinism, drawn from Charles Darwin's theory of biological evolution, and interpreted to mean that the world of business is a struggle for survival in which the fittest survive. As applied to the America of the late nineteenth century and early twentieth century, it meant no government regulation of or interference with economic affairs. There were exceptions, however, for government intrusion in the natural order of things if the result was to assist the trusts as in the case of land grants for railroads and tariffs on imported goods. The first significant challenge to big-business domination came from American farmers who had seen a long-term decline in commodity prices from 1870 to 1898. Railroad rates were high, the currency was deflated and could not grow, and the severe depression of 1893–1897 hit farmers hard. Farmers also felt a loss of status caused by urbanization and a tendency of urban America to think of its rural population as being unsophisticated and out of touch with modern society.

Farmers began to organize in the South and Midwest, and Arkansas farmers were active in these efforts to improve their economic conditions. The Granger movement appeared first, followed by the Farmers' alliances, and then the Populists in the 1890s. Midwestern Populists attempted to establish a separate third party, feeling that both the Democrats and Republicans were controlled by conservatives. Third-party sentiment was not as strong in the South because of the traditional loyalty to the Democratic party forged in the aftermath of the Civil War. Southerners who shared Populist views tended to concentrate on taking over state Democratic parties rather than beginning a third party.

The Populists wanted to nationalize the railroads and telegraph lines, break up the trusts, coin silver at the ratio of sixteen to one with gold (to inflate farm prices), create federal granaries where crops could be stored until market conditions were better, provide federal credit to farmers and support for crop prices, and adopt a graduated income tax. The Populist programs still spoke primarily for a rural-based, antitrust tradition that had strong overtones of localism and decentralized government. In fact, many Populists had serious reservations about an active role for government except to break up or regulate trusts. In Arkansas, this outlook was exemplified by Jeff Davis, while nationally it came to be identified with William Jennings Bryan even though he also belonged to the Progressive tradition.

Since the Democrats by 1896 had adopted so many of the Populist programs, especially the unlimited coinage of silver, most Populists abandoned a third-party presidential campaign and merged with the Democrats. The nomination of William Jennings Bryan for the presidency and his subsequent defeat in 1896 "marked the last bid of the nation's farmers for leadership of a national reform movement."[1] Even though the Democrats had supported many Populist programs and used Populist rhetoric, the Populists were destined to disappear as a political movement because farm prices rose, railroad regulations became reasonably effective, and times were relatively prosperous from 1896 to 1920. Populist ideas, traditions, and outlook would influence the Progressive movement, the next wave of reform, in which the emphasis would shift from economic to political concerns and the role of government from that of only a regulator to a provider of services.

Progressivism, which flourished for twenty years beginning about the turn of the century, was an urban rather than a rural movement that prospered in America's towns, both small and large, and appealed to small businessmen. It was popular in places like Conway, Arkansas, and with businessmen like George Donaghey.

Progressives accepted both capitalism and a continuing role for government in the economy. Their goal was to retain the benefits of an industrialized society while alleviating many of the excesses. Concerned with corrupt city political machines and the flagrant bribery of legislators at all levels of government, they tried to make the political system more responsive to the people. The Progressives advocated popular election of U.S. senators, primary elections, and initiative, recall, and referendum for both the city and state.

Rather than a unified political force, Progressives were a loosely connected group of people who frequently differed on issues. Teddy

Roosevelt was a fairly mild Progressive Republican while president, but as time went on, he became more radical and founded his own separate Progressive party in 1912. He and Woodrow Wilson, a Democratic Progressive, disagreed over how much power should be exercised by the national government and whether big business should be broken up or allowed to exist with some degree of regulation. Another example of this Progressive autonomy was the choice of most Progressives to exercise their growing political influence in whichever political party was dominant in their areas. Thus, George Donaghey of Arkansas was a Democrat, while Bob LaFollette of Wisconsin was a Republican.

Some groups such as tenant farmers, recent immigrants, and blacks escaped the attention of the Progressives, and although Progressive programs often benefitted those groups, there was little enthusiasm for making them part of this basically middle-class movement. For example, in the South, Progressives did not aim at any basic change in the racial situation and did not advocate voting for blacks.

In general, the goals of Progressivism can be summarized in three broad categories: (1) regulation of business, (2) reform of the political systems and the purification of politics, (3) social justice and the conservation of human and natural resources. Business reform meant antitrust legislation and the regulation of railroads, but Progressives were divided as to how far this regulation should go. Reforming the political system and purifying politics included an ambitious agenda to decrease the power of city political machines, party bosses, and corrupt state legislatures by initiative and referendum, city-commission and city-manager forms of government, and more regulatory commissions. They also wished to increase the power of the executive branch (mayors, governors, the president). The area of social justice and the conservation of human and natural resources embraced a wide variety of programs and approaches: the abolition of child labor, factory safety, wage and hour laws, prohibition of alcoholic beverages, game and fish laws, the cessation of convict leasing, woman suffrage, improvements in education and health, anti-gambling and anti-prostitution laws, and conservation laws.

All of these Progressive initiatives were undergirded by some philosophical assumptions such as their faith in progress and that purposeful action, either by private agencies or an active state, could improve the conditions of life. Another strongly held belief was, as one authority put it, "The fundamental assumption of progressives was their deeply held conviction that men and women were creatures of their environment."[2] Another motivating concept was scientific rationality, a belief that all problems will yield to the new social sciences with their attempts to discover laws governing human behavior and their emphasis on investigating a problem thoroughly and accumulating relevant data. In fact, there were overtones in the Progressive movement of curtailing politics drastically since the idea was "to remove as many areas of social and economic decision making from the realm of politics"[3] and leave decisions to people "who are skilled in business management and social sciences."[4]

Many Progressive themes and programs recur in the political life of Donaghey (1899–1915), which roughly coincided with the Progressive era in the United States (1900–1920). The issue of prohibition was of crucial concern to Donaghey and the Progressives, and "among middle class people in the Progressive era no cause was more respectable or ardently fought for. . . ."[5] They associated liquor with crime, violence, prostitution, and other evils. They linked liquor interests to saloons, which often in the rural areas were little more than shacks with a bar, a sawdust floor, and spittoons. In both the rural and urban areas, saloons were frequently places for voter manipulation as blocs of semi-sober and semi-literate men were herded to the polls to vote as directed. They also provided opportunities for bribing public officials due to the required licensing of saloons and the payment of licensing fees. The liquor interests opposed woman suffrage because they feared that women would vote for prohibition and initiative and referendum laws through which prohibition attempts could be put on the ballot much easier. It was quite common for Progressive advocates of prison reform, woman suffrage, and honest government to also work for state dry laws and the prohibition of saloons and the liquor trade since they saw the liquor interests as evil people who "diligently frustrated the process of law, order, and reform."[6]

Another shared belief between Donaghey and the Progressives was the desirability of isolating government as much as possible from politics and running it like a business. Donaghey was a problem solver rather than a person who could touch the emotions of Arkansans. He devoted much time to carefully preparing himself to be a governor who could solve long-standing problems.

Progressives were strong partisans of executive power and the executive branch of government. They regarded the legislative branch, especially at the state level, as the least competent, the most corrupt, and in greatest need of reform.[7] In his campaign for a third term as governor, Donaghey ran mainly against the state legislature, which he characterized as full of bribe takers and completely subservient to the liquor interests.

Donaghey shared the Progressives' firm belief in the influence of environment. Donaghey thought that even though we might be born "little brutes," we grow out of it and that "environment must account for 75 percent of the training of higher minded men and women."[8] Both Donaghey and the Progressives believed that an active state could shape the environment and improve the conditions and quality of life. Still other items on the reform agenda of Donaghey and the Progressives were improvements in education and health, prison reform, labor laws, regulation of banking, insurance, and railroads, and initiative and referendum so that the people could share law-making power with the legislature.

Southern and Arkansas Progressivism

In the South during the Progressive period, there were the same two traditions fighting for acceptability—the agrarian Populist tradition with its emphasis on antitrust legislation, aid to farmers, and the state as regulator versus the Progressive tradition finding its momentum in the towns and cities and the middle class, focusing on political rather than economic reform, and viewing the state more as a provider of services. Populist traditions probably hung on longer in the South than in the rest of the country because of the continuing agrarian distress there, but even so, "Southern progressivism was essentially urban and middle class in nature and the typical leader was a city professional man or businessman, rather than a farmer."[9] The origins of Progressivism were similar in the South and the rest of the country and were found in depressed farm prices, the dreadful depression of 1893–1897, problems caused by increasing industrialization and urbanization, and the rising importance of a more assertive middle class composed of business and professional people. Support for southern Progressivism, like its national counterpart, came from prosperous farmers, school teachers, editors, small businessmen, doctors, lawyers, and other professional groups.

In the South, as indicated earlier, Progressives accepted segregation and disfranchisement of blacks as promoting social stability and removing from the voting booth "those considered most open to corruption in the balloting process, thus helping to prevent vote selling and other practices which would cast doubt on the political process."[10] In Arkansas, many prohibitionists, including Donaghey, saw blacks as allied with the liquor interests. However, within the bounds set by white supremacy, segregation, and disfranchisement there was some improvement in conditions for blacks in such areas as prison reform, industrial education on the Booker T. Washington model, health, and anti-lynching laws. Southern Progressives, at least in some states, also fought legislation to limit state support for black schools solely to the money collected from black taxpayers. Given the disparity in wealth between the white and black communities, the results would have been appalling had such bills passed.

There were significant differences, however, between national Progressivism and its southern variety. There was much more need for reform in the South because it was so impoverished, with public school systems barely existing and with convict lease systems firmly established as money makers. Attitudes about government were also vastly different in the South. It was extremely difficult to sell white southerners with their memories of Reconstruction on the need for an active state government. Southern tradition pictured Reconstruction as a time of great abuses, when Republicans had controlled state government and used it to their advantage. Because of Reconstruction, state government was associated with intimidation and unfairness. Woman suffrage also had an uphill battle against the image of a venerated southern womanhood.

Prohibition was also a national movement, but it seemed to take on a special religious and moral fervor in the South. It "brought together such varying tendencies as the countryman's suspicion of urban institutions, the puritanism of the evangelical churches, the humanitarian concern of social justice reformers . . . and the economic argument that the saloon breeds disorder, and crime demoralizes the labor system."[11] It probably was "the most dynamic and passionately supported 'reform' in the South during the progressive era."[12] During an eighteen-month period between 1907 and 1909, six southern states adopted statewide prohibition, and the momentum was such that it seemed inevitable that all southern states would adopt. Most of them had by 1915, when Arkansas enacted prohibition, and "for the better part of three decades prohibition and progressivism usually traveled the same road. Their paths did not diverge until well into the 1920s."[13]

Progressivism in Arkansas faced the same handicaps found in the other southern states, in particular the negative view left over from

Reconstruction of the state and the office of governor. Once this period in Arkansas history was past, the "redeemers" and ex-Confederates who replaced the Reconstruction Republicans reflected the "popular view that a passive, low tax, inactive state government was much to be preferred over an interventionist and expensive one."[14] This view continued well into the twentieth century, but despite its pervasiveness, much of the Progressive agenda was enacted in Arkansas. By 1915, an antitrust law had been passed, a railroad commission had been created, party candidates were elected by primaries instead of conventions, and an initiative and referendum state constitutional amendment had been adopted. Suffrage had been extended to women in the 1918 primary election, a corrupt practices act along with a public disclosure of campaign expenses had been signed into law, the convict leasing system had been abolished, two federal constitutional amendments—income tax and popular election of senators—had been ratified, and statewide prohibition was in effect.[15]

Some Arkansas groups interested in at least parts of the Progressive agenda were the Arkansas Medical Society, the Arkansas Bar Association, the Farmers' Union, the State Federation of Labor, teachers, pharmacists, Woman's Christian Temperance Union, state Democratic party, state Republican party, the Anti-Saloon League of Arkansas, and many other business, labor, and professional organizations.

The proposed state constitution of 1917–1918 was the culmination of the Progressive movement in Arkansas. Its failure to pass "perhaps signaled that the great reform effort had reached its peak."[16] It was a model Progressive constitution that contained a liberalized initiative and referendum procedure, prohibition, woman suffrage, four-year terms for state constitutional offices, and restrictions on local legislation. It also permitted counties to adopt a county commission form of government, authorized a workers compensation law, made kindergartens and juvenile courts possible, and created the office of lieutenant governor.[17] One unusual feature, designed to strengthen the office of governor, was probably taken from the English parliamentary system. It required the governor to submit a complete budget to the general assembly containing estimates of revenues and expenditures. The general assembly could revise, increase, or decrease individual items within the governor's total budget but could not exceed the total amount requested. This would have placed impressive fiscal control in the hands of the governor.

A special election was called on Saturday, December 14, 1918, to decide the fate of the newly proposed constitution. The expectation was that a vote on Saturday would encourage a large voter turnout, but this was not to be because of freezing temperatures, severe floods along the White and Black rivers, and a raging influenza epidemic. There was only a light turnout of sixty-three thousand voters, and the proposed constitution that embodied so much of the Progressive philosophy was defeated by a landslide. The margin of defeat was 13,677 votes, or 60.8 percent against and 39.2 percent in favor. "The supporters of the 1918 Constitution had apparently counted on a heavy urban vote and a large turnout in eastern Arkansas to offset losses in western and southern Arkansas where the small farmers were concentrated. The large urban vote did not materialize."[18]

Progressivism in Arkansas was shaped by three governors, and in that day and time the governor "most often determined the nature and content of the reform legislation presented to the Arkansas General Assembly."[19] These governors were Jeff Davis (1901–1907), George W. Donaghey (1909–1913), and Charles H. Brough (1917–1921). Other governors in this period were either governors with short abbreviated terms such as John S. Little and Joe T. Robinson, or interim acting governors like X. O. Pindall and Allen Hamiter. One governor, George Washington Hays (1913–1917), was not in basic sympathy with the Progressives. Thomas C. McRae (1921–1925) could be labeled a Progressive but falls outside the arbitrary end of the Progressive period in 1920.

Jeff Davis was a blend of Populist and Progressive in ideology; in style, he was all by himself. He came from the Populist rural-based, antitrust, antigovernment tradition. According to Davis' biographer, Raymond Arsenault, Davis was a throwback to the anti-institutionalism of the nineteenthth-century frontier, and "he and his followers had limited faith in government as a problem-solving institution and remained wedded to the ideals of low taxes and small government. Most of the Old Guard put more stock in politics than government. They knew that good politics would make them feel better, but they were not sure what good government would do for them."[20] Davis did champion many issues that also found favor with the Progressives such as insurance regulation, a railroad commission, and antitrust legislation. The Rector Anti-Trust Law was passed in 1899 when Davis was attorney general, and he "filed 126 suits against fire insurance companies, and while he was in the mood he brought action against express companies, tobacco companies, oil companies, and cotton oil companies."[21]

As was often the case with Jeff Davis, the results did not always live up to his rhetoric. The final outcome of his frenzied antitrust activity was that insurance companies boycotted the state and the legislation had to be modified. None of this seemed to matter, since Davis had such an unbreakable hold over the emotions of his followers that any administrative failure or his constant pattern of being heavy on drama and short on results was passed over and forgotten.

Although Davis did see a role for government in the regulation of trusts and railroads, in general, he took a limited or negative view of it himself and played upon his followers' suspicion of government. He opposed building a new state capitol, purchasing a convict farm, and building a state railroad. "Davis conceived of the executive role as that of watchdog or chief obstructor. The governor must prevent others in government from carrying out wasteful or dangerous programs."[22] His adamant stand against a new constitution is another indication of his distrust of government.

This belief system clashed in many particulars with the political outlook of George W. Donaghey and Charles H. Brough, who are usually classified as business Progressives. "Arkansas Progressivism, after Davis' administration (1901–1907) displayed the same zest for reform, but it had become less bombastic. The Donaghey and Brough administrations emphasized orderliness, efficiency, scientific planning, budgeting, and regulation"[23] and were also characterized by an "increased respect for business ideals and methods. They also adopted a less negative view of the role of government in social and economic affairs."[24]

While Donaghey and Brough were leading the Progressive forces in Arkansas, "political reform movements were changing from movements aimed primarily at regulation to more concern with social uplift, efficiency, and expansion of services."[25] Both Donaghey and Brough believed that Arkansas could prosper only if business and investment money could be attracted to the state, but in order for this to occur, "Arkansas would have to make great improvements in its educational system, public services, and highways."[26]

Donaghey and Brough shared a common outlook but differed in the emphasis they placed on certain issues. Brough was governor four years after Donaghey left office, which means he caught Progressivism at high tide. In many cases, before acceptability of Progressive issues had arrived, Donaghey had fought the hard battles, but timing allowed Brough to claim the field. Brough was identified with woman suffrage, the constitutional convention of 1918, and the creation of a commission to regulate public utilities in the state. Brough's term of office coincided with America's participation in World War I. He took office in January of 1917, a few months before the United States entered the war, and had only one legislative session before the war began to displace the domestic agenda. "He was out of the state much of the time in the war years, making hundreds of speeches in which he extolled the virtues of Arkansas while pushing the war cause."[27]

There were broad areas of policy agreement between Donaghey and Brough—they were also close personal friends—and both governors were moderate and sensible alternatives to Davis and his politics of combat. "Progressives in the era of George W. Donaghey and Charles H. Brough assumed a more respectable tone. The businessman and the professor elicited support from those town folk who were weary of politicians, machines, and demagoguery."[28]

The Political Environment of Arkansas 1900–1920

In 1900 Arkansas was a very poor state with a population of about 1.5 million. It was overwhelmingly rural with only 200,000 people in urban areas (defined as communities of 2,500 or more) located in twenty-two cities and six towns.[29] The rural-urban ratio was 87 percent to 13 percent. With 38,307 people in 1900, Little Rock was by far the biggest city in the state. It had three times the population of Fort Smith, its nearest rival with a population of 11,587.[30] Little Rock, the state capital, was the "political, social, intellectual, and cultural heart of the state."[31] It served both as a center of conservative influence through its banking and business establishments and as headquarters for reform groups, especially those concerned with prohibition and woman suffrage.

Arkansas's black population, 28 percent of the total population in 1910,[32] was concentrated heavily in the delta counties and was sparse in the northwestern part of the state. In 1910 thirty-five counties had 10 percent or less black population while fourteen counties had more than 50 percent.[33] Foreign-born population was minimal, less than 1 percent.[34] In 1890 approximately one-fourth of the population was illiterate.[35] One-third of the farmers were tenant farmers; this proportion would rise to more than 50 percent by 1920.[36]

Although agriculture was the major economic activity, there were some nonagricultural industries in the state such as coal, timber, and bauxite. Coal, concentrated mainly in Sebastian County, ranked first in value among Arkansas's mineral products, but the coal deposits were thin and buried deep in the ground. Local markets were limited, and transportation costs were high, and by 1922 oil replaced coal as Arkansas's most valuable mineral product.[37] Bauxite mining began in 1899, and by the early 1900s "85 percent of all bauxite mined in the world came from Arkansas."[38] Most of this was controlled by the Aluminum Company of America. Timber was another natural resource. By 1909 Arkansas ranked fifth in the country in lumber production, and 60 percent of all Arkansas wage earners were employed in the lumber and timber products industry.[39] There were only 26,500 industrial workers in 1900,[40] including the lumber industry workers as well as the coal miners and railroad employees. The largest railroad in the state was the St. Louis, Iron Mountain, and Southern, owned by Jay Gould, which later became the Missouri Pacific. This railroad was unpopular either because of Gould or because of its high rates, and was frequently denounced.

Public education in the early 1900s was minimal, and the term "minimal" probably exaggerated the situation in Arkansas's favor. In 1902 there were more than 500 school districts with fewer than 20 students, and by 1912, the state still had 5,143 districts.[41] High schools were in short supply, and in 1910 "only 300 students were graduated from Arkansas high schools and only a small fraction of the school's teachers had anything more than an eighth grade education themselves."[42]

Arkansas had no standardized high schools until Donaghey's second term in 1911, when a State Board of Education was created and state assistance to high schools was furnished for the first time. Before 1911 the state was responsible for elementary schools and colleges but not for secondary schools. The result was that there were only a few good high schools, mostly in the larger cities, and "with rare exceptions there were no high schools outside the towns and villages; hence, secondary or high school education was denied the great majority of children of high school grade and age."[43]

Health conditions were equally poor in the state. Life expectancy for whites was forty-five years and was much lower for blacks.[44] The big killers in Arkansas were infectious diseases such as malaria, tuberculosis, dysentery, pneumonia, and typhoid fever, as well as sicknesses now associated with childhood, such as measles, whooping cough, and scarlet fever. Hookworm was present in fifty-nine of Arkansas's seventy-five counties,[45] and it was estimated that one-fourth of all Arkansas school children had it.[46] State institutions to deal with people in need were limited, consisting only of a hospital for the mentally ill, a school for the deaf, a school for the blind, a reform school, and a home for Confederate veterans. Other areas were not thought to be the responsibility of the state. Even roads were looked upon as mostly a local or county responsibility.

Contributing significantly to this lack of vital services was the property assessment system in Arkansas. State and local taxes were levied on real and personal property only. There was no sales tax or income tax. Although assessment at fair market value was required, county officials put land and property on the books at much less than market value. Some counties would put property on the books at 25 percent, while others might go as high as 60 percent.[47] The result was that counties with high assessments paid the biggest share of state taxes, and the natural tendency was for local officials to lower assessments. Many businesses escaped taxation altogether, and even if a county assessor tried diligently for fair market value, there was always the appeal to the county court (the county judge) who could usually be counted upon to be sympathetic. The revenue situation was made even more desperate by a reduction in state taxes recommended by Governor Davis and passed in 1905, at a time when the demand for state services was increasing. Donaghey paid a high political price when he tried to introduce some fairness and rationality into this system of uneven and inequitable county assessments.

The political culture or climate of Arkansas during this twenty-year period "reflected the state's frontier heritage, retarded economic development, and agrarian cast."[48] It also reflected the complete dominance of the Democratic party. Democratic candidates for governor won thirty-three successive times from 1900 to 1964, and the Republican percentage of the vote for governor was less than 15 percent from 1900 to 1948.[49] This same massive superiority was also reflected in presidential elections from 1900 to 1920. There was little common ideology among the state Democrats except a belief in white supremacy, low tariffs, low taxes, and limited government. Campaigns were consequently a choice between "competing individuals rather than between issues and par-ties,"[50] with the only issue being who is the best qualified.

The only serious challenge posed to the Democrats of the state occurred in 1888 when a coalition of Republicans and old-time Populists and agrarian dissenters, under the name of the Union Labor party, came close to defeating the Democratic gubernatorial candidate, who won by 99,214 to 84,213, a margin of only 54 percent to 46 per-cent. There was much fraud involved in this particular election as well as other elections in the state. In one race for representative in Pulaski County in 1891, a recount showed that one thousand fraudulent ballots had been cast, and in addition, six ballot boxes had disappeared.[51] The close election of 1888 and the fraud associated with it led to an election reform law and attempts to curtail the suffrage.

The election reform law passed in 1891 did contain many genuine reforms, such as providing for standard ballots, prohibiting last-minute changes in polling places, and taking election supervision away from the county judges.[52] However, it also curtailed the voting of illiterates, both black and white, since political symbols were removed from the ballot and only the precinct judge, rather than a friend, could assist in prepar-ing ballots. Illiterates represented 25 percent of the population at this time.[53] Another change, partly reform and partly partisan, took control of election machinery from the county judges and placed it in the hands of the State Board of Election Commissioners, which consisted of the governor, state auditor, and secretary of state, all of whom would be Democrats. The Board of Election Commissioners, in turn, appointed three election commissioners for each Arkansas county. These county commissioners had the authority to select election judges and clerks. Because two election commissioners were to be appointed from the majority party and one from the minority party in each county, these county committees were almost always dominated by Democrats. Even if the Republicans had a majority in a county, their two election commis-sioners would still be appointed by the solidly Democratic State Board of Election Commissioners. This change to a more centralized election sys-tem helped guarantee Democratic control and made access to the politi-cal system more difficult for non-Democrats.

A poll tax amendment to the state constitution was passed in 1892. It required that a dollar tax be paid in order to vote and a receipt be pre-sented at the time of voting. The poll tax requirement and the provisions in the Election Reform Act of 1891 regarding illiterates were major factors in dropping the voter turnout from 183,000 in 1888 to 133,000 in 1900.[54] One further barrier to voter participation was the adoption of the white primary in 1906 at the suggestion of Governor Davis. This device limited voting in the Democratic primary to whites only and was aimed exclusively at blacks. A "grandfather clause," a constitutional amendment limiting the right to vote to those who could read and interpret a section of the Arkansas Constitution or to those who had voted in 1866 or whose ancestors had voted in 1866, was defeated at the polls in 1912.

In Arkansas from 1900 to 1920, the only election that really counted was the Democratic primary. Until 1915, there were three elections in Arkansas. The Democratic primary was held first, usually in the last week of March of the even years; this was followed by a state general election, normally held in the first two weeks in September. In the state general election, Democratic and Republican nominees for state and county offices as well as proposed amendments to the state constitution and initiated acts would be on the ballot. There was then a third election in November, where Arkansans voted on federal offices, such as the presidency, presidential electors, and members of Congress. The reason for this awkward intrusion of the state general election between the primary and the national election was to minimize federal interference in Arkansas state elections since no federal offices were involved in the state general election.

Campaigning for office did not often involve issues, only personalities and who was the best qualified candidate. To illustrate this, it was usually necessary to demonstrate that your opponent was not only less qualified than you but probably belonged in prison. An absence of issues led to character assassination, wild and unfounded accusations, and mudslinging, all summed up in the phrase "bucket and bile." Campaigning for office did involve making contact with county and local leaders who would pass the word for a particular candidate. In some counties, groups of politicians would get together and form machines. This practice was especially prevalent in eastern Arkansas which, at that time, was looked upon "as the home of boss rule and machine politics."[55] Fraud was also a problem, even with the new reforms, because poll taxes could be bought *en masse* and distributed as needed.

In the field of political campaigning, Jeff Davis was a great democratizing influence. It was no longer sufficient just to go and see the important county and local leaders. "Davis broke the custom of organizing state campaigns around courthouse cliques and took his electioneering to the voters at the grass roots."[56] He transformed the political environment so that a candidate had to have popular appeal as elections shifted from conventions controlled by leaders to primaries where the popular vote was crucial.

No one could equal Davis in his appeal to the people, and the Democratic primary with its popular election meshed beautifully with Davis's public speaking talents. He loved to campaign and found running the government boring, so he started his campaign early during the first part of July, almost ten months before the March primary. In prior years, most Democrats announced in late September or early October. Davis's early start, which had to be matched, lengthened the campaign season by one-third. He also shattered another time-honored precedent which was not to get involved in other political races. Davis not only intervened in other political contests, but he ran a slate of state constitutional officers (secretary of state, auditor, attorney general, treasurer, and sometimes other offices) whom he supported and from whom he demanded unquestioned loyalty.

The result of all this was that for a period of almost ten years, Democrats in Arkansas were divided into Davis and anti-Davis Democrats. His personality and the issues that he raised dominated the state's political landscape. He had a volatile and domineering personality and seemed comfortable with the character assassination, wild accusations, and "bucket-and-bile" tradition of the times. He may even have added a few new pages to the bucket-and-bile tradition. With his insistence on personal loyalty and his opportunities for appointments, he built a formidable political machine, or as stated by a historian of that period, "Davis did not build a capitol, but he did establish a powerful political structure that dominated the state during his governorship and continued as a force in Arkansas politics even after his death."[57] Davis reached the peak of his power during the spring and summer of 1906.[58] He had just been elected to the U.S. Senate, and his endorsed candidates for both governor, John Little, and attorney general, William Kirby, had won. Even though Davis would be in Washington, D.C., he presumably could count on a sympathetic governor and attorney general in Arkansas and run the state by proxy.

However, Governor Little suffered a mental and physical collapse on the second day after his inaugural. He never recovered, and during most of his term X. O. Pindall, the president of the Arkansas Senate, was the acting governor of the state. Pindall had run for attorney general in 1906 against Kirby, whom Davis had endorsed. Needless to say, Pindall was a staunch and unwavering enemy of Senator Davis. Davis's carefully planned succession began to unravel as Pindall made his own appointments during the seventeen months (May 1907 through January 1909) that he served as acting governor. In trying to remedy this situation and regain control of the state, Davis suffered his first significant defeat. He and his followers met to decide whom they would support in the 1908 Democratic primary. They considered Donaghey because he had supported Davis in the past, but the decision was to go with Attorney General William Kirby.

Davis, as he had done on numerous occasions, took the stump for Kirby, who was running against Donaghey and former superintendent of public instruction John H. Hinemon. Davis spent six weeks campaigning the length of the state for Kirby. This time, however, Davis's campaigning was resented by Arkansans, who felt that Davis should spend his time in Washington representing his state in the Senate and not try to run the state from that distant city. Donaghey defeated both Kirby and Hinemon, and Davis suffered the most serious political reversal of his career. Jeff Davis would still have influence in the state, and if there was one constant in Donaghey's political career, it was that Davis would always be an implacable foe, automatically opposing anything that Donaghey wanted. Nevertheless, it was clear in 1908 that "the electorate had become weary with politicians and looked to the business community for a new leader."[59] The new leader was George W. Donaghey.

TWO

Early Years

Years at Lapile

Very little is known about Donaghey's grandfather, except that he was named William Donaghey, came from County Cork, probably left Ireland in 1815, and finally settled in Marion, Alabama. William Donaghey's son and George's father was born in Marion in 1827. His full name was Christopher Columbus Donaghey but he was called "Lum." George Washington Donaghey was proud of the family tradition of using historical names, but the tradition ended with him because he had no children.[1]

C. C. Donaghey probably arrived in northern Louisiana in the early 1850s. In 1855 he married Elizabeth (Betty) Ingram who was from Tennessee and originally of Scottish ancestry. She had two brothers, John and William, who eventually settled in Conway, Arkansas. "The Donagheys came west with other pioneers to settle the still underdeveloped country beyond the Mississippi"[2] and settled on lands that lay on both sides of the Arkansas-Louisiana border, partly in Union Parish, Louisiana, and partly in Union County, Arkansas.

George Washington Donaghey was born on July 1, 1856, in Oakland, Louisiana, a very small community about one mile from the Arkansas border. The only remnant of that hamlet today is the Oakland Baptist Church. The Donagheys moved to the Lapile community in Union County Arkansas in 1858.[3] The rest of the children were born in

Arkansas: Alice in 1858, Lenora in 1860, Columbus in 1862, Willie (sister) in 1868, and James in 1870. Since the Donaghey farm was located in both Louisiana and Arkansas, the family, according to George Donaghey, "always felt that both states were our home."[4]

Lapile Township was bordered on the east by the Ouachita River and on the south by Louisiana. It was an isolated pioneer community with the nearest railroad eighty miles away.[5] The area was so wild that a patrol had been appointed in 1847 to ride over the entire region twice a week to protect the settlers "from prowlers both four footed and two footed."[6]

Lum Donaghey was relatively prosperous before the Civil War. His farm was on rich, untouched alluvial land. According to his son, Lum "was a good manager and an excellent farmer"[7] who produced more cotton than his neighbors and who was successful enough to own six slaves. George Donaghey was unusually close to one of these slaves, Dinah. He later gave her the credit or blame along with his Irish mysticism for making him very superstitious.[8] George's mother, Elizabeth, was a good housekeeper who taught George how to cook, made the clothes for the family, loved music and piano, and presided over the family prayers every evening. He was very close to her and wanted her to be proud of him but worried that he would "have to achieve something very remarkable indeed to be worthy of her pride."[9]

All of the Donagheys' relative prosperity came to an end when the Civil War began. Lum volunteered for the Confederacy in March of 1862 and served in a Louisiana infantry regiment. He was wounded and captured at Vicksburg in 1863 and paroled home for a time. He later rejoined the army and was wounded and captured again and spent the last months of the war in a federal prison camp.[10] While Lum was gone, George and his mother had to take care of the farm and the younger children. Only six years old when his father left, George worked almost full time in the fields, never really had enough to eat, and didn't have any shoes in the winter since all the hides and leather had to be used for the Confederate soldiers.[11] Even when George's father came home from the war, things were never the same.

When Lum returned to the farm in Lapile, he found that all the farm profits and reserves had been consumed to keep the family alive during the war. What was worse, Lum had acquired a terrible drinking problem. George Donaghey later attributed this to the custom of the day to use whiskey in prison camps as an anesthetic for both pain and insufficient food.[12] Whatever the cause, from this point on Lum's behavior was unpredictable. There is some evidence that he was a mean drunk who would get drunk two or three times a year, but his drinking bouts sometimes lasted for weeks. When this happened, his wife had to take the children and hide in a closet until he calmed down.[13] It soon became clear that George or his mother would have to look after Lum for the rest of his life because drinking had made "my courageous, intelligent father a failure."[14]

There were some compensations, however. Lum seemed to recover quickly from these periods of drunkenness, and when sober, was an excellent farmer and provider. He even served in 1879 on the school board of the Tulip School, a school district in Union County close to the Louisiana border.[15] Betty Donaghey was quite supportive of him, never considered divorce (they stayed married for fifty years), and was always willing to believe in his good intentions for change even when he once returned from New Orleans with a twenty-gallon cask of whiskey.

Lum and Betty often argued about the value of education for a boy. Apparently they both agreed that girls should be educated so that they could develop poise and refinement. As to boys, Lum argued that only a smattering of education was needed since too much would spoil the future farmers. He once told George, "I don't want you to grow into a dandy. Lean on that plow."[16] George's mother argued to the contrary but to no avail. One person in Conway who knew Lum felt that he was very stubborn, independent, and difficult to deal with.[17] Donaghey, although admiring many of his father's qualities, such as hard work, good management, understanding, and humor, still felt his father was unpredictable and thought his drinking habit "took him out of the class of respectability."[18] In one unflattering comment about his father, Donaghey said he "was an uneducated man, a farmer . . . [who] soon forgot the legend of his own foreign connection."[19]

One other incident involving Donaghey and his father needs to be noted. On page nineteen of the docket book of the county judge, Faulkner County, Arkansas, is a short summary of an "insanity" hearing held in June of 1896 before Judge G. W. Rice. The first part of the pleading reads, "This day comes G. W. Donaghey and makes oath that C. C. Donaghey is insane and ought to be restrained of his liberty and sent to the Lunatic Asylum for treatment . . . ." Donaghey (George) was at the hearing as well as other witnesses (unnamed) and Dr. G. W. Ringgold, a practicing physician in Conway. Judge Rice found C. C. Donaghey to be insane and sent him to the asylum for treatment. The only other notation in the case is that C. C. Donaghey was sent to the Asylum but escaped. No family members in Conway had any knowledge of this incident, which is understandable since the incident would have been forgotten as quickly as possible and not mentioned outside the immediate family. No other official records of incarceration or escape can be found, and one can only speculate that a prolonged and destructive period of drunkenness may have been the cause. Be that as it may, Donaghey must have gone through a painful emotional experience before he found the will to commit his father.

Donaghey had a very short childhood and had only had approximately six months of schooling by the age of fifteen[20] due to hard economic necessity and his father's belief in the futility of education for future farmers.

There were some positive effects of his austere childhood. Donaghey learned how to cook, to hunt, to work hard, to avoid excessive drinking, to depend upon himself, and to look to his mother for guidance in religion and other areas of life. Still, despite these helpful attributes of his childhood, the fifteen or sixteen years that he lived at Lapile were not the best of his life. As he later put it:

> Once, many years ago, the world to me was a place of hardship and grinding poverty. The Civil War had just been fought. I was a child on a farm that was none too prosperous. I had to work long hours in the fields, often with insufficient nourishment. I could never adjust myself happily to life as I saw it then. And so I got out of it.[21]

First Texas Trip and Initial Move to Conway

Covered wagons on their way to Texas sometimes passed through Lapile, and Donaghey's mother, who kept a bed for overnight guests, would sometimes put them up. The boy's imagination was so fired by stories that these guests would tell that he decided before he was ten that he would "go to Texas and be a cowboy."[22] Texas had been little damaged by the Civil War, and by southern standards was prospering with its thriving cattle industry. Notwithstanding his limited education,

Donaghey still managed to read some Wild West stories, which increased his eagerness to go to Texas. When he told his mother about his longing to go to Texas, she was horrified and told him, "You're too young, George! You're only fifteen, and small for your age."[23]

Donaghey's obsession with Texas overcame his mother's warning. One day in February, probably in 1871, he took the saddle horse his father had given him, and without a word to his family or any money in his pocket, he set off for Texas. He must have been relying on the frontier tradition of feeding and sheltering strangers. Donaghey traveled west through northern Louisiana, and besides "the actual physical dangers of riding alone in a rough, roadless county, swimming streams, and enduring chilling rains, there was the danger of illness resulting from the daily wearing of water soaked clothing and . . . drinking from questionable creeks."[24] He finally reached the border of Texas and crossed into his hoped-for paradise.

He eventually discovered a friendly family by the name of Gatling who had a farm in Harrison County near Marshall. The Gatlings, whose son, Paul, was about Donaghey's age, offered Donaghey a job as a hired hand with room and board as his compensation. The Gatlings treated him almost as a member of the family, and he seemed to enjoy knowing and working for them. He stayed on their farm for four months before he had a fight with one of the other hands (which he lost) and realized that paradise was not yet at hand. He was homesick and ready to go home. He returned home, repentant, and a "serious minded youth, who was destined to be forever dissatisfied with the constricted life of an Arkansas farm."[25]

Lum Donaghey was understanding and sympathetic when his son returned and even offered him some rent-free land and a horse to see how well he could farm on his own. If Donaghey succeeded, he would have his father's consent to go anywhere he wanted to seek his fortune. Donaghey was successful enough to have accumulated two hundred dollars from his crop, and his thoughts turned to north Arkansas as an area in which to try his luck. He selected Conway as his future home because his uncle William Ingram lived there. To reach Conway, he traveled by horseback twenty-five miles to El Dorado, then by buckboard forty miles to Camden. There he stayed overnight to catch the stage the next morning for Prescott. He caught the train at Prescott and rode almost all day to get to Little Rock. Not knowing railroad schedules or procedures, he arrived two hours early at the Prescott station just to be sure that he did not miss the train.

Donaghey spent the night in Little Rock, which impressed him as a grand city with its population of ten thousand. He left for Conway the next morning with his two hundred dollars in capital. His uncle William Ingram, a successful farmer in Conway, also owned a gristmill and a cotton gin and had been an incorporator of the city of Conway in 1875.[26] He had another uncle in Conway, John Ingram, who owned a livery stable and was mayor in 1886,[27] and another relative by marriage, John H. Hartje (married to Sally Ingram, William Ingram's daughter), who was also an incorporator of Conway[28] and became postmaster in 1879.[29] Unfortunately, Donaghey lost his two hundred dollars capital through a poor investment, but this loss was cushioned by the fact that he was living with his uncle, William, and helping him in the fields and at the cotton gin.

Donaghey probably arrived in Conway in 1873 or 1874. The coming of the railroad in 1871 had given the community its first big boost, and it had become Faulkner County seat in 1873,[30] when Conway "had only two small stores, two saloons, a depot, a postoffice, and a few horses."[31] Donaghey later described Conway at this time as ankle deep in dust when it was dry and ankle deep in mud when it was wet. It was "so rude, so drab and poor that only a fertile imagination could picture an attractive town growing from it."[32]

As time passed in Conway, George Donaghey began to worry about what he could do to earn his livelihood so that he would not have to keep imposing upon his uncle. One day, he passed a carpenter working on a new house and was fascinated by his skill and the way in which he used his carpentry tools. Although Donaghey was too shy to ask any questions, he realized that the carpenter was doing the very work he "had always loved best."[33] Since mechanical things had always stirred his interest, he decided to repair the gates at his uncle's home as an experiment. He borrowed some tools and his aunt bought some lumber for him. Donaghey worked hard at putting both the gates in good condition. When the gates were repaired and painted, he was surprised at how successful he had been, and from that point on, he considered himself a carpenter.

His uncle praised the restoration of the gates in glowing terms, but even though Donaghey had shown a real talent for repairing and making mechanical devices, there was still not enough work in Conway for a young inexperienced carpenter with good potential but still undeveloped skills. Donaghey decided to begin farming on his own again. He persuaded his uncle to lease him some land along the Arkansas River and to furnish a horse and some farm tools. The debt was to be repaid when the crop was harvested and sold. William was reluctant at first for Donaghey to do this alone because of his age and small build, but he finally consented on condition that his nephew find a partner. This was done, and at least one good crop of cotton was raised.

Bad luck then struck when Conway suffered a malaria epidemic of unusual violence, and George Donaghey, like many others, fell victim to the disease. He did not recover rapidly and was sick and could do little work for almost six months. He had heard that the Texas climate, especially the prairie winds, would cure the most stubborn case of malaria. So in March of 1876, after arranging for someone to take care of his crop, George Donaghey began his second Texas trip, not so much for adventure as for health. This time, he was almost twenty years old and had fifteen dollars with him.

The Second Texas Trip

Donaghey rode the train to Waco, Texas, the end of the railroad line at that time. He then proceeded west through the Basque hill country. On his first day on the Texas prairie, a sudden attack of malaria disabled him for most of the day, putting him in a feverish sleep almost like a coma. At twilight, Donaghey awoke and managed to stagger to a farmhouse that he saw in the distance. The farmhouse belonged to Jeffrey McLane who not only took Donaghey in but offered him work at a salary of fifty cents a day. The work consisted of cutting down trees in some bottom lands ten miles from the McLane farm, shaping them so that they could be used for building, hauling the timber back to the farm, and building a barn with the timber. The work must have been exhausting in the extreme since Donaghey got up every morning before daylight, "hitched the horses to the wagon and drove to the timberlands. It required a day of heavy labor to chop down and hew out a load of timbers, and six weeks were needed to work up enough material for the barn."[34]

This does not seem like ideal therapy for a recovering malaria patient, but by the time Donaghey had left the McLane farm, he was no longer plagued with malaria attacks. He had also gained some good practical knowledge about how to build a structure as large as a barn. Talk with some cowboys on what Donaghey called the "Cow Trail" rekindled Donaghey's childhood dream for "to be a cowboy on this trail was the supreme ambition of most redblooded young Americans at that time."[35]

Donaghey was now only about seventy-five miles from the Cow Trail where thousands of Texas cattle were driven to railroad stations in Kansas to be shipped to eastern markets. The Cow Trail to which Donaghey referred was most probably the Chisholm Trail which began in south Texas, ran by Austin and Lampasas, crossed the Red River at Nocona and then on to Caldwell and Wichita, Kansas.[36] At any rate, Donaghey was only a four-day trip from satisfying his childhood fantasy.

At the end of the fourth day of walking, Donaghey reached a drover's camp on the cow trail. It consisted of five hundred head of cattle, twenty cowboys to act as herders, and assorted cooks, pack horses, and attendants. The herd was owned by two wealthy graduates of Harvard University, who had come west for experience and excitement, and Frank McMahan, a native Texan from Bastrop County.[37] Donaghey was hired as a packhorse attendant and was put through the usual initiation process to see if he really had the stuff to be a cowboy. The hazing included a mock serious discussion of whether new members of the group should be branded and a much more serious incident where he was directed to dismount and help with the roping of a bull. After he had dismounted, the bull charged, and Donaghey was urged to run, which he did. Actually, the cowboys had arranged all this, and the bull was driven back into the herd before it could reach Donaghey even as Donaghey was urged to run even faster (which he did). There were many such tests that tried a newcomer's courage and good nature and helped Donaghey acquire, as he phrased it delicately, "a picturesque and adequate cowboy's vocabulary."[38]

The cattle drives lasted from three to six months, and during this time Donaghey learned to lasso fairly well and to break wild horses. He often drew outpost duty, which could be extremely dangerous. When a storm or other disturbance stampeded the cattle, his duty was to ride about a hundred yards in front of the cattle to keep the herd as compact as possible. The danger was even greater because the stampedes seemed to happen mostly at night. There were also the inconveniences of lack of water—which meant no baths—and the use of dried cattle dung for fuel. Despite these problems and the great physical exertions required, which Donaghey characterized as "the hardest work he'd ever done,"[39] he delighted in being a cowboy.

As the days grew into weeks and weeks into months, I felt that I should be satisfied to follow the Cow Trail forever. The dangers were just enough to satisfy an adventurous boy. The life was so carefree, so unrestricted by forms and customs, that a rather dangerous contentment settled on all of us. No one progresses when he is too content.[40]

Just at this juncture, Frank McMahan sold his interest in the herd to the two Harvard graduates and planned to return to Bastrop County and collect another herd to drive to Kansas. Under the agreement among the herd owners, Donaghey and one other cowboy were to return with McMahan.[41] Donaghey had admired McMahan on the cattle drive, but on the trip to Bastrop County, he confided to Donaghey that he was a fugitive from the law because he had stabbed someone in Bastrop.[42] This would not have been that unusual in the Texas of the 1870s, but another incident helped to change Donaghey's judgment about McMahan. McMahan had gone to a dance some twelve miles from Bastrop and asked Donaghey to watch for any police officers who might be looking for him and also to hold his revolver belt and holster while he concealed a revolver inside his shirt. The police officers came and arrested McMahan and put him under bond for a court appearance. Donaghey was also arrested but released. This event and McMahan's pride in the notoriety of having been arrested caused Donaghey to think seriously about law and order and his duties as a citizen, and he terminated his relationship with McMahan. [43]

Donaghey had heard about a man named Voss who lived on the Colorado River several miles from Bastrop and was looking for a person to run his cotton gin. After the arrest of McMahan, Donaghey obtained this job as superintendent of the cotton gin at twenty dollars a month. The job required someone who could cook and was willing to sleep in the gin. Shortly after he began work, Voss injured his hand in the machinery, and the entire management of the cotton gin was left to Donaghey. It was his first executive responsibility, and he thoroughly enjoyed it. The employment lasted for sixty days, and the isolation gave him a chance to think and "to consider what the proper functions of life are. And I knew that my cowboy days were forever ended."[44]

After completing his employment with Voss, Donaghey moved back across the Colorado River in December of 1876. His luck held, and he was given a job by Captain J. W. Fitzwilliam, who lived two miles west of Bastrop. Fitzwilliam, a former captain in the Confederate army, had a plantation along the Colorado located on the main road between Mexico and the United States. The plantation was called "Wexford" in honor of the county in Ireland where Fitzwilliam had been born. Fortunately for Donaghey, Fitzwilliam had strong Arkansas ties since his wife, Nancy, had been born in Washington County, Arkansas, in 1837,[45] and Fitzwilliam, for a time, had been a blacksmith in Fort Smith, Arkansas.[46]

Fitzwilliam was a well-educated individual who lived with his family in a gracious two-story house that still stands today, and he and Donaghey got along well together. Donaghey admired the education of the older man and was intrigued by the scientific farming that Fitzwilliam employed on the plantation. Fitzwilliam also apparently sensed Donaghey's potential and even offered to pay his way through college if he would study hard and prepare himself. However, Donaghey was still in a wandering mood "and was too restless to accept so sound an offer."[47]

While staying with the Fitzwilliams, Donaghey had one last unpleasant contact with Frank McMahan, the fugitive from Texas justice. Donaghey had gone to Bastrop with a young and slightly retarded ward of Fitzwilliam's mother. They met McMahan in the city. He had been drinking, and Donaghey tried to avoid him, but somehow Craig, the ward, and McMahan got together, and when Donaghey was ready to leave, he found Craig with McMahan, and both were drunk. As all three rode out of Bastrop, Donaghey criticized McMahan for getting Craig drunk. McMahan pulled out a knife and threatened Donaghey. At the same time, Craig said something that offended McMahan, and McMahan then stabbed Craig who fell from his horse. Donaghey dismounted to help Craig. McMahan, who had also dismounted, again threatened Donaghey with the knife, but Donaghey pretended that he had a pistol. McMahan, who was drunk enough to believe the bluff, mounted his horse and left.

Donaghey, with the help of some other people on the road, put Craig back on his horse so that he reached home before he lost too much blood. Craig's wound soon healed, and McMahan was put on trial for the stabbing. Donaghey testified at the trial, and McMahan was convicted and went to the penitentiary. He escaped but was recaptured, and after finally serving his time, he returned home to Bastrop and was killed in a quarrel with one of his relatives. Donaghey never saw McMahan again after the trial but marked the whole experience as another significant milestone in his life and believed "my childhood ended after this unfortunate incident. Certainly I was more serious and thoughtful after that, I felt that I had sowed my wild oats, and that I should now set about the serious job of finding a more stable place in life."[48]

In the summer of 1877, Donaghey moved again, and his luck did not desert him. This time, he managed to find employment at the farm of E. B. Burleson, located on the Colorado River in the same general area as the Fitzwilliam place. Burleson came from one of the early pioneer families whose members had helped establish the Republic of Texas. Burleson's uncle, General Edward Burleson, was second in command to Sam Houston at the battle of San Jacinto and later became the vice president of the Republic of Texas from 1841 to 1844.[49] Before that he was a member of both the Texas House of Representatives and the Texas Senate.[50] E. B. Burleson's father was Jonathon Burleson who was an Indian fighter and captain of a scouting company during the Texas revolution against Mexico.[51] E. B. Burleson raised cattle on his large farm where he lived with his wife and six children.

Donaghey not only did his usual work as a farm laborer but also helped the young mother with the housework, did some cooking, and eventually fixed breakfast every morning. As with the Fitzwilliam family, Donaghey's relations with the Burlesons were exemplary. He was encouraged by the Burlesons to attend a local academy, which he did for six weeks during the summer of 1878 once the crops had been planted. In 1911, when Donaghey was governor, Burleson came to a Confederate reunion in Little Rock and stopped by the capitol to see his former hired hand.[52]

Donaghey was fortunate to have lived with the Burlesons and the Fitzwilliams—two families who had founded and helped build Texas. He does not say in his autobiography, but he must have seriously considered moving permanently to Texas as two of his brothers did.

After staying with the Burlesons for about eighteen months, Donaghey left their farm in December of 1878 and returned home on horseback through Texas and Louisiana to Union County, Arkansas. Donaghey probably spent about three years in Texas on his second trip and six months on his first trip. At twenty-two, Donaghey had passed around 15 percent of his life in the land of his boyhood dreams, and even if all his expectations had not been met, he had many achievements to his credit. He had mastered the rough cowboy life, was an accomplished farmer, had learned self-reliance, and had acquired a smattering of education. He seemed to inspire confidence in people since they valued his work and encouraged him to develop his potential. Perhaps what was most important, he had realized that the life of a cowboy or a farm laborer, while not to be denigrated, was not enough for him.

The Permanent Move to Conway

After returning to Union County in 1879, Donaghey decided to spend most of the year there reacquainting himself with his family. He and his father formed a partnership to work the family farm but he soon became bored and saw no future for himself on his father's farm. During 1879 Donaghey heard many accounts of the opportunities in north Arkansas. His relatives in Conway wrote often about the good prospects in that city, and he decided to try Conway again. He took the train and arrived in Conway a few days before Christmas in 1879. While impressed by the town's energy and the opening of new businesses there, Donaghey was less enthusiastic about the muddy streets, the lack of street lights, and "the seven or eight saloons, some of which remained open all night."[53]

Donaghey moved in with William Ingram again, and the 1880 U.S. census listed him as a nephew living in the Ingram household, whose age was twenty-three and who was born in Louisiana.[54] His occupation was given as carpenter. As soon as Donaghey reached Conway, he began looking for a construction job in which he could utilize what he had learned in building the barn for Voss in Bastrop County, Texas. He visited many construction sites but was too shy to ask for work until he encountered a friendly young carpenter who was impressed when Donaghey said that he was not yet a carpenter but wanted to be one and would work for very little while learning the trade. The young carpenter hired Donaghey for $1.50 a day (a day being from sunrise to sunset). Donaghey began by nailing shingles on a roof and progressed to other more complicated tasks. At the end of a month or six weeks, the other workmen were amazed at his skills with carpentry tools.

All seemed to go well for the would-be carpenter as the work was enjoyable and the salary, although small, was enough to take care of his living expenses with something left over to save. In the middle of February 1880, Donaghey began having nightmarish dreams in which he found himself stuck in a river of mud from which he could not get free. There was a superstition at that time in some areas of Arkansas that muddy water in a dream was a sign of death. Donaghey, who was always superstitious, woke up with a sense of impending doom which soon became reality. His uncle, William Ingram, came to his place of work with the news that one of his sisters, Lenora, had died of typhoid fever. Lum and Betty Donaghey had decided to move to Conway to be close to the Ingrams. The family had set out for the two-hundred-mile journey in covered wagons in the middle of February and took their drinking water from wells or streams along the way.

The first part of the trip was uneventful, but on the fifth day all the children—Alice, Lenora, Willie, Columbus, and James—came down with typhoid fever after drinking contaminated water. The party stopped at Rison in Cleveland County for a month to fight the disease and recover. Lenora died during the month at Rison, but the others seemed to recover, so they continued their travel to Conway. But Alice suffered a relapse, and Donaghey and William took a wagon and picked them up five miles south of Conway. They went immediately to the Ingram home, but Alice died within two days. Donaghey described the grief of his mother at the death of her two daughters as terrible to behold,[55] and he quit his promising job to spend sixty days with his family to try to help ease the pain and loss.

This dreadful incident in which two of his sisters—Lenora at the age of twenty, and Alice at the age of twenty-two—died and one brother, Jim, was weakened for the rest of his life[56] had a powerful impact on Donaghey. The effect on Donaghey was strengthened even further when his sister, Willie, died of tuberculosis at the age of thirty-one and he lost three uncles and one aunt to the same disease.[57] Public health would become a major concern of Donaghey's administration. The tuberculosis sanitarium at Booneville and a vastly strengthened state health department with the authority to issue and enforce sanitation regulations came from these unforgettable family deaths from what are now preventable or curable diseases.

Once Donaghey decided to resume work, the construction project on which he had worked prior to the family tragedy was finished, but he found a job building a frame house at Mt. Vernon, a small mountain community northeast of Conway. Still, work as a carpenter was hard to find, and he used the unfilled time to attend school for a while and even to dig a well. At last, he joined another carpenter in Conway who had a contract to build a cottage for $400. This was Donaghey's first participation in the business of contracting. In smaller cities like Conway, architects were virtually unknown. "Carpenters were both architects and contractors. The owners stated how many rooms and porches they wanted, and left the rest to the carpenter."[58] Carpenters became what might today be called "vernacular architects."

The next contract awarded to Donaghey to build a porch had unforeseen and very special consequences. Some of the detail work had to be done in John Pence's woodworking and cabinetmaking shop located on Front Street in Conway. After the contract for the porch was finished, Pence asked Donaghey to come to work for him at $1.25 a day plus the promise to teach him cabinetmaking. Donaghey eagerly accepted. The relationship between Pence and his new apprentice would last until Pence's death and was gratifying to both parties.

Pence was an undertaker as well as a cabinetmaker.[59] A family would bring the deceased and give the measurements to Mr. Pence. The family would then wait for the casket to be made. The casket was usually of pine or oak, the interior lined with flannel, handles attached on the outside, and "often an endearing epitaph was engraved and placed on the simple flattop of the casket."[60] Once a casket was finished, "Mr. John Pence would then send word to the family (often by young George W. Donaghey, who was an apprentice in this period) waiting at the wagon yard."[61] As well as carrying messages to waiting families, Donaghey helped to make the caskets,[62] which could be purchased in 1880 from the Pence Cabinet Shop for sixteen dollars.[63]

John Ingram, Donaghey's other uncle who lived in Conway, owned a livery stable. Being shorthanded one night just after Donaghey had come to Conway, Ingram asked Donaghey to drive one of the carriages to a big reception. He was to pick up and drive a Miss Wallace and her escort. The escort was a young lawyer named James H. Harrod who had offices above the Pence Cabinet and Woodworking Shop. It was rumored that Pence and Donaghey gave him his first case.[64] James Harrod and Donaghey would have very important personal and political ties through the years, but on this particular night, the most important person in the closed carriage, as far as Donaghey was concerned, was Louvenia Wallace.

She had been born in Darlington, South Carolina, in 1862 and had been educated in the local institutions at Darlington. Her parents were J.

G. and Eunice Wallace,[65] and in 1879, the Wallace family decided to move to Arkansas when Louvenia was seventeen. Her father had a farm at Carlisle in Lonoke County. Louvenia and Sally Hartje of Conway were very close friends at the time and remained so for the rest of their lives. Sally, the daughter of William Ingram, was Donaghey's first cousin. She had married John Henry Hartje in 1879, and Louvenia made frequent long visits to the Hartjes.

Because of her friendship with Sally Hartje, Louvenia was often in Conway. Donaghey was quite taken with her. He described her as very beautiful with blue eyes and brown hair. She had a vivacious personality and a scintillating wit as contrasted with his own shyness in a crowd and rather grave demeanor.[66] Be that as it may, they got along well and became engaged around 1880.[67] The relationship did not always proceed smoothly, however. Donaghey refers to several lovers' quarrels,[68] and Peggy Jacoway, a biographer of the wives of Arkansas governors, refers to the Donagheys traveling "a merged road, not always smooth, that presented hills to climb, but had a royal lining."[69]

Donaghey's attendance at college became a serious problem the engaged couple had to solve. He wanted to study at the state university at Fayetteville, and Louvenia encouraged him in this undertaking. In spite of his poor academic preparation, Donaghey had been interested in going to college for a long time. He had almost decided not to go because of his age (twenty-six) and his progress in carpentry, but a visit with two of his friends changed his mind. These two friends were John Puryear and H. B. Ingram (Donaghey's first cousin), both of whom were attending the university at the time. They came through Conway and encouraged Donaghey to go with them. He talked it over with Louvenia and decided to enroll.

Donaghey left for the University in September of 1882, and it was a grueling trip for him, both physically and mentally, to reach Fayetteville. The train ride from Little Rock to Fort Smith took ten hours. The passengers going to Fayetteville got off at Altus and took a stagecoach across the Boston Mountains. Another train then had to be taken to Fayetteville itself. Donaghey was overwhelmed with grave self-doubts on this trip. He was not sure that his academic preparation was adequate, his savings would be consumed, his wife-to-be was left behind not to be seen for a year (transportation was so difficult that very few college students went home for Christmas, and the holidays were very short), and this strange and difficult venture might be a disaster. When the stage-coach that had taken them from Altus across the Boston Mountains started back, Donaghey watched it, wishing that he might return also.[70]

Many Arkansas students in those days were, like Donaghey, poorly prepared for college work. The University itself had only been in existence for ten years, and good high schools in Arkansas were rare, so the university had created a preparatory department to help students compensate for their poor educational backgrounds. In 1882 there were 276 students in the preparatory department with only 87 doing college work,[71] and "the preparatory department for nearly forty years had an enrollment as large or larger than the collegiate enrollment."[72] As might have been expected when practically all of Donaghey's academic training had been in summer schools, the placement tests that all freshman had to take indicated that Donaghey should be in the preparatory department and that was where he was assigned. He is listed officially under the A class of the preparatory department in the 1882 catalog of the Arkansas Industrial University. Donaghey was mortified.

He was twenty-six years old and felt that he had been placed with children. Only four years earlier, the ages of students in the preparatory department ranged from nine to thirty-one,[73] but the minimum age had been raised to fifteen[74] by the time Donaghey enrolled, and it apparently was not uncommon for people much older than fifteen to be in the department.[75] The curriculum which began with a fourth-grade reader, the embarrassment that he could not join his two friends in taking college work, and his past life experiences of making his way as a cowboy all must have contributed to the humiliation that he felt in having to do grade-school work with students younger than he was. This set of circumstances and the encouragement of Ingram and Puryear, who thought he could do college work, fortified Donaghey's desire to ask permission for a transfer to the college department. This was initially refused, but when Donaghey offered to withdraw from school and return home if he couldn't keep up, and went even further and said that if he was not allowed to transfer, he would go home anyway, his offer was reluctantly accepted. With the help of his two friends and his own diligent work and fierce energy, he did satisfactory work which improved as time went on.

Donaghey roomed with Ingram and Puryear and frequently studied with them. Courses were offered in Latin, Greek, modern languages, English, sciences, agriculture, education, civil engineering, and mining engineering. Student life was spartan, and discipline was strict. "Most of the out-of-town students lived in private homes in Fayetteville, paid twelve to fifteen dollars a month for room and board . . . and walked to and from school, even from houses in the east part of town. Organized extracurricular activities were few."[76] In fact, a resolution of the board of trustees in June of 1881 stated that no student was to be permitted "to attend parties, circuses, theaters, or any place of social amusement, except at the close of each term when general permission will be granted to attend social parties."[77] Sunday school, chapel, and church were required of all students. Male students had to take military training. Military uniforms had to be worn at all times when the students were on campus. A student was expelled if he or she accumulated two hundred demerits. There were thirteen penalties from the use of profanity (ten demerits) to intoxication, however slight (two hundred demerits).[78]

Many weeks before commencement on June 7, 1883, Donaghey had exhausted his funds and did some part-time work repairing campus buildings and working in a furniture store to make ends meet. In both cases, his experience as a carpenter was valuable. His college work was proceeding smoothly, but relations with Louvenia were deteriorating.

Louvenia was living with Sally Hartje and her family during the winter of 1882–1883. Sally was the sister of H. B. Ingram, Donaghey's roommate. Despite what should have been opportunities for communication both directly and indirectly, Donaghey wrote a letter to a friend in Conway in November of 1882 saying that he had received only one letter from Louvenia since going to college and indicated that he didn't blame Louvenia because waiting was so hard.[79] He also began to receive letters from friends in Conway urging him to marry soon because other suitors were courting Louvenia. H. B. Ingram and Sally Hartje gave him the same advice.

Although Donaghey had planned to spend the summer of 1883 in Fayetteville preparing for the next year, he decided to return home instead. He had also planned to borrow money to finish his last three years of college, but the pleas of his roommate and his roommate's sister also persuaded him to go home to spend the summer vacation. Donaghey had a tough decision to make, and he did not make it right away. He wanted to complete college but felt that if he gave himself "a finished education I should probably deprive myself of her companionship throughout life. The fight was on between my love for her and ambition. And ambition was daily becoming more insistent."[80] However, they had been engaged for three years, and he couldn't bring himself even to raise the idea of another three years of waiting while he completed college, so he went home.

Surprisingly enough, once Donaghey was home, he did not see or write Louvenia, but instead took a teaching job at a rural school district near Conway. This lasted until the first part of September and was not a rewarding experience for Donaghey, and if he had been considering the idea of teaching as a profession, it vanished in that rural school district. At some time during the summer of 1883, Donaghey had decided to go back to college. He had planned to write Louvenia canceling their matrimonial plans. But before doing so, he went to see her for the first time since his return to Conway. All their problems were apparently resolved, and they got married on September 20, 1883.

It was seemingly a very happy marriage with both partners devoted to each other. Agreeing with the traditional role of the wife, Louvenia said she "was content with the efforts and achievements of my husband . . . my highest aim in life was to do what I could for his comfort and to assist and encourage him in every way that I could."[81] Her marriage role was much greater than this statement indicated. She was a political and financial adviser as well as supervisor of their home and sometimes a farm in Conway. Later in life, she seemed to be as devoted to education as he was. The Donagheys had no children, although on one occasion they offered to adopt the two youngest children of John Ingram when his wife died at the age of thirty-three.[82] Even though John Ingram was Donaghey's uncle, he was only four years older than Donaghey, and if the adoption had taken place, John Ingram would still have had three children in his family. But the oldest of the children, Lillian, dropped out of school at the age of fourteen to take care of the younger children and keep the family together, so the adoption was not necessary.

The only person who came close to filling the vacancy left by the lack of immediate family was Raymond R. Donaghey. He was the son of Donaghey's brother C. C. Donaghey and Kitty Chandler and was born in Chandler, Texas, in 1897. At the age of either eight or nine,[83] he came to live with the Donagheys in Conway and later accompanied them to Little Rock when Donaghey became governor in 1909. Raymond Donaghey attended public schools in Conway and Little Rock before he went back to Texas to finish high school.[84] His uncle encouraged him to seek further education and paid his way through Baylor University and the University of Texas Law School. Their relationship was very close, more like father and son than uncle and nephew. After Raymond graduated from law school in 1924, George Donaghey tried on numerous occasions to persuade him to come back to Little Rock and take over the family business.[85] Raymond declined because he thought he needed to prove himself and make it on his own without the advantage of his uncle's reputation and further help. He did have a successful legal career, and at the time of George Donaghey's death he had already been elected county attorney and state representative while living in Vernon, Texas.[86] He still maintained frequent contact with his uncle, arranging to travel to Little Rock usually twice a year to renew family ties. He once indicated to his sister-in-law[87] that looking back he regretted his decision not to manage the Donaghey properties.

George W. Donaghey at the age of 21, taken at Bastrop, Texas, in 1877.
Courtesy of the Arkansas History Commission.

Louvenia Wallace, taken in 1879, when she and Donaghey first met. *Courtesy of the Arkansas History Commission.*

Drawing of the Washington County Courthouse in 1903. Donaghey was the builder. Construction was completed in 1905. *George Washington Donaghey Papers. Special Collections, University of Arkansas Libraries, Fayetteville.*

"Donaghey Day," at Morrilton, opening of his campaign for governor, October 7, 1907. *Courtesy of the Arkansas History Commission.*

Louvenia W. Donaghey at the Democratic National Convention in Denver in 1908. *George Washington Donaghey Papers. Special Collections, University of Arkansas Libraries, Fayetteville.*

Home of the Donagheys in Conway until they moved to Little Rock in 1909. *Courtesy of the Arkansas History Commission.*

William Jennings Bryan campaigning for initiative and referendum at Harrison on September 10, 1910. *Courtesy of the Arkansas History Commission.*

Donaghey standing to the right of William Jennings Bryan on the special train at Leslie, Saturday, September 10, 1910. *Courtesy of the Arkansas History Commission.*

Donaghey (center) with his nephew, Raymond R. Donaghey, and Raymond's wife, Lucille Donaghey. *George Washington Donaghey Papers. Special Collections, University of Arkansas Libraries, Fayetteville.*

Former President Theodore Roosevelt (center) speaking at the state fair in Hot Springs on October 10, 1910. Behind Roosevelt is an American flag formed by fifteen hundred school children dressed in red, white, and blue. *George Washington Donaghey Papers. Special Collections, University of Arkansas Libraries, Fayetteville.*

President Theodore Roosevelt and George W. Donaghey at the state fair in Hot Springs in 1910. *Courtesy of the Arkansas History Commission.*

All 1910. 1. September 6, progress of stone work on dome; 2. May 4, main stairway on north end; 3. June 6, corridor to senate chamber being prepared for finishing; 4. May 4, main stair, south end; 5. June 2, looking into the house of representatives; 6. June 2, putting up partition walls in the house of representatives; 7. finishing attic; 8. September 5, finishing main stairway, north end. *Courtesy of the Arkansas History Commission*

1. January 2, 1911, house of representatives being made ready for legislature; 2. December 1, 1910, further progress on east front steps; 3. April 28, 1911, at south end of building looking north from senate door; 4. March 1, 1911, main rotunda after completion; 5. April 28, 1911, northwest front showing improvement of outside grounds; 6. April 28, 1911, main rotunda, showing central section completed; 7. Governor Donaghey standing in governor's office ready for the convening of the 1911 legislature; 8. February 3, 1911, balcony railing around the inside of dome. *Courtesy of the Arkansas History Commission.*

The first day in the new state capitol, January 1911. (From left) Hamilton Moses, assistant secretary to the governor; George W. Donaghey, governor; Bruce T. Bullion, secretary to the governor; Miss Birdie Wilson, assistant secretary to the governor. *Courtesy of the Arkansas History Commission.*

Donaghey in what is now called the governor's conference room sometime early in 1911. *Courtesy of the Arkansas History Commission.*

Donaghey (second from left in coat and tie) standing on dome of state capitol, 1915. *George Washington Donaghey Papers. Special Collections, University of Arkansas Libraries, Fayetteville.*

Donaghey (right) on the Broadway Bridge, December 25, 1922, with other Broadway–Main Street commissioners. *Courtesy of the Arkansas History Commission.*

Five-story building built by Donaghey and located at Seventh and Main streets in Little Rock. Now called the Waldron Building. *George Washington Donaghey Papers. Special Collections, University of Arkansas Libraries, Fayetteville.*

The Donaghey Building. This fourteen-story building at Seventh and Main streets in Little Rock cost over one million dollars and was the largest structure in Arkansas at the time. *Courtesy of the Arkansas History Commission.*

Six of Conway's oldest residents in 1928. From left to right: Jo Frauenthal, R. B. McCullock, Dr. George S. Brown, George W. Donaghey, John J. Hartje, and P. H. Prince *George Washington Donaghey Papers. Special Collections Division, University of Arkansas Libraries, Fayetteville.*

Governor W. Donaghey signing the deed to their property which created the endowment for the Little Rock Junior College, July 1, 1929. *Courtesy of the Arkansas History Commission.*

Mrs. George W. Donaghey signing the deed to their property which created the endowment for the Little Rock Junior College, July 1, 1929. *Courtesy of the Arkansas History Commission.*

Donaghey seated on the steps of his old home site near Oakland, Louisiana. *George Washington Donaghey Papers. Special Collections, University of Arkansas Libraries, Fayetteville.*

Donaghey standing next to a monument built in his honor at the Donaghey State Park in Union County, 1933. *George Washington Donaghey Papers. Special Collection, University of Arkansas Libraries, Fayetteville.*

Donaghey monument at the Donaghey State Park, 1991.

Donaghey on his pony, riding over his Chickasaw plantation near McGehee, 1934. *Courtesy of the Arkansas History Commission.*

George and Louvenia Donaghey at their home in Little Rock on his eightieth birthday, July 1, 1936. *Courtesy of the Arkansas History Commission.*

Donaghey seated in his car in front of the state capitol. *George Washington Donaghey Papers. Special Collections, University of Arkansas Libraries, Fayetteville.*

Residence of Mr. and Mrs. George W. Donaghey at 2109 Gaines Street, Little Rock. *Courtesy of the Arkansas History Commission.*

Donaghey in the flower garden at his Little Rock home. *Courtesy of the Arkansas History Commission.*

George W. Donaghey. *George Washington Donaghey Papers. Special Collections, University of Arkansas Libraries, Fayetteville.*

THREE

Conway Years

After George and Louvenia got married in September of 1883, they spent about a month visiting relatives and friends, a customary honeymoon in those days. In January of 1884, Donaghey found himself with a young wife, $75 in debt, and living in a rented house. Donaghey resumed the job he had left to go to college, in John Pence's cabinet shop and undertaking establishment, for $1.25 a day.[1]

For several months, things went well until Louvenia had to go to Lonoke County to help care for some sick relatives. While nursing her relatives, she caught pneumonia, and Donaghey, in turn, had to go to Lonoke County to be with her. Her illness lasted two weeks, and according to Donaghey she was never as strong as before and her health was often precarious. This turn of events forced Donaghey to draw upon the housekeeping and cooking skills that he had learned. The two-week loss of wages, doctor bills, and other expenses involved with his wife's illness again put Donaghey seventy-five dollars in debt.

This recurring pattern of accumulating just enough money to get ahead and then some event, tragic or otherwise, consuming his savings haunted Donaghey during his early efforts to get ahead. He had lost two hundred dollars he had saved and brought to Conway just before his second Texas trip, the death of his sisters had wiped out a promising start in carpentry work, college tuition had taken the two hundred dollars he had saved up to that point, and his wife's illness had put them back in debt again.

The Donagheys joined the Methodist church in Conway. The

Methodist identification stayed with the Donagheys for the rest of their lives and when they settled in Little Rock in 1908, they joined the First Methodist Church of Little Rock.

Business Successes in Arkansas

George Donaghey was beginning to be successful again in 1885, and one year later, he had once again reached the magic figure of two hundred dollars in capital.[2] He was prosperous enough to buy on an installment plan the complete works of Charles Dickens and Bulwer-Lytton so that he could as he said "recreate myself from the unlettered backwoods boy I had been."[3] In the spring of 1886, Pence's partner, who was named Carter, decided to retire from the business, and Donaghey was offered the chance to buy his share of the business for five hundred dollars. Terms were arranged, and Donaghey became part owner of the cabinet shop and undertaking parlor. Financial security always seemed to elude the young businessman at this stage in his life, and shortly after he had sunk all his capital in this new investment, a devastating fire struck Conway in November of 1886. Most of the Conway business district was constructed of wooden one-story structures and the fire destroyed 80 percent of the town, including the Pence shop and everything in it.

In the fire, Donaghey lost his investment and all his tools, and was $250 in debt. Louvenia had to do needlework and take in boarders. Donaghey's optimism was tested by this fire since he had always thought that some day he would "find a way to build a little fortune for myself. Rebuffs and losses only spurred me on to greater outbursts of energy. But this fire was the greatest disappointment I had ever borne."[4] Pence and Donaghey moved to an old building outside the business district and set up shop temporarily in that new location. Pence, who still owned the land on which the destroyed place of business had been situated, decided to rebuild the store with brick. Since the cost was so high, Pence decided to curtail some of his activities and proposed to Donaghey that they agree to a division of labor in which Pence would supervise the undertaking business and Donaghey would operate the cabinet shop. Donaghey further agreed to rent the lower floor of the rebuilt building. With this kind of arrangement between the two men, business boomed, and the fire that had been so destructive had a more positive side for

Donaghey, because everyone in town had lost doors, windows, and furniture, and needed Donaghey to replace them.

Times were prosperous enough for Donaghey to build a small house for himself and Louvenia. He had soon saved a thousand dollars beyond his liabilities, and with the experience of building his small home behind him, he tried to obtain a contract for a large building. Donaghey had been part of a Conway group of businessmen who had been instrumental in persuading the Hendrix board to move that college from Altus to Conway. He approached the college building committee, headed by W. W. Martin who was a good friend of Donaghey's, about getting the contract to construct the first building on the Hendrix campus. The committee rejected his request, however, because he had not yet had enough building and contracting experience.

This disappointment was short-lived since Donaghey was given the job of building the Bank of Conway by a group of incorporators headed by the same W. W. Martin. The bank was badly needed since all the Conway business firms had to bank in Little Rock. Donaghey, himself, when he first started to work for Pence, left any surplus he saved with Pence because there were no banks in Conway.[5] The bank, which was a fairly small structure, was built by Donaghey in 1890 and was a complete success. The Bank of Conway "was the turning point in the life of George Donaghey. It was his first important construction contract."[6]

After the successful completion of the bank, Donaghey decided to become a full-time contractor and sold his furniture business. With Martin's approval and encouragement, Donaghey again approached the Hendrix building committee and was successful. He contracted to build the second building[7] on the Hendrix campus. Notwithstanding his wife catching typhoid fever, and his sister, Willie, developing tuberculosis during the building of College Hall, Donaghey completed it in time for the fall 1891 semester. At about the same time, Donaghey and Pence obtained the contract[8] to build Main Hall at Central Baptist College in Conway, starting work in 1892. That building lasted until 1980 when it was torn down.[9] Pence and Martin were Donaghey's great benefactors in the early Conway years, and both maintained good relations with him until their deaths.

Donaghey's next project was almost a disaster. The Faulkner County courthouse had burned in 1890, and in 1893 he made a bid of twenty-five thousand dollars to build a new courthouse. There were two problems that hampered this contract. One was that county scrip was issued for all county obligations, and it could be redeemed for cash when and if cash was available. Merchants usually discounted county scrip by 25 percent,[10] but Donaghey had taken that into consideration in his bid. The second problem was related to the first and was the crippling depression of 1893–1897 that began after the contract was drawn up and brought the scrip discount closer to 85 percent.[11] Donaghey had to delay completion of the courthouse until he could realize more money from the scrip and find other jobs. He managed to obtain a contract, probably in the early part of 1894, to erect a building at the School for the Deaf in Little Rock. It is not clear which building this was, but there is an advertisement in the *Conway Log Cabin* on June 27, 1895, for Donaghey, that states that he is the "Builder of Hendrix College, Faulkner County Court House, Chapel of the Arkansas Deaf Mute Institute, and buildings at Camden, El Dorado, and other points." Whether the chapel or another building, Donaghey made $1,500 on the new contract for six months' work and came back to Conway to finish the courthouse job. With this $1,500, the judicious sale of some scrip, and the extension of his personal credit to its furthest limit, the courthouse was completed.

Building the Faulkner County courthouse consumed Donaghey's savings and left him heavily in debt at the age of thirty-eight. It never seemed to bother Donaghey that, as had so often been true in his life, he once again had to start from the beginning. He secured a job in late 1894 to supervise the repairs to the State Hospital for the Insane at a salary of ten dollars a day. The hospital had been damaged by a tornado that struck Little Rock in October of 1894.[12] Donaghey answered an advertisement placed in the local newspapers on October 4, 1894,[13] asking for contractors and builders to make bids for the needed repair work. The work on the hospital went well, and Donaghey was commended by Governor James P. Clarke, who said that Donaghey's bid cost less than any of the other bids and "anyone seeking the services of an experienced and conscientious workman will not regret having procured the services of Donaghey."[14]

Donaghey's success with the hospital led to other commissions in Arkansas. He built six new buildings in El Dorado and a Methodist church in Camden in 1895.[15] Louvenia became sick again during the Camden contract and had to be taken to New York City for an expensive operation. This took two months away from Donaghey's work in Camden, but the setback this time was not as serious as the others, and Donaghey quickly recovered as did Louvenia. Donaghey's next construction project was an ice plant in Texarkana for the Anheuser-Busch Company of St. Louis.[16] These profitable ventures enabled Donaghey to buy a new and bigger house in Conway along with sixty acres of land. His mother and father moved in with him and Louvenia as well as his sister, Willie, who was dying of tuberculosis. His father, Lum Donaghey, farmed the sixty acres, while George continued his contracting.

By 1899 or 1900, Donaghey had become a successful businessman in Conway mainly through contracting and building. Of all the structures that he contributed to Conway, not many are left today. The Bank of Conway still remains in rebuilt form on Front Street, the Ott building located at Parkway and Oak was constructed by Donaghey and was formerly called the Donaghey Building, the Old Main building at UCA still stands and was Donaghey's last construction project in Conway (1917). There is also a main thoroughfare in Conway called Donaghey Avenue and a street called Louvenia that branches off several blocks to the west of Donaghey Avenue. Louvenia Street leads to the location of what was once the Donaghey home. In addition, there is a chifforobe at the Conway Public Library from Donaghey's days as a furniture maker (as well as a cradle at the Ted Hiegel home). There are probably other pieces elsewhere in the city. The Kenneth Fuchs residence, now remodeled, was originally built by Donaghey.

There is one other rather strange reminder of Donaghey in Faulkner County. He bought over a period of time some one thousand acres of swampland southwest of Conway[17] and worked for many years to make it profitable. It was sold in 1916,[18] but Donaghey left a concrete monument behind in the middle of the field that gives advice to future owners. It is dated November 1916. The base is ten feet by seven feet, and the part containing the inscription is five and one-half feet tall and six feet wide. The message that should last forever says, "The struggle for its [the tract of land] reclamation has been the greatest task of my life. Future owners should greatly enlarge the levee, tile drain the land, and provide an adequate pump for rain or seep water during excessive overflows. . . ." This advice set in concrete for future generations is signed "George W. Donaghey."

The Conway Colleges

In less than twenty years, the people of Conway brought three major colleges to their city by local organization and financial generosity—Hendrix in 1890, Central Baptist in 1892; and the Arkansas State Normal School, which later became the University of Central Arkansas, in 1907. Donaghey was involved in each of these efforts and played the major role in bringing the State Normal School to Conway. The three colleges "definitely modified the personality of the city"[19] and had a major impact on Donaghey in a variety of ways. Not only did he help financially to bring the colleges to Conway, he also built at least one large structure on each campus: College Hall at Hendrix, Main Hall at Central Baptist, and Old Main at State Normal. He benefitted greatly from the exposure that his role in bringing these three colleges to Conway gave him, especially among the Methodists and Baptists in the state.

Hendrix College was given its present name in 1889, when it was still in Altus, Arkansas, a small town of five hundred people situated in the foothills of the Ozark Mountains. The president of the college, Dr. A. C. Millar, felt that a more central location was needed. There was also some conflict between the college and the townspeople, so the decision to move was reached easily. The Methodist conference, by January 1, 1890, had granted the power to the Hendrix Board of Trustees to decide the future location of the school.[20] The board met and decided to establish it "at that place which shall offer the greatest inducements in the way of land, money, geographical position, accessibility, healthfulness, morality, and patronage."[21] Bids were requested from any interested Arkansas city, and a decision was to be made in March of 1890.

According to Donaghey, the possibility of bringing a college to Conway united all its citizens "in one great ambition . . . to secure a college for our community."[22] The leadership in this effort was taken by W. W. Martin and Reverend Edward A. Tabor, the same two crusaders who had led the campaign to close the saloons in Conway. W. W. Martin pledged $10,000 immediately which "was thought to be the largest contribution by an Arkansan to higher education up to that time."[23] Martin added another $1,000 later and was joined by other residents of Conway, including Donaghey who pledged $1,500, one-third of his assets at the time.[24] All of the pledges were converted into a fund of $55,000, co-signed by Donaghey and others and guaranteed by a committee of which Donaghey was also a part. Donaghey later had to add another $750 to his original contribution.[25]

Conway had to compete with six other cities for Hendrix. Presentations were made on March 19–21, and all cities stressed the absence of saloons, a healthy environment, good road connections, and a large population in the area. One member of the Stuttgart delegation brought his son along who weighed over 300 pounds and who was presumably there to demonstrate the wholesome environment in Stuttgart, since he had been raised on milk furnished by cows that had grazed on the Grand Prairie.[26] An *Arkansas Gazette* reporter, obviously bored after so many presentations, said facetiously that each city claimed to have been the birthplace of Homer.[27] There were forty people in the Conway delegation, including W. W. Martin, Reverend Tabor, John Ingram, John Pence, and Donaghey. James Harrod made the appeal for Conway and pointed out that when donated land was counted as well as money, the citizens of Conway had pledged over $72,000 to secure Hendrix.[28] Harrod also emphasized that the saloons had been closed in Conway. This was a point made by all the cities, even Van Buren, which had saloons but promised to close them.[29] The attitude of higher education backers toward saloons is illustrated by a passage in the college catalogue when Hendrix was still in Altus that praised Altus because "the town was free of saloons, theatres, and other places so alluring and pernicious."[30]

After three days of turmoil and fifty-seven votes[31] (a two-thirds vote of the board was required) Conway was chosen by the Board of Trustees to be the permanent site of Hendrix. About seven hundred people were at the depot to greet the victorious Conway representatives, and a sign in the front of the depot said "$72,000—nothing cheap about Conway."[32] Reverend E. A. Tabor and W. W. Martin were seated in a double buggy, followed by the rest of the delegation in buggies, and bringing up the rear was a German brass band. Although Donaghey played a role in the successful campaign, it was minor compared with the efforts of Tabor and Martin. Donaghey served on the Hendrix board from 1906 until his death in 1937.

In the same year that Hendrix came to Conway, a committee had been appointed by the State Baptist Convention to look at the feasibility of establishing a "Female College" at some place in Arkansas. This committee reported to the 43d Annual Baptist State Convention at Arkadelphia in October of 1891 that a female college would be feasible. It recommended that a seven-person board be appointed as a board of trustees for the new college, with the power to solicit bids from interested localities and make the final decision as to site.[33] This recommendation was later adopted by the full convention. It is interesting to speculate how much, if any, of this Baptist activity was stimulated by the publicity surrounding Hendrix, since the Methodists and Baptists not only were the two largest denominations in Arkansas but "were rivals, so that almost any noteworthy move made by one group would be matched by the other."[34]

The procedure followed was very similar to that used for the selection of Hendrix. The main Conway booster was G. W. Bruce, a prominent attorney and Baptist in Conway who served as the first president of the board of trustees for Central Baptist College for Women. As before, a building committee was created to raise money for Conway's bid. Donaghey was a member and subscribed $5,000. In this case, Conway had to compete against three other cities, but their bid of $27,582 plus a guarantee from Bruce that the new college building would be furnished with everything required "except for carpets, chinaware, and pianos"[35] carried the day. In the spring of 1892, ground was broken for the foundations of the first building, and the first classes began in October of 1892, even though the building was unfinished.[36] Bruce personally guaranteed up to $30,000 that the subscribers would make their pledges.[37] Unfortunately, the depression of 1893 intervened, and Bruce suffered great financial losses. He undoubtedly played the major part in bringing Central Baptist College to Conway, and Donaghey's efforts, while increasing in significance, were still secondary.

The third college to find a home in Conway was the State Normal School (later State Teachers College, and still later, the University of Central Arkansas). It was founded some fifteen years after Central Baptist, and by this time Donaghey was a wealthy person, largely due to his railroad contracting in Oklahoma. Act 317 of 1907 created an Arkansas State Normal School with a board to be composed of seven people, four of whom would be appointed by the governor. The board was to ask for proposals from different parts of the state "provided that no donation shall be considered which does not include the offer of at least twenty acres of land . . . and the sum of fifteen thousand dollars ($15,000) for the construction of proper buildings. . . ."[38] and then decide which city had won.

Donaghey was the "executive manager of the organization that was formed to secure the college for Conway."[39] He met with ten leading citizens of Conway first without asking for money. Then he got the ten together again and $40,000 was raised in less than forty minutes, and still more was raised later.[40] Donaghey subsequently presided over a mass meeting at the Faulkner County courthouse[41] to raise subscriptions. Conway was competing with four other cities. When the board came to Conway on June 27, 1907, for its presentation, Donaghey made the case for Conway.[42] Conway's bid of $51,753 was the highest,[43] and once again, Conway triumphed "because it pledged more local support than its rivals."[44] Nolen Irby, the president of Arkansas State Teachers College in 1943, wrote a letter to Mrs. Donaghey asking her to come to Conway and celebrate Founder's Day. His letter said that "Governor Donaghey was perhaps the outstanding person in this matter."[45] There seems little reason to doubt Dr. Irby.

Conway's incredible achievement of snaring three colleges in seventeen years, in which Donaghey fully participated, must have left a strong impression on him. This feat is all the more impressive when it is realized that Conway's population in 1890 was 1,207, barely over 2,000 in 1900 and only 2,794 by 1910.[46] By 1907 the people of Conway had raised $139,000 for the three colleges—an amount nearly equal to half the assessed valuation of all real estate in Conway in 1905.[47] These successful undertakings undoubtedly reinforced Donaghey's confidence in himself and blended nicely into the Progressive outlook that all problems yield to investigation, study, and effort. His problem-solving and coalition-building skills were sharpened, and his belief in the positive effect of prohibition and higher education on a community surely became part of his political outlook. The remarkable civic spirit of Conway in completely changing the nature of the town was an example that inspired him to try to do the same thing for the state of Arkansas.

Work Outside Arkansas

By the time he was forty, Donaghey had achieved a reasonable degree of success as a builder and contractor in Conway. He began to branch out beyond Arkansas when his brother, Columbus, who lived in Longview, Texas, became very ill. Donaghey went to Longview to nurse him, probably in 1896 or early 1897. While helping to take care of his brother, Donaghey learned that a new courthouse was being planned there.

Longview, a small town of about two thousand, had floated a bond issue to build a new courthouse. In spite of the presence of twelve Texas contractors all bidding for the job, Donaghey was the low bidder and was awarded the contract for $27,450 on May 10, 1897.[48] Somehow, Donaghey managed to avoid lawsuits from the disappointed Texans, was not driven out of town, and even got other contracts in Longview.

The courthouse was completed in 1897 and is described in a history of Texas courthouses as "a two-story brick. . . . the contractor agreed to build. . . . and tear down the old one for $27,450."[49] Donaghey also built an annex to the State Mental Hospital in Terrell, Texas, in 1898. Donaghey stayed in Texas intermittently for two years (1897–1898) and made a profit there of $40,000.[50]

Donaghey returned to Conway after finishing his building projects in Texas. He had been there only a short time when he found that he had been recommended to F. A. Molitor, who was in charge of railroad construction for the Choctaw, Oklahoma, and Gulf Railroad (later to become the Rock Island). This was the time when the Oklahoma Territory was first opened to homesteaders and other settlers. The company was building a railroad from Little Rock west into Oklahoma, and "it needed depots, section houses, and other buildings along the route."[51] Molitor gave Donaghey his first assignment, building a section house near Shawnee, Oklahoma, with the understanding that if he passed this first test, he would then get more work. Donaghey met this first challenge easily, because being a railroad contractor "was the dream of every contractor"[52] and he was not going to miss the opportunity.

It is not possible to determine precisely how much time Donaghey spent on railroad work in Oklahoma, but he was in Oklahoma, off and on, from 1899 to 1903. The work consisted of constructing bridges, stations, section houses, water tanks, pipe lines, and stock pens. Donaghey especially enjoyed the erection of water tanks that held fifty thousand gallons. He had 150 to 200 men reporting to him and they would often work twenty to thirty miles ahead of the tracks. He didn't object to living in tents since "it was a rough virile life that had something of the exciting flavor of my Texas cowboy days."[53]

At one time or another in his railroad work, Donaghey had offices and depots at Oklahoma City, Muskogee, Tulsa, and Pawhuska in Oklahoma; McLain and Amarillo in Texas; Hartford and Fort Smith in Arkansas; and Silverdale in Kansas.[54] His extensive railroad work in these states is summarized by one historian, who said that "he was one of the principal contractors in the building of the Choctaw, Oklahoma, and Gulf Railroad (now a part of the Rock Island system); the Midland Valley Railroad from Oklahoma into Kansas; and the Hot Springs branch of the Chicago, Rock Island, and Pacific, which runs between Benton and Hot Springs."[55] With his usual drive and energy and his increasing skills in building construction, Donaghey mastered railroad building. When he left Oklahoma, he was a highly successful contractor who was also much wealthier than he had been when he had first entered the Sooner state. Even with this lucrative performance in Oklahoma, he still was not satisfied with his work, because as he said, "I realized that this railroad construction was only an interlude in my life, and that even yet I was not in the right niche."[56]

While still in Oklahoma, Donaghey was the low bidder ($100,000) on the contract to construct the Washington County courthouse in Fayetteville. The cornerstone was laid on October 1, 1904; Congressman Hugh Dinsmore gave a speech, and the University of Arkansas cadets were present at the ceremony.[57] The plaque on the courthouse today lists Charles Thompson as the architect and George W. Donaghey as the builder. At about this same time, Donaghey was again successful as a low bidder for six buildings to be erected on the University of Arkansas campus in 1905. The buildings included Ella Carnall Hall for girls ($35,000), Gray Hall for boys ($20,000), a chemistry building ($18,000), an agriculture building ($9,000), a dairy building ($5,000), and an infirmary ($5,000).[58] Gray Hall and the dairy building have been torn down, but the remainder of the buildings still exist.[59]

Politics in Conway

During the ten-year period from 1880 to 1890, Conway evolved from a frontier village with a rough railroad heritage to a city whose future direction was shaped by the acquisition of two colleges and the imposition of city prohibition. Although there is disagreement among Conway historians as to the degree of influence exercised over city politics by saloons and saloon keepers in the 1880s, they do agree that saloons were an integral part of Conway. There were five licensed saloons in the city of one thousand people, and Conway at one time was no different from other frontier towns in America where "life . . . was boisterous, rugged, and dangerous, and no institution in that bygone era more aptly fits that description than the American saloon."[60]

Conway in the 1880s was little changed from the town that Donaghey had first seen ten years earlier. The streets were muddy when it rained, dusty when dry, with "no sewers and no healthful water supply"[61] and hogs and other livestock wandered through the streets. These were manageable problems compared with Conway's major problem—"the dominance of the liquor and gambling interests. With five licensed saloons in the town, open gambling, public drunkenness, and street brawling marred Conway's reputation. In addition, the liquor interests also dominated both city and county politics."[62] One writer even described Conway, at one time, as having "had more saloons than churches."[63]

Many of these descriptions may be exaggerated, but there seemed to be general agreement that Conway was a wild and disorderly town, and many people began to take steps to correct what they viewed as a harmful environment. In 1884 the Union Sunday School Convention was organized, consisting of one representative from each of the city's church denominations. The mission of this organization was to fight liquor, gambling, and other societal evils. They were aided in their fight by two laws dealing with the liquor question—one requiring the question of prohibition to be present on the ballot in every township or city ward at every general election[64] and the other, and more important law for Conway, prohibited the sale of alcoholic beverages within a three-mile radius of a church or public school when petitions to that effect were signed by a majority of the adult inhabitants of the area.[65] This second act was called the "three mile" law, and unlike most Arkansas statutes of that historical period, "adult" inhabitants rather than only "male" inhabitants could sign and present petitions.

A campaign was started against the saloons in 1884. Donaghey was part of the movement and was elected town marshal in 1884.[66] As town marshal, he would patrol the streets from eight o'clock in the evening until eleven making sure that the drunks were kept within civilized bounds. There were few lights on the streets, and the stores barricaded their doors with huge padlocks every night. "Walking home, by lantern, one would not see another human being even though the hour be short of nine,"[67] but it is hoped, a sense of security was present since "George W. Donaghey was . . . protecting the public peace each evening from eight till eleven."[68]

Donaghey apparently ran for mayor one year later, in 1885 on the anti-saloon ticket, but was defeated.[69] Unfortunately, there are no accounts of that race, either official or unofficial, but according to Donaghey, the drys did increase their vote.[70] There is an incident connected with this unsuccessful campaign that shows, on occasion, that Donaghey would lose control, and his "Irish" temper would take charge. There was a sizeable German population in Conway in the 1880s[71] who not only voted wet but organized a brass band on election night to serenade the person who had defeated Donaghey.[72] Since the winner lived near Donaghey, the band disturbed Donaghey's rest, and the next morning when he was approached to contribute a quarter to meet the expenses of the band, he was not in a mood to be magnanimous. The man who approached Donaghey asking for the gift had been a supporter of Donaghey's opponent. Donaghey must have interpreted this as ridicule or taunting, because as described by Donaghey "a sheet of fire seemed to flame behind my eyes. The next moment my tormentor was lying in the gutter. I had knocked him down. I was ashamed of it afterwards. But I believe he had it coming. . . ."[73] The man later sued Donaghey for five thousand dollars but lost the suit.[74]

The campaign to close the saloons in Conway was aided immeasurably by the arrival on the scene in 1887 of Reverend Edward A. Tabor, who was the new minister of the First Methodist Church in Conway. Tabor joined W. W. Martin and others in an organized effort to shut down the saloons. Public irritation was rising as drunken men were "reeling and fighting in the streets,"[75] and gambling was carried on in the rear of the saloons. As has been noted earlier, there is a disagreement among Conway historians about whether Conway was controlled by the liquor interests. One school of thought was that the "politics of the town and county [was] under complete domination of the liquor interests."[76] The other point of view was that Conway was not controlled by the liquor interests, but that once their livelihood was threatened, they were prepared to fight.[77] Both views agreed that the frontier tradition was still strong in Conway and a rough and noisy environment was often present. One resident, who was a young girl at the time, recalled Saturday night as a particularly bad time since the men from the surrounding area came in to visit the saloons. She spent "many Saturday nights hiding under the bed in fear as she heard the country men staggering up and down the railroad tracks . . . singing at the tops of their intoxicated lungs."[78]

Tabor intended to use the three mile law with the help of Martin and others, including Donaghey, to prohibit the sale of alcoholic beverages in Conway. There was a small four-room schoolhouse located about half a dozen blocks from the center of town, next to Tabor's First Methodist Church. Tabor circulated petitions to prohibit the sale of liquor within three miles of the schoolhouse. He received valuable assistance in this petition drive from women in the area who could not vote but could sign petitions. In part, the drive went smoothly since "most Conway residents had grown weary of the saloons and the problems they brought with them"[79] and because "the steadily growing influence of the more progressive and civic-minded element in the town's population had gathered enough strength by 1888 to assert its will in the face of opposing forces which had dominated the town from the beginning and which had never been seriously challenged."[80]

Even though Tabor had little trouble in obtaining enough signatures, there was some personal danger involved since at one time W. W. Martin allegedly "faced a drawn and loaded pistol."[81] Martin, however, could cope with such crises because he carried a navy 45 caliber pistol to protect himself.[82] The petitions were challenged, but the circuit court on August 8, 1888, held for the petitioners, finding that a majority of the adult inhabitants living within three miles of the schoolhouse had signed valid petitions and that liquor could not be sold for two years within three miles of the schoolhouse.[83] The two-year limit was required by the Local Option Law of 1879. However, saloon keepers with valid licenses were allowed to operate until December 31, 1888, but at midnight on that date "the saloons closed their doors and never reopened."[84] An *Arkansas Gazette* correspondent reporting from Conway said that "the contest over the whiskey business here has been very bitter, and it is with some relief that we view the end of it."[85]

What can be seen in this battle over saloons in Conway, Arkansas, is the Progressive movement in miniature. Nationally, it was a movement led by middle-class business and professional people who were residents of small towns or cities. They wanted to reform the political system, purify politics, and conserve human and natural resources. More specifically, they hoped to rid the big cities of their corrupt political machines, which were often supported and maintained by the saloon keepers and the liquor interests. One way to do this was by enactment of local and later national prohibition. The urban middle-class reformers were joined in this effort by churches, women, and teachers.

Conway fits this model in most respects. Businessmen like W. W. Martin, John Pence, and Donaghey were active in the reform cause as well as church groups, ministers, and women. The reformers viewed the liquor and gambling establishments as impediments to the growth of a well-run and progressive town. They felt that the prohibition campaign would rescue Conway from the clutches of evil saloon keepers and their allies and restore a normal and healthy environment where human potential would not be wasted in drinking and gambling. The campaign was successful, and national Progressives could point to Conway as a model city where the ideas of the Progressive philosophy had been tested and found successful. The closing of the saloons helped produce a sea change in Conway. Within three years, the two largest religious denominations in Arkansas would both have colleges in Conway. Conway "had rather suddenly obtained a reputation for culture and progressiveness which was recognized and respected throughout the state."[86]

The impact on Donaghey of this successful battle must have been profound. He had been a member of a group that had challenged entrenched interests who had insisted that driving the saloons out of Conway would bankrupt the city. He had seen a linking of prohibition and higher education with great benefits for his home town. Undoubtedly, both prohibition and higher education now ranked even higher in his personal scale of values. In a tribute written in 1915 to W. W. Martin for his role in the reform movement and bringing Hendrix to Conway, Donaghey said that "a well endowed college has proven to be the most permanent as it is the most productive institution of man."[87] Donaghey also must have been impressed with the way in which politics in his town had been purified, another Progressive theme. This may have been the starting point for his strong support of initiative and referendum, which was quite unusual in the South. Initiative and referendum were devices that Progressives hoped would keep politics permanently purified since the people could use it any time they wished. Lastly, Donaghey surely must have drawn inspiration and optimism for the future from this exhilarating experience that saw a town reverse directions and undergo real and lasting change. He may have thought—if it's possible in Conway, why not Arkansas?

FOUR

The First Term (1909–1910)

Donaghey's success as a building contractor in Arkansas, Texas, and Oklahoma made him a wealthy man. His wealth attracted considerable attention in the state's political community since Donaghey had some interest in politics and was a person who might be willing to spend money on campaigns. He was appointed in 1899 to the first State Capitol Commission by Governor Dan Jones. This appointment and Donaghey's highly publicized criticisms of the way in which the state capitol was being constructed made him a potential candidate for some statewide office. The building of the state capitol itself and Donaghey's involvement with that project are subjects too detailed and too complicated to include here in the text so they are included in an appendix at the end of this book.

The state capitol was probably the most influential factor in Donaghey's decision to run for governor and must have outweighed everything else. In a way, a political career seemed unsuited to Donaghey's skills and temperament. He could not speak well in public; he did not have that outgoing "back-slapping personality" often associated with politicians; he had a temper; and his tendency was to pursue the immediate objective to the exclusion of all else.

On the other hand, he was not a stranger to politics since he had run for office in Conway and was an active participant in the Conway liquor battles. Since 1905 Donaghey had been the most outspoken critic of the state capitol venture. He denounced the cost, the materials used, the length of time that construction was taking, and the building expertise and even the integrity of Caldwell and Drake, the contractors for the state capitol. There had been much press comment about how the state capitol would be the most important issue in the 1908 campaign[1] and that a businessman was needed to bring some order and efficiency to the state.[2] At any rate, Donaghey decided to run.

The political climate in the state approaching the 1908 election favored the candidacy of someone like Donaghey. Many unforeseen events also helped prepare the way. Governor John S. Little, who had been elected with the support of Governor Jeff Davis in 1906, suffered a "mental and physical collapse"[3] on the second day after his inauguration in January of 1907. X. O. Pindall became president of the Arkansas Senate in May of 1907 and served as acting governor for most of the remainder of Little's term. Pindall, who had run for attorney general in 1906, had a long-standing grudge against Jeff Davis who had backed William Kirby for attorney general. Kirby, with Davis's support, won the nomination at the state Democratic Convention in June of 1906, which was the way party candidates were still selected until 1908. Pindall's defeat was particularly galling since he had a ten thousand popular vote majority in the counties that held elections and elected their convention delegates by popular vote.[4] Donaghey benefitted greatly from having a confirmed anti-Davis man in the governor's mansion during most of 1907 and 1908.

Davis and his supporters had been planning for the 1908 election since the spring, when Governor Little seemed unlikely to recover from his illness. They discussed several candidates, including Donaghey who had helped Davis both financially and personally in 1905.[5] In fact, Davis opened his campaign for senator on July 6, 1905, in Conway[6] and mentioned Donaghey at that time as being "a man who has stood lone-handed and fought the biggest gang of grafters and thieves that ever invaded our state. He has saved the taxpayers of Arkansas hundreds and thousands of dollars."[7] In case there was any doubt about who the person was, Davis ended his comment by saying, "I refer to honest George Donaghey of your own city."[8] Davis's reference was to Donaghey's opposition in 1905 to a special appropriation of $800,000 (SB 370) requested by Caldwell and Drake to complete the state capitol.

Despite these flattering remarks made in 1905, Davis chose William F. Kirby, the attorney general, to receive his endorsement. Kirby had a progressive record as both a representative and a senator, and as attorney general he tried faithfully to enforce the antitrust legislation that Davis had championed so vigorously when he was attorney general and governor. Davis also needed someone he could trust, because, as a U.S. senator, he would be spending much time in Washington, and "Kirby was loyal to a fault."[9] Donaghey was much more independent, and he and Davis had had disagreements in the past over the state capitol. Kirby was a poor speaker,[10] but so was Donaghey, and Davis could tour the state and compensate for Kirby's mediocre platform manner. Davis "not only wanted to see Kirby elected, he also wanted to demonstrate his power to sway the electorate. If he could save Kirby and destroy Donaghey, the boys at the county courthouses would think twice before they challenged his authority again."[11] Davis's choice of Kirby would turn out to be a blessing in disguise for Donaghey, who now made his campaign against Davis and machine politics rather than against Kirby.

There were other factors that made it easy for George Donaghey to run in addition to a possible "complete-the-capitol" campaign. He was, relatively speaking, a political amateur, which was a nice contrast to the character assassination and unsubstantiated charges which were the stock-in-trade of many Arkansas politicians. He was also a businessman and builder, an ideal background for anyone who pledged to clean up the state capitol mess. His career as a businessman seemed to hit just the right idealistic note and separated him from the professional office seekers. Donaghey's business success also meant that financing a campaign was not a problem. The *Arkansas Democrat* in an editorial on September 15, 1907, thought that the state needed to elect more successful businessmen "who are not chronic seekers after office, making office-holding a vocation. The businessman may not be able to make as great a speech on the hustings as the politician who does very little else, but he will more closely safeguard the interests of the state, the county, or the city."

Another significant influence on Donaghey's decision to enter the race was Ben Griffin and the Farmers' Educational and Cooperative Union of America. The Farmers' Union was begun in Texas, and the first local was established in Arkansas in 1903.[12] Griffin was the secretary-treasurer of the group. Its first statewide meeting was held in Hot Springs in 1905, at which time it claimed 50,000 members in Arkansas.[13] Griffin had once been a supporter of Davis,[14] but as was often the case, there had been a disagreement and a parting of the ways. Griffin was also a close friend of Donaghey, and Donaghey was invited to speak to the 1906 meeting of the Farmers' Union on the topic of the state capitol.[15] By 1906 the Farmers' Union had 1,831 active chapters in the state and 64,085 members.[16]

At about the same time, Griffin must have transferred fully to the Donaghey camp. Sometime in 1906 or 1907, the office of the Farmers' Union was moved from Little Rock to Conway into free office space provided by the Conway Chamber of Commerce. One writer about the Farmers' Union said that "some political understandings were involved in the move"[17] because Donaghey was preparing to run for governor. Donaghey gave the welcoming address to the group when it met in 1907 for its annual meeting in Conway.[18] He also eagerly embraced one of the main projects of the Farmers' Union, the establishment of four agricultural schools[19] in the state, and made it part of his platform. Although the Farmers' Union as a group had a policy of not endorsing political candidates, Griffin made his own personal preferences clear and was the first to announce that Donaghey would be a candidate for governor.[20] This enthusiastic political help from Griffin and the distinct possibility of many members of Arkansas' largest and fastest-growing agricultural organization looking with favor on his candidacy certainly encouraged Donaghey.

The relationship with organized labor developed favorably along the same lines. Just as in the case of the Farmers' Union, the State Federation of Labor could not endorse individual candidates, but L. H. Moore, secretary-treasurer of the State Federation, was as strong for Donaghey[21] as Ben Griffin of the Farmers' Union. Labor was interested in an initiative and referendum amendment to the state constitution,[22] which became another one of Donaghey's platform planks. The State Federation also favored agricultural schools as did the Farmers' Union, and as time went on, a close working relationship developed between the Farmers' Union and the State Federation of Labor.[23]

Donaghey was, of course, eager for the reaction of his friends and associates in Conway. According to Bruce Bullion, Jr., son of Donaghey's private secretary and chief of staff, Donaghey approached the Frauenthal law firm in Conway,[24] which included Bruce Bullion, Sr., a young and politically active lawyer who had been chair of the Faulkner County Democratic Committee. Sam Frauenthal (later appointed to the Arkansas Supreme Court by Donaghey in 1909) and Bullion both agreed to do what they could for Donaghey. It is quite likely that other friends from Conway, such as W. W. Martin, John Pence, James Harrod, H. B.

Ingram, J. H. Hartje, and Frank Robins participated. Donaghey gave special credit to Jo Frauenthal, brother of Sam Frauenthal, and a successful department store owner and banker. Jo Frauenthal had moved to Conway about two weeks before Donaghey and in 1907 was at the top of the Conway power structure. After Donaghey met with Jo Frauenthal about running for governor, they decided to call in others to get their reaction. Jo Frauenthal had "caused lots of men to do things because he believed they could do them,"[25] and if Jo Frauenthal believed that Donaghey could be elected, "they all got to believing it and then the whole of Conway got to believing it and then Faulkner County and it then spread out over the state and the thing was done."[26] Donaghey expressed his gratitude to Jo Frauenthal in a letter some thirty years later—with a little dig at the end—when he said, "It was your brains and master judgment that directed the campaign which put me in the Governor's Office. Aside from that, our association has been long and pleasant."[27]

Donaghey announced that he would run for governor on September 7, 1907.[28] In his statement, he said that he had never been an office seeker or a politician, would be a strong friend of education, would run primarily on the issue of the state capitol, and that he believed "in the old Democratic doctrine of the greatest good to the greatest number and special privileges to none."[29] His campaign was to open in Morrilton on October 7.

Before the Morrilton speech, R. W. McFarlane, who had announced for governor on September 11, had written to the other candidates (Kirby and Donaghey were candidates in the Democratic primary by that time) asking them to join in a joint canvass or debate. This was the customary method of campaigning in Arkansas. Donaghey responded by declining to join the canvass and gave as his reasons the possibility that other candidates would soon enter the race and that he had already scheduled a formal opening for Morrilton on October 7.[30] The real reason was that he could not yet speak well, and he emphasized this in responding to the request from Morrilton that he open his campaign there. He said, "I am not an orator, have never studied that art . . . I am only a plain businessman and can make no claim to the distinction of a platform entertainer or a great political spellbinder."[31] He made this apology in advance so that no one would be disappointed. By the decision to avoid joint canvassing or debating, Donaghey gave his opponents an issue that they would use effectively against him, but he felt that this was a risk that had to be taken.

Donaghey had decided to open his campaign for governor at Morrilton in Conway County in response to petitions signed by 500 people living in the area.[32] The Morrilton and Conway bands were to be there, six thousand pounds of meat were to be roasted, and 6,000 to 8,000 people were expected, including 250 from Conway.[33] Unfortunately for Donaghey, it rained all night on October 6 and intermittently the next day. The Conway *Log Cabin Democrat* estimated that the rain had driven away about 75 percent of the crowd[34] so that only a few thousand remained. Among them was Senator Jeff Davis who "listened attentively to Donaghey's speech,"[35] which lasted approximately two hours.

Donaghey's speech was vintage southern Progressive as he called for abolishing the convict lease system and putting the convicts to work on the public roads, establishing agricultural schools since "we can never have a great people without excellent schools,"[36] enacting initiative and referendum, no retreating on antitrust legislation, and completing the state capitol in twelve months. He defended labor unions, stating that "the right to strike is as sacred as the right to work."[37] His most inflamed rhetoric was directed at the state capitol commissioners, the architect, and the contractors on the state capitol job—all of whom he felt should be discharged. He concluded his remarks on the state capitol by pledging to the taxpayers of the state to keep watch on the capitol job until it was "redeemed from the unscrupulous grafters who are now in charge of it."[38]

In a more general sense, Donaghey said that he was not identified with any faction in the state Democratic party, sought nothing beyond the office of governor, and stood for a much needed businessman's administration. The *Arkansas Gazette* commented in an editorial on October 9, 1907, that Donaghey had opened his campaign with a businesslike statement of his platform, and despite the reduced attendance because of rain, his "campaign was successfully launched."

William Kirby, who had been elected attorney general in 1906 with Jeff Davis's support and probably could have had another term as attorney general, decided instead to announce for governor on September 1.[39] He had served in both the Arkansas House of Representatives and the Arkansas Senate as a representative from Miller County and was generally thought of as a Progressive. Kirby favored abolishing the system of convict leasing, completing the state capitol speedily, and changing the management of the penitentiary. He was supported fully by Senator Davis, which turned out to be his greatest asset and greatest liability at the same time.

R. W. McFarlane from Sebastian County, a member of the State Capitol Commission and a close friend of Governor Little, announced on September 11.[40] He also wanted to eliminate the leasing of convicts, supported the agricultural schools, and promised that "the next regular session of the Arkansas legislature will be held in a completed new state capitol building."[41] Because of his membership on the State Capitol Commission, McFarlane had to defend the commission, and to a lesser extent, the contractors who worked under their guidance and control. He became the champion of the status quo, and the state capitol was a clear-cut issue between him and Donaghey.

A surprise entry into the race was John H. Hinemon, a former school superintendent and state superintendent of public instruction for five years, who was the president of Henderson College in Arkadelphia. Hinemon announced on September 22.[42] Like the other candidates, he wanted the agricultural schools, speedy completion of the capitol, and an end to convict leasing. In addition, he urged more liberal appropriations for the university and the state charitable institutions. Newspaper accounts indicated that he was not in the same mold as the "bucket and bile" politicians and was not inclined to resort to character assassinations and half-truths.[43]

There was speculation in late September that Judge W. M. Kavanaugh, president of the Southern Trust Company, would file for governor, but he decided not to join the contest. His decision not to run helped Donaghey more than the other candidates, since Kavanaugh would also have campaigned on the "businessman is needed" theme.

Hinemon, Kirby, and McFarlane campaigned together and debated each other, and Donaghey took his lumps, since he was not on the stump with them. Not appearing with the other candidates allowed Donaghey to "campaign after his own style, under his own arrangements, and without the aid or consent of any other candidates on or off the earth."[44] Although he spoke often throughout the state, Donaghey still preferred to use printed material since "oratory takes away from the facts."[45] Reprints of speeches, platforms, and newspaper clippings were "sent out in large quantities usually by the tens, twenties, or even hundreds to trusted lieutenants all over the state to be placed where it will do the most good."[46] He opened two headquarters, one in Conway and one in Little Rock, and put Judge Frank Millwee of Monroe County and Bruce Bullion in charge.

Until the middle of January, Kirby, Hinemon, and McFarlane still campaigned together and debated each other at various courthouses. Early in the campaign, Davis expressed his support for Kirby by asking a farm group in White County in October to do all they could for Kirby since he was "the best man in the race."[47] In January Davis announced that he would spend a month in the state making speeches for Kirby, beginning at Ozark on February 17 and concluding in Little Rock on March 24. It was actually to be a thirty-six-day effort at fifty-seven locations in the state.[48]

Once Davis returned from Washington and began his whirlwind tour for Kirby, the joint campaign involving Hinemon, McFarlane, and Kirby was called off, but it continued until a few days before Davis's Ozark speech. All three candidates criticized Donaghey for spending too much money and for failing to debate. Kirby stressed that it had been his opinion in August of 1907, later sustained by the Arkansas Supreme Court that had stopped the construction on the state capitol, and although he wanted the capitol completed, he wanted it done by honest men. He also urged a three-person penitentiary commission and an office of lieutenant governor. McFarlane defended the construction of the state capitol and the State Capitol Commission. Hinemon pushed state support for high schools, maintained a dignified demeanor on the stump, and complained that there was "an ugly and unseemly wrangle between Kirby, Donaghey, and McFarlane, charge and counter-charge are made. The people are tired of such campaigning."[49]

In late December of 1907, an incident happened that showed that Davis's heretofore unbeatable political magic was wearing thin and his attempt to dictate state politics from Washington was creating hostility instead of acquiescence. A group of Davis's supporters from east Arkansas, which had always been a Davis stronghold, met with him on December 28, 1907,[50] to express their strong reservations about his support for Hal Norwood in the race for attorney general. Davis was supporting Norwood and also J. C. Clary for secretary of state because of the influence of those offices on the Penitentiary Board and the Board of Election Commissioners. This east Arkansas delegation was backing P. R. Andrews of Augusta for attorney general and resented Davis's interference.

According to one newspaper account, Davis was told to "go back to Washington and keep up the good work in the United States Senate, but keep your hands off state politics and let someone else have a chance."[51] A member of the delegation was quoted as saying in even stronger terms that there needed "to be a change from the style of politics that has prevailed in recent years. The backwoods element has dominated politics long enough."[52] Shocked by this rebellion in his heartland, Davis agreed to stay out of the attorney general's contest.

The very next day another delegation from east Arkansas met with Davis about the same issue and must have driven the point home. The second delegation asked him to keep out of the governor's race altogether, indicated that they favored P. R. Andrews for attorney general, and urged him to stop interfering with the policies of acting-Governor Pindall who was from Desha County in eastern Arkansas. The *Arkansas Democrat* summarized the serious message of the two delegations to Davis as a warning that his political machine in east Arkansas was "broken and there is evidence that it will be permanently ruptured if he does not wash his hands of state politics . . ."[53]

The threat from east Arkansas caused Davis to modify his tactics only slightly. He left the attorney general's race alone but still campaigned vigorously for his candidate for secretary of state and pulled out all the stops for Kirby and against Donaghey. Davis made a famous speech at Ozark on February 18, 1908, which was the beginning of his campaign for Kirby and a pivotal event in the governor's race. It was a typical Davis performance in which he attacked not only Donaghey, McFarlane, and Hinemon, but also Ben Griffin, O. C. Ludwig (candidate for secretary of state), Pindall, and others. His endorsement of Kirby was strong and unequivocal; Kirby was "the only candidate in the race who would carry out the policies and principles of government which I have inaugurated."[54]

As was his custom, Davis savaged his enemies, and Donaghey, despite his past support for the senator, was now a member of that class. Donaghey "had an itching palm to get charge of the Statehouse contract,"[55] and was "flooding the State with his literature, written by paid attorneys, not willing to meet his opponents on the stump in open, fair discussion."[56] Davis wanted to know how anyone could trust Donaghey who was "worth $500,000 . . . and had never yet in any contract that he has ever had employed union labor as his workmen."[57] He portrayed

Donaghey as a "political novice who lacked the manhood to meet his opponents in fair open debate."[58] Even if elected, "Donaghey would be as perfectly controlled by the ringsters and politicians of Little Rock . . . as your little boy would be controlled by you."[59]

Donaghey countered these charges in two effective ways. One was to challenge Davis directly about these accusations as Davis was speaking. Donaghey stood up and said that the charge about never employing union labor was false and was being spread by carpenters working for Caldwell and Drake. He also said that he had never been in business with Thomas Cox, a Little Rock lobbyist, as Davis was charging.[60] In both cases, the crowd was with Donaghey when he interrupted Davis and shouted, "Hurray for Donaghey. . . ."[61] This was not really a debate with Davis, but it served to refute the charge that Donaghey was afraid to debate, particularly when the headline in the *Arkansas Democrat* on February 18, 1908, was "Donaghey Defies Davis."

The second way in which Donaghey challenged Davis was to make the race between himself and Davis rather than between himself and Kirby, the Davis surrogate. After the Ozark speech, Donaghey portrayed himself as one man fighting an entrenched political machine.

Davis reprinted 100,000 copies of his Ozark speech,[62] and that was only the beginning. "For six weeks Davis stormed across the state, venting his spleen at Donaghey, the trusts, the penitentiary ring, and other enemies of Jeff Davisism."[63] Davis did not travel with Kirby, but Kirby quit the joint campaigning with McFarlane and Hinemon after the Ozark speech.[64] The campaign accelerated after the Ozark speech to such an extent that R. W. McFarlane, the state capitol commissioner, withdrew on February 29 with a blast at Donaghey for setting such a demanding financial pace. McFarlane said that he had already spent $1,500 and would have to spend $4,000 more to still be a serious contender.[65] His leaving the contest was not unexpected, and it was generally thought that he was running last.[66] Officially, McFarlane did not endorse any of his opponents, but it was assumed that unofficially he would try to swing his support against Donaghey and probably for Hinemon.[67]

Perhaps sensing momentum from McFarlane's retirement from the primary, Hinemon began to emphasize statewide prohibition as an issue. Donaghey was equivocal on this issue, apparently at one time supporting both nationwide and statewide prohibition,[68] but later pulling back to a more defensible position of being willing to sign a statewide prohibition bill if the legislature passed it. He also recalled his role in the Conway prohibition fight.[69]

The campaign continued with Davis and Kirby attacking Donaghey for his refusal to debate and for the money he was spending. Donaghey in turn assailed Kirby because he accepted Davis's support, and Hinemon because he would allow Caldwell and Drake to finish the state capitol contract and was splitting the anti-Davis vote. Hinemon blistered Donaghey for his unclear stand on prohibition and saw himself as the courageous warrior against the Davis political machine and the Donaghey money machine. Donaghey was worried about a late surge on Hinemon's part. To help meet this problem, an advertisement was placed in the *Arkansas Gazette* on March 22, signed by several prominent people, such as ex-Governor Dan Jones, Ashley Cockrill, W. L. Terry, and Thomas McRae. The advertisement said that the signers were switching from Hinemon to Donaghey because he was the only person who could beat Kirby.

A variety of campaigning techniques were used in 1908. Most of the state was covered either in a joint canvass such as that by Kirby, Hinemon, and McFarlane, or individually as was the case with Donaghey. Speeches would usually last at least forty-five minutes and often as long as two hours. They were normally held in the county courthouse or one of the local schools. The number of speeches per day increased as election day came closer. In the closing days of a primary election, a candidate might make four to five speeches a day. Donaghey complained about the number of speeches he had to make because his throat was often sore and he needed two shirts for every speech.[70]

Donaghey's real love was "literature" which in this case meant speeches and pamphlets. Speeches often had grandiose titles, such as "Shot and Shell from the Fortress of Truth."[71] But Donaghey distributed these speeches and other printed matter in quantities never seen before.[72] The pamphlets, speeches, and platforms were given out personally by volunteer and paid workers in each county. In addition, candidates acquired mailing lists of voters, often approaching 140,000 to 150,000 names. A mailing of 150,000 letters or speeches with a one-cent stamp cost $1500. This was called a "swing"[73] and had to be done two or three times during a campaign. More elaborate mailings with a personal letter and a sealed envelope cost four cents per letter, but most swings cost one cent or two cents per speech. In the 1908 campaign, Donaghey used the

Conway post office for most of his mailings. This gave the postmaster at Conway a raise in salary, since Conway was a post office in which salary was based on the volume of mail.[74]

Newspaper advertising was also used extensively by all the candidates, beginning usually about six weeks before election day. A full-page advertisement in the *Arkansas Gazette* or *Arkansas Democrat* cost eighty dollars. Such campaign advertisements almost always contained a picture of the candidate and a message. Quite often, editorials from newspapers that endorsed the candidate were included. Cartooning was not that popular, but the *Arkansas Gazette* did run a series of political cartoons, including one for each candidate. The cartoon about Kirby, for example, had him labeled "The Jeff Davis Candidate," and pictured him working a machine cranking out opinions underneath a big picture of Jeff Davis.[75]

The amount of money spent by the candidates for the office of governor in the 1908 primary is not known exactly. Listing of campaign expenditures was not required until two years later. There are some educated guesses, however. The deputy superintendent of education, W. A. Crawford, who could be regarded as a neutral and impartial source, estimated that the three candidates for governor spent a total of $50,000 with one candidate alone spending $30,000.[76] This candidate was obviously Donaghey. Some supporters of Hinemon ran an advertisement after the election was over asking that people contribute toward a goal of $10,000 to help Hinemon pay his expenses.[77] It can be assumed from this that Hinemon spent at least $10,000 in his unsuccessful race. McFarlane left the contest because he thought $1500 was too much. The *Arkansas Democrat* editorialized on August 9, 1908, about the amount of money that had been spent and noted "that some defeated candidates in the last election spent nearly $10,000 while the amounts spent by some of the successful ones are really stupendous." If Donaghey did spend $30,000 in the 1908 Democratic primary, and that seems to be a good estimate, the amount would translate into $351,000 in 1990,[78] which seems fairly reasonable until one considers that in 1908 there was no radio, television, or public opinion polling to consume the budget.

The Democratic primary was on March 25. Frank Millwee, Donaghey's campaign manager, made a pre-election forecast that was close to the mark. He predicted, assuming a total vote of 125,000, that Donaghey would have 62,000 (49 percent), Kirby 40,000 (32 percent), and Hinemon 23,000 (18 percent).[79] The actual results, with a total vote of 133,838, were Donaghey 55,589 (42 percent), Kirby 41,745 (31 percent), and Hinemon 36,504 (27 percent).[80] Donaghey led from the very beginning, and the early returns left little doubt that he would win the nomination. Another even surer indication was that the first baby born in the state was named for him on March 28[81] (George Washington Wells) even though the final vote was not yet in. Donaghey was delighted that his home county of Faulkner gave him a vote of 92.4 percent (Donaghey: 2,767; Kirby: 183; Hinemon: 43).[82] O. C. Ludwig was also elected secretary of state in preference to the Davis-backed candidate. The only encouragement that Davis and his followers could draw from the results was the election of Hal Norwood as attorney general, and even he distanced himself from Davis as the campaign progressed.[83]

Donaghey carried forty-eight of seventy-five counties, took Davis's east Arkansas stronghold by carrying Mississippi, Poinsett, Crittenden, St. Francis, Lee, Phillips, Desha, and Chicot while losing only Craighead and Cross. Donaghey also won twelve of the sixteen Ozark Mountain counties[84] and added the four largest urban counties, Pulaski, Sebastian, Jefferson, and Garland. Davis's biographer described the 1908 primary as "a bitter pill for Davis to swallow. More than a third of the Old Guard [strong Davis supporters] had ignored his advice and voted for Donaghey and Ludwig. Although most farm voters had kept the faith, village and town voters had defected in droves."[85]

The normal concession statements were made by Kirby and Hinemon congratulating Donaghey and pledging support to him in the state general election in September. Jeff Davis also congratulated Donaghey and pledged support, and then in a typical Davis ploy, he tried to place a self-serving interpretation on the outcome. His telegram to Donaghey stated that he was pleased with the results and if the statements of some of the candidates in the race were to be believed, it was "simply a choice between two Jeff Davis men—yourself and Kirby, I selected one Jeff Davis man and the people selected the other which [sic] they thought to be a Jeff Davis man. I bow to the will of the people."[86] The two Jeff Davis men had reference to a campaign theme by Hinemon that because of Donaghey's past support of Davis there were two Davis supporters in the race. Donaghey responded to this distorted reading of the election results by Davis with the statement, "I wear no man's collar."[87]

Newspaper reaction to the primary ranged from almost ecstatic to just favorable. The *Log Cabin Democrat* in Conway, as might be expected, congratulated Donaghey for his splendid support in Faulkner County and said that "Davisism will never again be an issue in a state campaign. Arkansas has been redeemed."[88] This redemption theme was also expressed in a telegram from a Donaghey voter in Clarendon to Donaghey headquarters in Little Rock; it read, "Hail Donaghey for us as the modern Moses who delivers the children of Arkansas out of the bondage of the Davis ring."[89] Some time later, an editorial in the *Arkansas Democrat* on August 4, 1908, entitled "The Carpenter from Conway," expressed the opinion, "The people have spoken, and in the carpenter rests the hope of their emancipation from bad politics and worse politicians." The *Arkansas Gazette* was more restrained, and after congratulating Hinemon for a good showing, it commended Donaghey for his stand against Davis and his machine and predicted that Donaghey "will be one of the most popular candidates that has ever been put at the head of a state ticket."[90]

In the absence of public-opinion poll taking it is difficult to say what issues or events played the biggest role in Donaghey's victory. A variety of factors contributed: the support of Ben Griffin of the Farmers' Union and L. H. Moore of the State Federation of Labor, which meant voting strength in both those organizations; the working arrangement with Ludwig and acting-Governor Pindall, which helped hasten the break between Davis and his followers in east Arkansas; Donaghey's wealth, which made possible the distribution of thousands of pieces of literature that assisted greatly in giving him political visibility and name identification (he probably outspent his nearest rival by three to one); the fine organizational job done by Millwee and Bullion; the appeal of a businessman and a contractor who made credible promises to run the state efficiently and finish the capitol; the need for stability after a string of six governors and acting governors in two years, and the doubt as to whether a Davis-endorsed candidate or a political unknown could provide that; and the denominational gratitude that Donaghey had earned through his efforts on behalf of Hendrix and Central Baptist colleges and his active participation in the Methodist church.

There was also the political attractiveness of a non-political, non-office-holding amateur who was obviously not a professional politician and who identified with the progressive trends of his day and had the good political instincts and judgment to focus his campaign on the state capitol and opposition to Jeff Davis, the boss of an infamous machine.

After listing all these presumably causative factors in Donaghey's success, it still probably should be considered more a negative than a positive victory, more a vote against Jeff Davis than a vote for George Donaghey.

Donaghey recognized that Davis was the issue and stated in his autobiography that although his three opponents "seemed a formidable array of competition against that 'carpenter from Conway,' . . . my most important opponent was . . . United States Senator Jeff Davis . . . who left his seat in Washington to campaign in Arkansas for his favorite."[91] Davis's decision to come to Arkansas to campaign was a serious tactical blunder that played into Donaghey's hands and helped him win the primary. The best summation of the impact of Donaghey's victory on Jeff Davis and his control of the state is furnished by Arsenault:

> Nothing did more to ensure Donaghey's victory than Davis' heavy-handed tactics. By leaving his post in Washington to campaign against a former ally, Davis had violated the electorate's sense of fair play. Jeff the martyr had become Jeff the bully. For the first time in his career, he had made a serious mistake in political judgment. That one mistake cost him dearly. Even though he retained a loyal core of followers, the myth of his invincibility had been dispelled. For many voters the Davis mystique was irrevocably broken.[92]

Travel and Conventions

Once Donaghey had won the Democratic nomination for governor in the March 1908 primary, he had almost ten months to wait before taking office. There would be a state general election in September against a Republican opponent, but in those days, the Democrat always triumphed. The first major decision he had to make was to advise acting-Governor Pindall not to call a special session in April of 1908 to consider the unfinished state capitol. As Donaghey saw it, a special session would cost too much, and it would be better if a new legislature dealt with the state capitol.

In May of 1908 Donaghey and Pindall attended a conference in Washington, D.C., on land drainage. Congressman Joe T. Robinson arranged for them to go to the White House to meet President Theodore Roosevelt.[93] Donaghey was impressed with Roosevelt and mentioned an incident in which Roosevelt, after being introduced to Secretary of State

Ludwig and told that he and his wife had seven children, presented him with two American Beauty roses as a gift for Mrs. Ludwig.[94]

Late in April, the state Republican convention met and nominated Judge John Worthington of Harrison as the Republican candidate for governor to run against Donaghey. Worthington had also run for governor in 1906. The Republican platform endorsed statewide prohibition, perhaps anticipating that the Democrats would not follow suit because of Hinemon's defeat.[95] They also asked that there be at least one Republican judge and clerk at each polling precinct and that the county Republican committee be allowed to name the third member of a county election commission (usually two were Democrats because in virtually all counties the Democratic party was the majority party) rather than the State Board of Election Commissioners that consisted of the governor, the attorney general, and the secretary of state, who were all Democrats. Worthington was selected unanimously, and the prohibition plank was cheered.[96]

The biggest immediate challenge confronting Donaghey was the state Democratic convention which was scheduled to meet in early June. Even though there was always traditional deference to a newly elected Democratic nominee, Donaghey had to be careful to avoid the bulldozer tactics often used by Davis to intimidate institutions and individuals, because he did not think that kind of approach would fit with a relatively non-political businessman's administration. At the same time, he had to let the Democrats of the state assembled in convention know that he was in charge. The initial problem at the convention, as might be expected, was Jeff Davis. The specific issue was the election of delegates from Arkansas to the Democratic National Convention to be held in Denver in July of 1908.

The Arkansas delegation to the Democratic National Convention in 1908 was entitled to eighteen delegates, two from each of the state's seven congressional districts, and four at-large delegates. It was customary that two of the four at-large seats be reserved for the state's two U.S. senators (Davis and Clarke).

In early May, acting-Governor Pindall, a Donaghey ally, announced that he would be a candidate for one of the at-large seats and suggested Donaghey, Senator Clarke, and O. C. Ludwig for the other three.[97] He went on to say that he opposed Jeff Davis and could not serve in the same delegation with him and asked the delegates in picking the fourth delegate at large to "choose between Senator Davis and myself."[98] He continued that he knew this broke a precedent but that Jeff Davis had also broken many in his day. Donaghey must have supported Pindall in his campaign, and although he was normally very gracious to his opponents, he may have reasoned that political generosity would be lost on Davis.

Davis campaigned mightily for an at-large position, flooding the state with letters and making strong personal appeals for support. The *Arkansas Democrat* said that "the fight made by Jeff Davis to nominate Kirby is nothing to the appeal that he is now making to the Old Guard to stand by him."[99] Before the convention began, Pindall withdrew, and James Harrod, an old friend of Donaghey from Conway, announced almost immediately that he would be a candidate for an at-large position.[100] Although Donaghey denied that he was backing an approved list of candidates and said, "I have no 'slate' in the common acceptance of the term,"[101] all the evidence was to the contrary. It was generally assumed that Clarke, Ludwig, Harrod, and Donaghey for the four at-large positions, Pindall for temporary chair of the convention, Joe T. Robinson for permanent chair, Frank Millwee for chair of the state Democratic party, and Bruce Bullion for secretary of the state party, had all been endorsed in advance by Donaghey. These individuals were subsequently called the "Pindall-Donaghey" slate by the newspapers.

The first day of the convention, June 2, contained most of the fireworks. There had been a meeting of about thirty delegates the night before at the Marion Hotel. This group contemplated an opposition slate to run against the Donaghey-Pindall "machine" as they called it.[102] Nothing tangible seemed to come from this opposition meeting, as both Pindall (temporary chair of the convention) and Joe T. Robinson (permanent chair) were selected overwhelmingly. Pindall in a short talk said that the state had turned not to "oratory or scholarly attainment" but to a "man who could heal the wounds."[103] In the same vein, Robinson said that Arkansas had demonstrated "that no political boss, however crafty or aggressive, can dominate its politics."[104] Donaghey still had to go through the formality of being nominated and approved by the convention, and he was nominated by Sam Frauenthal from Conway, who said, "The time is ripe for a business administration of our state."[105] Donaghey made a short acceptance speech asking the delegates to condemn him if he did wrong but to help him if he was trying to make the right choice.

After these preliminaries were concluded, nine candidates were nominated for the four at-large slots. Only eight, however, could really be considered serious candidates since one got only nine votes. The candidates and the number of votes for each were: Clarke (408), Donaghey (389), Harrod (329), Ludwig (301), ex-Senator Berry (279), Hinemon (279), Davis (196), and Tompkins (179). Davis finished seventh in a field of eight, a dramatic indication of his reduced status. The voting took an hour, and surprisingly enough there was not much block voting since only nine counties voted the entire slate, while thirty-four counties voted for Davis either in whole or in part.[106] The split voting indicated that Donaghey did not lean on the delegates; this made the victory over Davis all the more enjoyable because the "Wild Ass of the Ozarks"[107] had been tamed without the use of Davis methods.

On June 3, the second day of the convention, Frank Millwee was chosen unanimously as chair of the party and Bruce Bullion as party secretary.[108] The only discordant note that day was brought about by a contest for the position of Democratic national committeeman between Guy Tucker, the Democratic nominee for the office of commissioner of mines, manufacturers, and agriculture, and part of the Donaghey slate, and W. M. Kavanaugh of Little Rock. Tucker won easily, 422 to 177,[109] but this must have led to friction between Donaghey and the Kavanaugh family. The platform was also adopted unanimously on June 3, and it contained most of the items that Donaghey had recommended to the platform committee the day before.[110]

The platform was the epitome of Progressivism. It called for the four agricultural schools, increased powers for the state Railroad Commission, no further leasing of convicts, bank guarantee laws to protect depositors, an initiative and referendum amendment, laws for the conservation of natural resources, publication of itemized expenses for all candidates in primary and general elections, liberal appropriations for the entire educational system of the state, safety laws to protect people engaged in mining, manufacturing, and other industries, no free railroad passes except for railroad employees, increased pay for the judiciary, and no more special or local legislation. Two other planks are of special interest. One in effect turned the state capitol construction over to Donaghey carte blanche by calling for the passage of such laws "as will remove all persons and officials connected with or engaged in the construction of the building at once and pass such laws as may be recommended by the nominee of our party for governor."[111] The other was the compromise over prohibition and recommended "that the next legislature pass such laws as will ascertain, during the year 1909, whether the people favor local option or statewide prohibition, and we pledge the Democratic Party to execute the people's will when it shall have been ascertained."[112]

After the convention had adjourned, late on the afternoon of June 3, Donaghey must have been pleased with what had taken place. He had put his own people in charge of the party machinery, the platform was a Donaghey document, and Davis had paid the price of losing a campaign—an experience new to him.[113] All of this had been done without employing steamroller tactics, and Donaghey had not been overbearing and had not yet lost his status as a political novice and nonpolitician. His first big political test was passed with honors, and the *Arkansas Gazette* praising Donaghey's leadership in an article on June 4, 1908, stated that "in not one particular was the so-called Donaghey 'slate' broken from the time the convention opened until it closed," and concluded that the convention "was the most harmonious session the Democrats of Arkansas have held in years."

Governor-elect Donaghey, as one of the four at-large delegates, went with the Arkansas delegation to the Democratic National Convention held in Denver from July 7 through July 10. A special train, five sleepers and a dining car, left Little Rock on July 3 with more than one hundred[114] people on board. The Arkansas delegation had been instructed by the state convention to vote for William Jennings Bryan, who was duly nominated on the first ballot. Donaghey was pleased with the national convention, was enthusiastic about Bryan, and had great hopes for the outcome of the presidential election.[115]

Louvenia had accompanied her husband to Denver, and they took a combined pleasure and business trip after the convention. Counting the time spent at the Democratic National Convention, the Donagheys were gone for about a month. Most of the time was spent traveling through a dozen western and northwestern states to "get information and ideas on such matters as public roads, taxation, and agricultural schools," so that Donaghey could prepare himself "for making some great and needed reforms in Arkansas."[116] Donaghey visited and studied the irrigation projects in Montana, the famous agricultural school at Ames, Iowa, the Colorado system of employing convicts to work on public roads, the revenue system of the Dakotas, the state capitol at St. Paul, Minnesota, and the penitentiary at St. Cloud.[117] Donaghey wrote a full-page article for the *Log Cabin Democrat* describing his five-thousand-mile journey.[118] The trip through the West to prepare himself for office was in the best Progressive tradition of investigating problems. The trip was not all work as the Donagheys spent three and a half days at Yellowstone Park, for which they paid $17.50 for hotel accommodations.[119]

The state general election, held in Arkansas on September 14, 1908 was created originally to place a state general election between the state primary and the national general election in November to minimize federal control of Arkansas elections, since only state and county offices and no federal offices were elected in the state general election. Since Democrats invariably won all the contests for state constitutional offices, the only challenge was to see if the winning total of two years before could be surpassed. Nevertheless, Donaghey took his Republican opposition seriously. A campaign headquarters was opened in Little Rock, a speakers' bureau was formed, and Democratic officeholders and nominees as well as county committees were assessed to help pay for the campaign against the state Republicans.[120]

The Republicans began their campaign on August 8 in Ozark, with John Worthington from Harrison as their gubernatorial candidate. He tried as much as possible to make prohibition the issue since the Republicans had gone on record for statewide prohibition and the Democrats had simply left the matter to a vote of the people in a special election in 1909. Worthington also mentioned a reduction of taxes and a new state constitution, but prohibition was the "one question on which the two great parties have joined issue."[121]

The Democrats opened their campaign two weeks later. Party regulars, including Kirby and Hinemon, made about 250 speeches during the campaign.[122] Donaghey himself made about twenty speeches,[123] even though he had to leave Arkansas for four or five days during the last part of August and the first part of September to attend a hearing before a federal court of appeals in St. Paul, Minnesota, on an Arkansas law that reduced railroad passenger rates. Donaghey was an elusive target for the Republicans because he said that he had always voted for prohibition but now backed the party plank calling for the special election.[124] He even agreed to the Republican request that they be allowed to name one election commissioner in each county and one judge and clerk at each polling place because "an absolutely fair election"[125] was essential. To compensate for this civilized treatment of Republicans, he did refer to the Democratic party as the "white man's party"[126] and said that Negroes represented two-thirds of the Republicans in the state.

Despite the efforts of both parties and the issue of prohibition, there seemed to be little interest in the election. Donaghey had improved greatly as a speaker. An article about the closing Democratic rally in Little Rock took special note of Donaghey's progress as a speaker and mentioned that he was now much more at ease, used few notes, and spoke forcefully.[127] He still, however, had a strong aversion to self-dramatization, and at the same closing rally where his smoother style of speaking was mentioned, Donaghey said that he did not want "to be elected governor for the purpose of going on dress parade, but instead to give the people of Arkansas a good, sound business administration."[128]

The returns must have been disappointing to Donaghey, since he only increased the Democratic margin by 667 votes over Governor Little's defeat of Worthington in 1906.[129] On the more encouraging side for Donaghey, the Republicans carried only two counties (Newton and Searcy), and the chair of the state Republican Central Committee, F. W. Tucker, said in an election-eve tribute to both Donaghey and Worthington that "both candidates for governor are gentlemen, and have conducted their debates along the lines of the needs . . . of the state with due consideration and without personalities. I predict Arkansas will have the best governor she has had for many years, no matter which one of them is elected."[130] There were also nineteen counties that voted wet in the 1908 state general election.[131]

Between the state general election in September and the national general election in November, the Arkansas penitentiary was again in the news, and it became a frustrating problem for Donaghey. During the 1908 Democratic primary, all the candidates seemed to agree that the Penitentiary Board, consisting of five state officials (governor, secretary of state, auditor, attorney general, and commissioner of mines, manufacturers, and agriculture) should be replaced by three appointed or elected commissioners who could devote their full attention to the penitentiary. Dr. A. C. Millar, a Methodist minister and friend of Donaghey, who was the associate editor of the *Arkansas Methodist,* was selected as a special master by the Penitentiary Board to investigate charges of maltreatment of prisoners. Millar found convicts living in terrible conditions and being treated inhumanely, but blamed the system more than individuals and stated that the prison could not be properly managed under a board composed of state officials.[132] Another indictment of the penitentiary came only three months after Millar's investigation when the superintendent's report issued in December of 1908 reported that 2,000 convicts had been in the prison at one time or another from 1906 to 1908 and that 276 had been pardoned, 214 had escaped, and 95 had died—a total of almost one-third had been pardoned, escaped, or died.[133]

In April of 1908, Donaghey attended a meeting of the Conference for Education in the South held at Memphis. At a luncheon held in connection with the conference, he talked about some problems that he faced as governor-elect. One problem in particular was that he needed an educational plan for Arkansas, or as Donaghey phrased it in his autobiography, "I am looking for an educational architect."[134] He was surprised when an individual across the table from him not only expressed interest in what Donaghey wanted to do but offered to come to Arkansas and discuss it. The person in question was Dr. Wallace Buttrick, who was the executive secretary of the General Education Board, a Rockefeller-endowed project to promote education in the United States. Buttrick was also associated with the Southern Education Board, which focused mainly on education in the South and was financed by the General Education Board. Buttrick and Donaghey almost immediately developed a close personal and professional relationship, but more than this, Buttrick had the energy, financial resources, and confidence in Donaghey that eventually led to unprecedented gains for education in Arkansas.

On September 7, 1908,[135] Donaghey invited Dr. Buttrick to come to Arkansas and arranged for him to speak to about thirty Arkansas educators at the Hotel Marion in Little Rock. Buttrick talked about the latest educational developments but stressed that no state or institution could be helped by the General Education Board unless it also was willing to help. His main theme was that northerners out-produced southerners, not because they were inherently more able, but simply because they were better educated. The outcome of the meeting was a tour of the outstanding agricultural institutions in Wisconsin, Minnesota, and Illinois to garner ideas for similar schools in Arkansas. The trip was jointly financed by Buttrick and Donaghey.[136]

The trip lasted about ten days in late September and early October, and included Donaghey; Buttrick; George B. Cook, the superintendent of public instruction; and J. N. Tillman, president of the University of

Arkansas. They visited the University of Chicago and its agricultural department, Illinois State Normal, and agricultural schools in Minnesota and Wisconsin. At the University of Chicago, Donaghey was introduced to an elderly man who had left his entire fortune to that institution. Donaghey was impressed with how happy he seemed to be and credited this incident with being the catalyst for his later bequest to Little Rock Junior College.[137] George Cook, the superintendent of public instruction, spent several additional weeks visiting agricultural schools in the North. He commented at the end of the trip that the result was "to determine definitely what we want and what we need in the way of similar schools in this State."[138]

The November presidential election in 1908, between the Republican, William H. Taft, and the Democrat, William Jennings Bryan, was predictable, and Bryan carried 60 percent of the Arkansas vote.[139]

Donaghey was extremely busy with preparations for the beginning of his administration during the two and one-half month period from the November general election to his inauguration on January 14, 1909. One unsettling factor during this period was the report of the state auditor, which showed that the state had been living beyond its means for the previous two years and was likely to face a deficit of sixty thousand to eighty thousand dollars in the first quarter of 1909.[140] This problem had not been visible because the county collectors, who were required to make their payments to the state by July each year, were willing to make their payments of money already collected earlier than required (usually in January or February) so that state warrants could be redeemed. The state had been borrowing these advance payments to tide itself over, but by the first quarter of 1909 the deficit would arrive so early that the usual method of borrowing would not be sufficient. The auditor's report about a forthcoming state deficit was a harbinger of money problems to come.

A more soluble problem was the question of office staff. Bruce Bullion, who was now the secretary of the state Democratic party, had served as Donaghey's private secretary during the Democratic primary and was persuaded to move to Little Rock and become Donaghey's chief of staff. According to his son, also named Bruce Bullion, his father did not want to leave Conway, but the salary of $2,200 a year was the clincher.[141] Bullion was an ideal choice since he was someone from home who could be trusted, had statewide contacts through his work in the 1908 elections, and was both efficient and diplomatic.

Another encouraging development took place shortly after Donaghey was inaugurated. Dr. Buttrick made his fourth trip to Arkansas in three months and announced that the General Education Board would donate $75,000 to Hendrix College with the understanding that Hendrix would raise an additional $225,000.[142] He also announced that the General Education Board would share the cost of an additional faculty position with the University of Arkansas. The person selected would have faculty rank as a professor of secondary education at the University of Arkansas but would stay in Little Rock and work with the State Department of Education to promote public high schools in Arkansas.[143] The salary was to be $3,000 per year with the General Education Board contributing most of the money.

Donaghey deserves most of the credit for this interest by Buttrick and others in Arkansas's educational system. Although the amount of money involved was small by today's standards, it was a significant breakthrough that came at just the right time. The only outside organization to contribute to Arkansas's education was the Peabody Fund, which had spent only $129,000 from 1868 to 1897 for teacher institutes, the third lowest amount in the southern states. The Peabody Fund was diminishing[144] because the state had not been willing to match it. In addition, the image of the state as one of perpetual chaos under Davis created an environment that frightened away national philanthropic organizations interested in education. Donaghey reversed this image, and he commented in his autobiography and the facts back him up, "Until I had made my fortunate contact with Dr. Buttrick, Arkansas had received nothing from Mr. Rockefeller nor from anyone else."[145]

As the time for Donaghey's inauguration approached, he began putting the ideas and recommendations that he had gathered from his trips throughout the country into written form. His preparation was impressive and, in 1909, unprecedented. Few officeholders would spend that much time and money in educating themselves for political office. During the primary campaign, he had talked about many progressive issues that would surface in his inaugural speech. In the September general election, he added woman suffrage[146] but later qualified this by suggesting that women vote at home away from the drunks and the grubby atmosphere of most polling places.[147] During November and December of 1908, Donaghey spent most of his spare time incorporating these thoughts into an inaugural address. He worked in a vacant office in the upper story of the Faulkner County courthouse saying that there were very few interruptions there.[148]

The 1909 Legislative Session

The 1909 legislature contained seventy-five new members in the house of representatives and fifteen new members in the senate,[149] which was probably encouraging for Donaghey, since he would present some innovative proposals to the legislature. Donaghey adopted a "hands-off" attitude toward the legislative leadership races and said that the legislature was a distinct branch of government and it was not his "place to intrude on that body in any way."[150] The *Arkansas Democrat* commended him for this decision, commenting that Donaghey was "not a dictator and has scrupulously kept himself in the background during the organization of the legislature."[151]

Epps Brown of Des Arc (Prairie County) was elected speaker of the house of representatives, and although Donaghey was not involved, Frank Millwee, Donaghey's campaign manager in 1908 and chair of the state Democratic party, served as Brown's campaign manager.[152] Notwithstanding Donaghey's neutrality, it would have been hard for Brown not to have been reasonably sympathetic to Donaghey's legislative program given Millwee's role in the speaker's race. Jesse Martin of Russellville (Pope County) was selected as president of the senate.

Given the large number of legislative items mentioned by the Democratic state platform in 1908 and the reforms supported by Donaghey in the 1908 campaign, the legislative agenda promised to be both long and time-consuming. The session would last 122 days. Donaghey was prepared for the session, even though he was to be inaugurated earlier than usual, and had finished writing his inaugural address by the first week in January. He did complain, however, about the hordes of office seekers who besieged him constantly wanting appointments to state boards or state jobs. The appointments that the governor could make were limited in number, and Donaghey, some twenty-eight years later, made the same point in a letter to J. N. Heiskell that "too much of the governor's time is consumed by parties seeking jobs, when, as a matter of fact, the Governor of Arkansas actually has very few jobs at his disposal."[153]

X. O. Pindall, who had been acting governor from May 14, 1907, to

January 11, 1909, made a thirty-minute farewell address to a joint session of the house and senate on January 13, 1909. It contained many of the same legislative concerns (the state capitol, a state tax commission, hiring lawyers to plead the state's cause in the railroad cases, and the state penitentiary) in which Donaghey was also interested. Donaghey gave his two-hour inaugural speech (approximately twenty-eight thousand words) on January 14. It was frequently interrupted by applause and was watched by about five hundred[154] spectators as well as members of the house and senate. There was a special section reserved for Mrs. Donaghey and twenty of her friends; a number of Donaghey's close friends from Conway also were present.[155]

Donaghey's lengthy message to the legislature with forty-three legislative recommendations read like a bible of Progressivism. It began with a revealing quote about his philosophy of government: "Having seen what efficiency can accomplish in industrial and business affairs, I am now prepared to believe, after all, that even so important a work as statecraft is only an intensely practical matter."[156] Putting most of Donaghey's proposed legislation into Progressive categories such as social justice and the conservation of natural and human resources, reforming government and purifying politics, and regulation of business and economic justice should help measure his program against the Progressive movement in the United States and give some ideological guidance as to what he was trying to do.

Into the category of social justice and the conservation of natural and human resources fell such requested legislation as the four agricultural high schools, creation of a state board of education, a program to teach trades to inmates of the state reform school, a severance tax on coal, timber, and stone, comprehensive game and fish laws, the prohibition of convict leasing and putting convicts to work on state and county roads, a new penitentiary board that consisted of three full-time people appointed by the governor, a tuberculosis sanitarium, a new hospital for mentally disturbed patients at a location other than Little Rock, and generous appropriations for the blind and deaf schools and the existing hospital for the mentally disturbed.

In the category of reforming government and purifying politics were such proposals as initiative and referendum, abolishing the State Land Office, requiring the itemization of campaign expenses in all state primary, special, and general elections, increasing the salaries of the state treasurer and auditor and circuit and chancery judges, and limiting free railroad passes to railroad employees. Donaghey also recommended that state officials should not serve on so many boards (twelve in some cases) and that election laws should be revised so the party in power could not take advantage of the minority party, but no specifics were suggested on these two matters.

In the category of regulating business and securing economic justice were such items as a minimum of forty thousand dollars to hire lawyers to prosecute the state's case against the railroads, enlarging the powers of the Railroad Commission, creating the office of state bank examiner, amending the state antitrust laws to be certain that labor unions and farm organizations were not included, authorizing the governor to appoint a state tax commission, and establishing a state insurance commission.

There were several other important subjects, such as the state capitol and the special election in 1909 to decide whether the people of the state wanted local option or statewide prohibition. The *Arkansas Gazette* thought that Donaghey had treated comprehensively every public question facing the state[157] while the *Arkansas Democrat* felt the inaugural address was "a most able and statesman-like document" and that Donaghey was "a man of ideas who has since the election devoted considerable time to a close and thorough study of governmental affairs."[158]

Once the legislative session began, as might have been anticipated, Donaghey won some and lost some. On the matters of convict leasing and the penitentiary, Donaghey was generally unsuccessful in the 1909 session. The attempt to outlaw the leasing of convicts failed by a vote of thirty-three to fifty-seven in the house of representatives,[159] even though Donaghey had been willing to accept an amendment to outlaw leasing after one year.[160] The attempt to change the Penitentiary Board so that it would be composed of five commissioners to be appointed by the governor met a similar fate after an amendment was passed, by forty-seven to twenty-seven[161] to keep the present penitentiary board unchanged.

Two victories in this general area were not on a par with the defeats. One allowed adjoining counties to form road improvement districts[162] and use convicts in the county jails or from the state penitentiary from the counties forming the district to work on the county roads. This was mild reform, but it did provide that the county would assume responsibility for the care, maintenance, and supervision of the convicts, mandated a ten-hour working day, and required some reduction of sentence if the prisoner's work was good. The county road act was passed after it was known that the legislature would not stop convict leasing. The other victory involved a ten-year contract with the Arkansas Brick and Manufacturing Company to lease convicts from the state at fifty cents per day.[163] The contract expired on January 1, 1909, and all the convicts were to be returned to the state. The Arkansas Brick and Manufacturing Company refused to return the prisoners, claiming that the state had not furnished them three hundred convicts per day as required by the contract. The Penitentiary Board, on January 17, canceled the contract and ordered all convicts returned to the state. The Pulaski County Chancery Court had enjoined the Penitentiary Board from putting this order into effect, and Donaghey, in a special message to the legislature on January 18,[164] asked the general assembly to ratify the action of the Penitentiary Board. Both houses stood behind the Penitentiary Board by unanimous votes.

The matter of referring to the people the question of state-wide prohibition or local option became ensnared in political crosscurrents. The prohibition forces, who had great influence in the house of representatives, pushed for a state-wide prohibition bill without any submission to a vote of the people, but the senators wanted a popular vote. The final outcome was the passage of a house bill (HB 114) requiring state-wide prohibition, which was then amended in the senate to make this contingent upon a special election on July 14, 1909.[165] The amended bill was then returned to the house of representatives, but the opposing forces were at stalemate, and the bill died despite a special message from Governor Donaghey urging action.[166]

Legislation containing a $160,000 appropriation ($40,000 each) for the construction and maintenance of four agricultural high schools open to both male and female students, and located in four specified regions of the state, passed easily. The Farmers' Union, which had a prior commitment from Donaghey that a majority of the board of each of the four institutions would be members of the organization,[167] worked energetically for passage. The measure was a significant triumph for Donaghey that placed state support for the first time behind high schools, and it proved to be so successful that over a period of time, these four agricultural high schools eventually became junior colleges and then colleges. Today they are Arkansas State University in Jonesboro, the University of Arkansas in Monticello, Arkansas Tech University in Russellville, and Southern Arkansas University in Magnolia.

Another precedent-shattering piece of legislation was the creation of the Arkansas Tax Commission, another special project of Governor Donaghey and one that was the epitome of the Progressive idea that experts could settle very complicated problems. The need for such a commission came not only from the state's financial deficit but also from the erratic way in which property was assessed in different counties. Some counties assessed at 25 percent of actual value and some at 60 percent. The average was estimated to be between 20 and 30 percent of actual value.[168] This was important for the state because in those days most state revenues came from a millage levied against real property. The counties that assessed higher and closer to actual market value paid the biggest share of state taxes, which created a natural tendency to lower assessments.

The Tax Commission was a powerful body with general supervision over county assessments and the power to act as an equalization board. It was to have three purposes: (1) put on the rolls property that was escaping taxation; (2) equalize assessments throughout the state, and (3) increase the value at which property was being assessed. It was composed of three salaried commissioners appointed by the governor and was to visit every county in the state at least once in every two years. The commission was also to assess railroad property, a job that had formerly been done by the State Railway Assessment Board composed of the governor, the attorney general, and the state auditor. Considering the drastic changes in the fiscal structure of the state that were possible with the Tax Commission, it is surprising that it passed both houses by overwhelming margins.[169] The appropriation (HB 511) to pay the expenses of the commission, including the salaries of the commissioners,[170] passed the house and was still pending on the senate floor when the session adjourned. Failure to pass the appropriation bill was not thought to be a fatal defect since it was hoped that the commissioners could be paid out of a contingency fund that would later be reimbursed by the 1911 legislature.

Governor Donaghey was extraordinarily successful in passing what he wanted for the state capitol. The State Capitol Act contained an appropriation of $795,000 to complete the capitol and a section allowing the governor to appoint a new State Capitol Commission. Another act discharged the present commissioners and the architect and annulled the contract with Caldwell and Drake. It also established an arbitration commission to adjudicate the claims of Caldwell and Drake against the state and vice versa. Donaghey missed a complete and total victory on the state capitol only because the appropriation bill (SB 443) of $175,000 for payment of claims found to be valid by the adjudication commission did not pass because of legislative hostility toward Caldwell and Drake.

Much time in the 1909 session was devoted to the railroads. The jurisdiction of the State Railroad Commission was expanded to cover the furnishing of cars, speed limits for trains, and the building of passenger and freight depots in cities of the first or second class. Another bill appropriated fifty thousand dollars to pay for legal counsel to fight the new rates imposed by the railroads. The railroads had obtained a temporary injunction from the U.S. Circuit Court in St. Paul, Minnesota, enjoining the rates imposed by the State Railroad Commission and the Arkansas legislature in 1907, which were two cents a mile for passengers and a standard freight distance charge. Under the temporary injunction granted in September of 1908, the railroads were allowed to again set their own rates, which they did in the amount of three cents a mile for passengers and increased freight rates.

Legal counsel hired by the state to fight these new railroad rates were Chief Justice Joseph M. Hill of the Arkansas Supreme Court, who would be chief counsel after he resigned from the Arkansas Supreme Court, and two assistants were James H. Harrod, Donaghey's friend from Conway, and William F. Kirby, Donaghey's chief opponent in 1908. Although selection of the lawyers was made jointly by the governor and the attorney general, the appointment of Kirby was a brilliant move by Donaghey to heal wounds and earn the loyalty of a former opponent. Arkansas sued in the federal court for the eastern district of Arkansas, challenging the new railroad rates as unreasonably high and confiscatory and asking the court for relief since the State Railway Commission had been temporarily enjoined from enforcing rates. Judge Jacob Trieber ruled that the freight rates were too high but that the three cents per mile passenger rate did not need to be changed. He also urged compromise on the part of all parties.

Compromise was finally reached along these lines: the passenger rate would be lowered to two and a half cents per mile, the freight rates would be sizably reduced from the new railroad rates but still above the level set by the State Railroad Commission in 1907, the temporary injunction against the State Railroad Commission was to be dissolved, and both parties were free to bring suit again after one year.[171] Even though rates were higher than 1907, there was a considerable reduction from the rates imposed by the railroads in September of 1908. The new compromise rates began on June 1, 1909. Hill, chief counsel for Arkansas, estimated in 1911 that these new compromise rates had saved Arkansas shippers and consumers $1.5 million over the previous two years.[172] This was not a perfect victory for Donaghey, but the railroads had been forced to pull back.

A tuberculosis sanitarium was approved with little trouble, even though one senator voted against the bill on the grounds that "there can be no cure."[173] Donaghey obviously had a strong personal interest in the sanitarium because of the death from tuberculosis of his sister, Willie, at the age of thirty-one, as well as three uncles and an aunt. He regarded the new sanitarium, at least in part, as a monument to his sister.[174] One doctor testified in a committee hearing that at least three thousand Arkansans died annually from tuberculosis.[175] The legislature appropriated fifty thousand dollars to build the sanitarium and thirty thousand dollars for maintenance and operations. Donaghey had also recommended construction of a second hospital for people who were mentally ill, called the State Hospital for Nervous Diseases, No. 2. Legislation was passed to do this, but it was not funded because of the budgetary crisis in the state.

Another measure closely identified with Donaghey was a proposed amendment to the state constitution allowing initiative and referendum. National Progressives regarded this as the key to purifying politics, but it found little acceptance in the South. Even in the 1990s Arkansas is the only southern state with both initiative and referendum. Democrats in the South initially ridiculed initiative and referendum as Populist ideas. The proposal received only one vote when first introduced in the Arkansas General Assembly in 1891.[176] The situation had not improved measurably in 1907, when it gained only nine votes in the senate.[177] But by 1909, because of Donaghey support and adoption in the platform by the state Democratic party, the reversal was so dramatic that initiative and referendum passed by a vote of 28 to 1 in the senate[178] and 78 to 4[179] in the house. There was, however, a serious problem. The House Committee on Constitutional Amendments had added a poorly drafted amendment to the initiative and referendum proposal the purpose of which was to permit cities and counties the use of initiative on local laws.

Instead, the wording, if read literally, allowed counties and cities to propose state-wide laws and constitutional amendments and to reject at the polls any act of the legislature.[180] As a proposed constitutional amendment, it had to be ratified in the September 1910 general election, and this badly drafted change would be a burden in the ratification campaign.

Other important acts passed in 1909 included Act 13 that required that employees be paid twice a month, Act 38 that raised annual salaries of circuit and chancery judges from two thousand to three thousand dollars—the first raise since 1874—and Act 165 that compelled candidates for most offices to file an itemized account of all election expenses. Donaghey also apparently appointed on his own in 1909 a State Conservation Commission to find ways to preserve the natural resources of Arkansas.[181]

William Jennings Bryan addressed the general assembly in April. He was introduced by Donaghey as the "greatest Democrat that ever lived since the days of Andrew Jackson."[182] Bryan praised the general assembly for the enactment of the initiative and referendum proposal and urged passage of a bank guarantee law and a campaign-expense disclosure bill. At the end of the thirty-seventh general assembly Donaghey considered calling a special session immediately[183] to consider crucial matters left unresolved, such as convict leasing, a special election on prohibition, and financing for the Tax Commission. He later decided not to do this presumably because the legislature had already been in session from January 11 through May 12.

The *Arkansas Democrat* was complimentary of Donaghey's performance as governor both in the 1909 legislative session and in other matters, praised his hard work, and found him very much at ease in being governor.[184] The newspaper expressed amazement at how he could handle the administrative duties of his office, sit on twelve state boards, and still keep on top of legislative matters. Donaghey, who believed the governor should exercise strong legislative leadership, met in his office with legislators and legislative committees, dispatched messengers to round up administrative support, and sent eight special messages on legislative topics to the 1909 general assembly. His close attention and persistent lobbying on behalf of the three state capitol bills is a good example of how he interpreted a governor's unofficial role as legislative leader.

The meeting of the thirty-seventh general assembly was one of the most productive legislative sessions ever held in Arkansas, and the failure

to pass certain bills such as convict leasing, a new reorganized penitentiary board, and the special election on prohibition does not detract from
this favorable verdict. Donaghey's first 120 days as governor compare
favorably with the term of any American Progressive governor of this
period and set a standard by which past and future Arkansas governors
can measure themselves.

Administrative Events (1909–1910)

Because the state did not provide a residence for the governor at that
time, anyone elected governor usually moved to Little Rock and bought
a home there.[185] Donaghey rented his home in Conway, which eventually burned down, and later sold his land in Conway so that most of his
ties were gradually transferred to Little Rock. He first lived at 314
Gaines, but later moved to his permanent home at 2109 Gaines Street.
To finance his staff and office, Donaghey was allowed annually $2,200
for a private secretary, $900 for a clerk, and $1,000 for contingent
expenses.[186] His own salary was $4,000 a year, and he was provided with
a housing allowance of $2,000 for two years and a fund in the amount of
$3,000, also for two years, to offer in rewards leading to the arrest of
fugitives.[187] Bruce Bullion, although classified as a private secretary, was
actually Donaghey's chief of staff and ran the office. The Arkansas tradition of cutting costs by giving people paid with state money as many
jobs as possible was followed in the case of the governor's private secretary who was also the adjutant general of the militia. Bullion, who had
previous military experience in the Spanish-American War, was able to
handle this extra duty with a great degree of professionalism.[188]
According to Bruce Bullion's son, his father took charge of any legal matters, made appointments for Donaghey, helped write speeches, and, in
general, acted as a buffer for Donaghey. Donaghey and Bullion got along
well. Since Bullion lived near Donaghey, they usually walked to work
together, going early and staying late. Bullion described Donaghey as
diligent and hardworking. Although he didn't hesitate to criticize when
he felt it was necessary, Donaghey was still a hero to him after four years.
Bullion thought that politics was no place for intellectual honesty, but he
believed that Donaghey at least approached it.[189]

Office assistance at various times was furnished by Wallace Rose—
the son of U. M. Rose—who later became a doctor. C. Hamilton Moses

joined the staff to type, write speeches, and serve as an assistant to Bullion. Moses eventually became legal counsel to the Arkansas Power and Light Company and then the president in 1941. Another member of the staff during Donaghey's tenure was Bertie Wilson, a secretary. She married C. H. Murphy of El Dorado, Donaghey's close friend from Oakland, Louisiana,[190] C. H. Murphy was the founder of Murphy Oil Company, and his and Bertie's son, C. H. Murphy, Jr., later became the chairman of the board of that company. Donaghey's staff would eventually be very successful in their own right, but they all maintained frequent contact with their former boss.

Administrative duties of the office included filling vacancies in state and local offices, requesting governors of other states to return to Arkansas people accused of crimes in Arkansas, issuing commissions for justices of the peace and notaries public, calling special elections, appointing county election commissioners along with the secretary of state and attorney general, selecting delegates to various conferences, and granting pardons. There were also ceremonial duties to perform, speaking before various groups, giving out diplomas at graduations, and meeting visiting dignitaries. In a fairly typical week in his first year as governor, Donaghey went to Pine Bluff to make a speech, addressed the county assessors in Little Rock, traveled to Fayetteville to attend commencement and to meet with the University of Arkansas board, and ended with a meeting of the State Capitol Commission in Little Rock.[191]

There was occasionally a lighter side to these official duties. Donaghey had received a large Arkansas gourd as a gift during the campaign. He decided that if people wanted to see him and had personal calling cards, they could put their cards in the Arkansas gourd instead of a silver platter.[192] He also, in his capacity as governor, married C. A. Walls, who was the private secretary to Congressman Joe T. Robinson, and Antoinette Long. The wedding took place in the governor's office; the couple chose this method of marrying to surprise their friends.[193] He also greatly treasured and kept in his office a mosaic table made for him by one of the patients at the state hospital, a man who had great woodworking skills and had become Donaghey's friend when Donaghey repaired tornado damage at the hospital in 1894.[194]

Official responsibilities as governor, either light or heavy, did not hamper his work with the Methodist church. He was appointed, while governor, chair of a committee of twenty-four prominent Methodists to establish complementary roles for three Methodist schools, Henderson, Galloway, and Hendrix.[195] This appointment must have been made in recognition of the role that Donaghey played in securing the seventy-five-thousand-dollar challenge grant for Hendrix through his friendship with Wallace Buttrick of the General Education Board.

Donaghey took great pride in his appointments to state boards and commissions, feeling that they were in a sense "the Governor's special cabinet and advisors."[196] He expected them to work hard and to attend meetings regularly, and he planned to ask them to resign if they did not.[197] His business background encouraged him to search diligently for the most qualified people and to resist appointing someone just because that person had applied for the position or had been recommended by others. He valued the element of surprise. Often people whom he would appoint would have their first knowledge that they were being considered when Donaghey called or when their names appeared in the newspapers. He even seemed to prefer people whom the press had not known were under consideration. He tried to make practical rather than political choices, as he had always done in his business life, seeking people from all walks of life. His State Capitol Commission, which he selected in 1909, included a farmer, an architect, a lawyer, and a businessman.[198] It also included by statute the governor, a contractor.

However, Donaghey was not always above making predominantly political appointments. He picked his personal and political friend from Conway, Sam Frauenthal, to fill a vacancy on the Arkansas Supreme Court, ignoring the recommendation of the other members of the court.[199] From all indications, Frauenthal was a good judge, but there may have been a hint of favoritism in his choice. Some more typical examples were the appointments of Tom McRae of Prescott, the president of the Arkansas Bankers Association, and Dr. John Dibrell, to the Board of Trustees for the Charitable Institutions, which included the schools for the deaf and the blind and the state hospital. Dibrell was one of the leading physicians in Arkansas who could help with the medical needs of the state institutions, and McRae was selected to put some business methods to work. After Donaghey had filled seven vacancies on the Board of Trustees, the board instituted a new system of accounting and made a complete inventory of property and supplies on hand.[200] Donaghey's most nonpolitical appointment, which many Democrats found incomprehensible, was that of Harmon Remmel to the State

Capitol Commission. Remmel at the time was the leading Republican in Arkansas who had served as chair of the Republican party for years and had run for governor three times. The selection of Remmel was an attempt by Donaghey to take the State Capitol Commission out of politics, but to many Democrats in the state, it was almost like the return of Reconstruction.

Pardons were another administrative nightmare that consumed valuable time and energy. Justice in Arkansas was often high-handed and uneven, with vastly different sentences in different counties for the same crime. This situation cried out for the use of pardoning power. There were other occasions, however, where the well-connected had been convicted and sentenced and wanted some relief through pardon. One famous case was centered around W. Y. Ellis,[201] the nephew of a millionaire lumberman, who had shot and killed Nathaniel Willis in court while a custody trial involving the child of Willis and Mary Ellis (Willis's ex-wife) was taking place in the Pulaski County Courthouse. There were certain mitigating factors on W. Y. Ellis's side. Nevertheless, Donaghey did not bend to the pressure of three hundred letters and ten thousand petitions and refused to pardon Ellis, who had pled guilty to manslaughter. As one reason for denying the pardon, Donaghey said, "We all know that the taking of human life has been too lightly considered in Arkansas."[202]

Donaghey set aside one day each month to consider pardons. Some of the cases were easy since they simply involved restoring the rights of citizenship once a person had served his time, but many others were complex and difficult. Almost thirty years later in a letter to J. N. Heiskell, editor of the *Arkansas Gazette,* Donaghey recommended a procedure for future governors to use in considering pardons that included open and public hearings before the governor in which all concerned parties would participate.[203] In the same letter, he mentioned favorably a technique he had seen Theodore Roosevelt use that had application to pardons and other matters. At a certain time each day, Roosevelt would leave his office and go out to his reception room and greet callers waiting there and find out what they wanted.[204] It seemed to be a way to humanize administration.

The greatest administrative crisis of Donaghey's first term was the budget deficit, both past and that anticipated for the future. There was a $200,000 deficit left over from 1907–1909 when expenditures had been approximately $1.8 million and receipts had been only $1.6 million.[205] Much of this was due to the cutting of the tax rate for state general operations in 1905 from 2 1/4 to 1 3/4 mills and the consequent loss of $150,000 a year.[206] The deficit had been masked by using up the surplus in the general operations fund and because counties were willing to turn in their tax receipts to the state in January six months earlier than the legally required July deadline. For a time, the state was able to borrow against its future, but finally the deficit became too large and appeared too early in the year for this to help. As of April 1, 1909, there was only $1.00 in the general operations fund. The cashing of state vouchers had to be postponed for several days until a county check for $2,750[207] arrived.

Donaghey estimated that with the $200,000 deficit for 1907–1909 and expenditures of $566,000 above revenues in 1909–1911 (tax revenues were assumed to be the same as in 1907–1909—$1.6 million), the state was faced with a deficit of about $700,000, after some adjustments. He moved quickly to cut $440,000 from the state charitable institutions and to eliminate the $200,000 for the second state hospital. These cuts necessitated one- or two-month reductions in the school terms for the blind and deaf schools.[208] The Board of Trustees for the State Charitable Institutions, with Donaghey's new appointees present, voted to support Donaghey in his attempt to keep the state solvent.[209] During the next several days, he cut smaller amounts from other state agencies and even reached agreement with the University of Arkansas Board of Trustees on May 23 (referred to as the third day of the guillotine) not to use $50,000 in funds already appropriated.[210]

A grand total of $623,600 was vetoed, withheld, or pledged not to be used. This was about 40 percent of the state revenues in 1907–1909. The agricultural schools were not touched, but many other programs sponsored by the governor suffered. Donaghey did hope to obtain some additional revenue in 1909–1911 through the operation of the State Tax Commission. This was a good example of a businessman using administrative and management skills to ward off bankruptcy. Donaghey met personally with the board of every agency that had to be cut, explained the necessity for what he had to do, and was often rewarded with solid support for even drastic reductions. The Arkansas Democrat noted approvingly that rigid economy was "the only course for a business executive to assume."[211]

In addition to staffing his office, making appointments, issuing pardons, and other administrative duties, Donaghey pushed hard to implement his recently passed legislative program and see that it was functioning properly. The State Tax Commission was appointed. Because no appropriation for the commission had been passed, the commissioners agreed to work without salary, on the assumption that the next legislative session in 1911 would reimburse them for their work from 1909 to 1911.[212] Assessments were raised from $327 million in 1908 to $375 million in 1909,[213] mainly from railroads, corporations, and large property owners who had been assessed too low or not assessed at all. Donaghey said that $317,250 in new state revenues was raised,[214] but this had to be split among the school fund, Confederate pensions, and the state capitol, as well as the general operating fund. Thus the state general operating fund received only a little over $82,000.[215] In spite of this gain, Donaghey was disappointed that the Tax Commission was still dependent upon county assessors to correct the assessments of individual property owners, and even when assessments were raised, county judges would frequently reduce them.[216]

The boards for the four agriculture schools were selected, five board members for each school. Donaghey paid his debt to the Farmers' Union, as most of the twenty board members "were active Farmers' Union members."[217] Actually, Donaghey even stated some two years later that all but two or three board members were selected from the Farmer's Union even though they had only asked for three out of five on each board.[218] As noted before, the governor did not cut the appropriation for the agricultural schools, and hoped to have them in operation by September of 1910. Although the legislation specified the four regions of the state in which the schools would be located,[219] the actual sites would be chosen by the new boards on the basis of competitive proposals from communities within the four regions.

Unlike the agricultural schools, the eighty-thousand-dollar appropriation for the tuberculosis sanitarium had been withheld in 1909, but enough was released in 1910, along with a loan from Little Rock and Fort Smith banks, that construction at Booneville could begin in February of 1910.[220] Donations for rooms and cabins were also solicited from the public. The sanitarium was officially opened and dedicated on September 1, 1910, with a crowd of 1,500 present.[221] On January 23, 1911, the first patient was released and declared cured.[222]

The success of the agricultural schools and the tuberculosis sanitarium was not duplicated with the law[223] permitting counties to use convicts from the state penitentiary to work on the roads in the same county in which they had been sentenced. By the standards of the day, this was looked upon as a reform. However, if counties chose to use the act, they had to pay for guarding and maintenance. Due to the expense, Pulaski was the only county that chose to participate. An *Arkansas Gazette* editorial stated that "building roads with convicts is something that may have a slow growth in Arkansas where the practice is almost unknown."[224] Donaghey was equally frustrated in his attempts as a member of the Penitentiary Board to prevent any further convict leasing. He was joined in this position by John Jobe, the state auditor, but they were constantly outvoted, three to two, by Hal Norwood, the attorney general; O. C. Ludwig, the secretary of state; and Guy Tucker, the commissioner of mines, manufacturers, and agriculture, who presumably felt that such leasing was still needed because of the state's fiscal situation.

Donaghey was also active in helping to build the image of Arkansas and gaining acceptability from educational and philanthropic organizations domiciled outside the state. Donaghey wrote an article for *Colliers Weekly*[225] extolling Arkansas and mentioning, in particular, that it was the only state that produced diamonds and bauxite. One great breakthrough from a public relations point of view was the holding of the thirteenth annual meeting of the Conference for Education in the South in Little Rock in April of 1910. It was the first meeting of this group ever held west of the Mississippi. The conference was financed indirectly by the General Education Board and worked for free popular education, professional training of teachers, and an eight-month term in every school district.[226] The theme of the conference was agricultural education. More than 1200 delegates from twenty-five states were present as well as 23 representatives from the Federal Department of Agriculture.[227] In his welcoming address, Donaghey said that this meeting was "by far the most important event that has ever occurred in the history of educational affairs in the state of Arkansas."[228] Attending the conference were Donaghey's old educational friends, Dr. Wallace Buttrick of the General Education Board, and Dr. Wickliffe Rose of the Peabody Fund, which was now taking a renewed interest in Arkansas. Rose was also the administrative secretary of the Rockefeller Sanitary Commission.

Within a month after the Conference for Education in the South had adjourned, Donaghey appointed a state educational commission to study school laws and recommend changes. The commission was also to wage a campaign for education throughout the state to create a friendly climate for their recommendations in the 1911 general assembly. The Peabody Fund and the Southern Education Board helped make this commission possible by donating $3500[229] to hire an executive director for one year and for other commission expenses. This commission of twenty-one people, including Judge Trieber and the editors of both the *Arkansas Gazette* and the *Arkansas Democrat,* made a preliminary report on September 25, 1910, in which they suggested the creation of a state board of education, the consolidation of small schools (931 of these schools had 35 or fewer students) into larger and more centrally located institutions, and state assistance to nonspecialized high schools.[230]

Recognition of Arkansas's and Donaghey's efforts in the field of education by outside philanthropic institutions such as the Peabody Fund and the General Education Board had progressed to such a point by 1910 that the superintendent of public instruction reported that "much of the activity of the Department of Public Instruction during the biennial [1909–1910] term has been made possible by appropriations from sources outside the State, aggregating $18,500."[231] This amount included $3,000 for school improvement and extension work (PTAs), $3,500 for the Arkansas Education Commission, $7,000 to pay the salary of a professor of secondary education for two years, and $5,000 to assist the Agriculture Department at the State Normal School in Conway. For a poor state like Arkansas, which had to rely almost exclusively on its own resources, this was considerable assistance.

In 1909[232] John D. Rockefeller made $1 million available to fight hookworm in the southern states. The Rockefeller Sanitary Commission was established to carry out this project, with Dr. Wickliffe Rose as executive secretary. Rose was already familiar with Arkansas through his work with the Peabody Fund. He approached the State Board of Health to find someone to head the Arkansas campaign against hookworm. It was an honorary board with almost no power and no appropriation from the state,[233] but the requirement of a Rockefeller grant was that some state money had to be furnished to the state board to fight hookworm. Rose indicated, however, that this condition might be waived if the proper person could be found.[234]

Eventually Rose and the Board of Health announced that Dr.

Morgan Smith of Little Rock would direct the Arkansas campaign, with his salary to be paid by the Rockefeller Sanitary Commission. The campaign was mainly educational with twenty thousand pamphlets distributed by October.[235] Smith did try to organize hookworm eradication committees in some counties with the cooperation of the county medical societies. The Arkansas Medical Society at its annual meeting in May of 1910 urged the Arkansas legislature to appropriate money to take advantage of the Rockefeller hookworm offer.[236]

Several other events offered the state opportunities to promote itself as progressive and enlightened rather than as a stagnant backwater. One was the visit of President William Howard Taft to Arkansas in October of 1909. Taft had been visiting some western states and came back through Arkansas at the suggestion of ex-Senator Powell Clayton and Harmon Remmel, chair of the state Republican party and Donaghey's appointee to the State Capitol Commission.[237] Taft made short talks at Texarkana, Arkadelphia, and Benton. His major speech was in Little Rock where fifteen to twenty thousand people met him at Union Station.[238] By this time his voice was almost gone, and very few people could hear him. His talk lasted less than twenty minutes, and the headline in the *Arkansas Democrat* on October 25 read "Speech Short: Reception Great." Donaghey, who introduced him at Arkadelphia and traveled with him by train through the state, found his good humor and sunny disposition to be contagious and felt that Taft's visit had gone well.[239]

One year later, another distinguished visitor came to Arkansas, but this time more advanced planning was possible, and consequently, a more elaborate state observance was arranged. The distinguished visitor was ex-President Teddy Roosevelt, who had been invited to Arkansas to open the state fair in Hot Springs by John Greenway, a former Rough Rider.[240] Roosevelt had been touring the South and agreed to spend most of a day in Arkansas to open the fair officially with a speech on October 10, 1910. Donaghey, who introduced Roosevelt, walked across the platform and was met by someone dressed as Uncle Sam. Roosevelt entered through a double line of Spanish-American War veterans and then greeted Uncle Sam and Donaghey. In addition, there was a human American flag formed by 1,600 children dressed in red, white, and blue.[241] Roosevelt liked the human flag very much.[242] Crowd estimates ran as high as twenty-five thousand. The *Hot Springs Sentinel-Record* called it "the greatest gathering in the history of the state."[243] Donaghey introduced the ex-president as the most distinguished citizen in the country who was engaged in a mighty struggle "to secure more purity in private life and more honesty in public life."[244] Roosevelt reciprocated by calling Donaghey a "square man and a game man."[245] In his address, Roosevelt committed himself to finding national assistance for the drainage and reclamation of Arkansas swamps and urged the conservation of Arkansas timberlands. He also advocated a greater use of the power of the national government to help solve the nation's problems.

Donaghey was deeply impressed by Teddy Roosevelt and his magnetism. On one occasion, Roosevelt was so animated and so enthusiastic that Donaghey thought he might be drunk,[246] but was later reassured that this was not the case. While touring Hot Springs, Roosevelt told Donaghey that he was thinking about forming an independent party called the National party.[247] Donaghey and Roosevelt seemed to like each other, and Roosevelt's visit had gone even better than Taft's brief appearances, although Donaghey probably felt closer to Taft judging by his descriptions of both men. Donaghey's contacts with the state Republicans had probably facilitated both presidential visits.

As Donaghey's first term drew to a close, he could look back on some impressive achievements. He had defeated Jeff Davis and his political machine. Most of his important legislation had passed, such as that on the agricultural schools, the tuberculosis sanitarium, the State Tax Commission, the state capitol, and initiative and referendum, although he did lose on convict leasing and the prohibition election. His relations with the legislature were generally good during his first term. He met the state fiscal crisis head on and made painful but necessary cuts, which, surprisingly enough, were often endorsed by the boards of the institutions whose budgets were being reduced.

Donaghey also managed to reduce Arkansas's isolation from the rest of the country, and the image of the backward state filled with illiterate hillbillies was being challenged by the governor's new contacts with national philanthropic institutions that were willing to put money into Arkansas education. Donaghey's staff functioned smoothly and helped him grasp the reins of government with authority. In fact, it appeared that Donaghey's intention of running the state like a business was coming true. Unfortunately, however, as is often the case when politics is involved, things would get muddled as time went on.

FIVE

The Second Term (1911–1912)

Normally, in the Arkansas of the 1900s, in the absence of some cataclysmic political event in the first term, a Democratic governor was granted a second term without opposition. Donaghey, therefore, should have been able to look forward to a second term without Democratic opposition, but such was not to be, even though his victory in 1908 and his success with the legislature had put him in a strong position. Also, Donaghey's speaking abilities had improved, and he obviously had the financial capacity to wage an expensive campaign if necessary.

Donaghey analyzed in a reasonably accurate manner in his biography the groups, individuals, and issues that generated opposition to him in his bid for a second term. He mentioned people with ties to the state capitol contractors, Caldwell and Drake; members of the old state capitol commission, which had been abolished by a law supported by Donaghey; Jeff Davis and his supporters; and others offended by his attempts to end convict leasing, the appointment of Harmon Remmel, his veto of many state appropriations, and increased tax assessments.[1] By July the newspapers were speculating about who would run against Donaghey in the Democratic party. The four named most often were C. C. Kavanaugh, the former sheriff of Pulaski County; John McCaleb, a member of the old State Capitol Commission; John Hinemon, who had been a Democratic candidate for governor in 1908 and who would have strong prohibitionist support; and C. C. Reid, the congressman from the Sixth Congressional District.

On August 12, 1909, Donaghey announced for a second term. In a one and a half hour speech,[2] he spoke with satisfaction of the agricultural schools, the state capitol, the reduction in the railroad rates, good appointments, improvements in the revenue system, and his efforts to keep the state from going bankrupt. By December of 1909, the possible contenders against Donaghey had been reduced to two, Hinemon and Kavanaugh, who were trying to avoid a three-cornered race against the governor.[3] Hinemon finally decided not to run because of financial problems but agreed to support C. C. Kavanaugh.[4] Kavanaugh announced on December 11 and was Donaghey's only opponent in the Democratic primary.

C. C. Kavanaugh was the brother of William M. Kavanaugh, the founder and president of the Southern Trust Company, a successful Little Rock bank. W. M. Kavanaugh had also organized the Southern Construction Company to build the Southern Trust Building in which the bank was housed. Caldwell and Drake were shareholders in the Southern Construction Company; their interest in this company was worth $120,000 when they sold it in 1909.[5] The business ties with Caldwell and Drake plus W. M. Kavanaugh's defeat in his race for Democratic national committeeman by a Donaghey-endorsed candidate at the 1908 State Democratic Convention[6] left him with little love for Donaghey. W. M. Kavanaugh also had sufficient financial resources to help his brother in a campaign for governor.

C. C. Kavanaugh moved to Arkansas from Kentucky in 1892, several years after his brother had come to Little Rock. He first worked for his brother, W. M. Kavanaugh, who was the sheriff of Pulaski County. He served for four years as deputy sheriff under his brother and four years in the same capacity under another Pulaski County sheriff, and then was elected in his own right as sheriff for two terms, from 1904 until he retired in 1908. When he announced for governor, he was employed as a receiver for the T. H. Bunch Company.[7] C. C. Kavanaugh had also served as secretary of the State Association of Sheriffs, which gave him a statewide political network.[8]

The first advertisement for Kavanaugh set the campaign tone and highlighted the issues on which he hoped Donaghey would be vulnerable.[9] Donaghey was criticized for not completing the state capitol as he had promised, for granting too many pardons, for cutting appropriations to the charitable institutions, and above all, for appointing Harmon Remmel to the State Capitol Commission. Kavanaugh often closed his speeches to great crowd approval with the statement that his first official act would be to fire Remmel. He was a good speaker and challenged Donaghey to joint debates which the governor refused. Kavanaugh also had the good political sense to keep Davis in the background, although it was clear that "Davis partisans and recognized leaders were lined up to a man for Kavanaugh."[10]

The issues in 1910 were not as sharp or divisive as those in 1908.[11] Neither candidate backed statewide prohibition, which removed from the 1910 campaign one of the most emotional issues of the 1908 election.[12] In addition, Kavanaugh got a late start, was from Little Rock (Being from the largest city in the state, people assumed that he might be out of touch with the problems and concerns of ordinary people. Little Rock was also considered a center of sin and corruption.) and had never run in a statewide race before. His speaking ability and well-financed race could not overcome these handicaps. Donaghey even thought that his opposition had tried to find someone from outside Little Rock to oppose him but could not find anyone who was willing.[13] The *Arkansas Gazette* editorialized on December 13, 1909, that even though Kavanaugh had integrity and an enviable place in the community, he would have "to move mountains" to defeat Donaghey. Approaching this second campaign with confidence, Donaghey did not start campaigning until February 1, 1910,[14] and his first advertisement was on February 20. He also took a significant part in other campaigns for state constitutional offices, supporting John Jobe for reelection as state auditor and Earle Hodges for secretary of state so that the deadlock on the penitentiary board could be broken.

Probably Kavanaugh's most effective issue was Donaghey's appointments of Republicans to state boards. The appointments included not only Remmel but Frank Mayes, a Republican and U.S. marshal, to the State History Commission. Kavanaugh said that Donaghey might be entitled to a second term as a Republican but not as a Democrat. These appointments cost Donaghey the support of both George Murphy,[15] the former attorney general who had been his ally in the state capitol struggle against Davis, and Dan Jones, the former governor who had backed Donaghey in 1908 but now said in an advertisement that Donaghey had insulted every Democrat in the state and was not fit to be governor.[16] Donaghey countered by pointing out that other Arkansas governors had appointed Republicans, and the choice of Remmel was to take the construction of the state capitol out of politics. One of Donaghey's most popular ploys was to accuse the so-called Little Rock Ring of campaigning for Kavanaugh. The "Little Rock Ring" was allegedly made up of three groups: the Little Rock contractors who hired convict labor; employees and supporters of the charitable institutions located in Little Rock, such as the schools for the deaf and the blind and the State Hospital whose budgets had been reduced; and the Little Rock Railway and Electric Company whose assessment had been raised and whose board included Kavanaugh's brother.[17]

Campaigning techniques and strategies were not too different from those in the 1908 campaign. There were still "swings"—a mailing of 150,000 circular letters or speeches throughout the state that cost $1500 with a one-cent stamp—two or three times during a campaign. Speech titles were still grandiloquent. A typical Donaghey speech was entitled "Shall Political Pirates Scuttle the Ship of State?"[18] Newspaper advertising was used extensively, with Kavanaugh purchasing twenty-one advertisements in the *Arkansas Gazette* and twelve in the *Arkansas Democrat*. Most were full-page with a picture and a message and cost $80. Donaghey had only eight ads in both papers, five in the *Gazette,* and three in the *Democrat*. Given his front-runner status, Donaghey seldom mentioned Kavanaugh's name but did give up to three speeches a day beginning in early February. Kavanaugh did the same and tried to use the sheriff in each county to his advantage. Both candidates rode handcars or walked when no railroad line was available.[19]

Notwithstanding the best exertions of both Donaghey and Kavanaugh, the *Arkansas Democrat,* in an analysis of the election, judged that there was "less excitement than has ever been known in either local or state politics in the history of Arkansas."[20] This was an exaggerated verdict, but the general sentiment was that the turnout was going to be lower than in 1908. Donaghey's headquarters predicted that his majority would be 40,000 if 125,000 votes were cast and that he would carry sixty-seven out of seventy-five counties.[21] William M. Kavanaugh, speaking for his brother, thought that C. C. Kavanaugh would carry forty-nine counties and would pick up 70,000 votes to Donaghey's 46,000 if 116,000 people voted.[22] Turnout predictions were pretty much on target, as only 115,577 voted as compared with 133,838 in 1908,[23] a drop of over 18,000, or about 14 percent.

Donaghey won an overpowering victory, receiving 69 percent of the vote and a majority of 44,079 as well as carrying 73 out of 75 counties.[24] As usual, he won his home county with 88 percent of the vote and even carried Pulaski County, where Kavanaugh lived, with 57 percent of the vote.[25] Donaghey's candidates, Jobe for state auditor and Hodges for secretary of state, also won, which gave him two reliable allies on the Penitentiary Board and other important boards. Donaghey's election triumph was so complete that speculation started immediately that he should take on his sworn enemy, Davis, in the senatorial race in 1912, with Congressman Joe T. Robinson possibly running for governor.[26]

For the first time in Arkansas, candidates had to reveal how much they had spent seeking office in 1910. Kavanaugh reported spending $15,188, with most going for printing of speeches and circulars ($2,719.09), newspaper advertising ($2,529.54) and postage ($3,818.45).[27] Donaghey listed about half as much, with only $7,805 spent. This included postage ($3,451.23) and printing and advertising ($2,762.50).[28] The *Arkansas Gazette* complained about expense reporting not being uniform because some candidates reported every penny spent and others reported only totals. It doubted that many candidates really revealed all they spent.[29] There were, however, two exceptions of refreshing honesty—one Pulaski County candidate recorded $6.15 for whiskey[30] and a legislator from Augusta wrote on his account $1.15 for "treats."[31]

Donaghey's spectacular primary victory was due to many factors. Even though Kavanaugh spoke well and outspent Donaghey two to one, his issue of Donaghey appointing Republicans to public office, which appeared to have the most popular appeal and did cost Donaghey the support of some prominent Democrats like Murphy and Jones, was softened somewhat by the acceptance, at least in Little Rock, of Harmon Remmel. Remmel was not regarded in the same way as Powell Clayton, who had come to symbolize all the evils, both real and imagined, of Republican Reconstruction in Arkansas.[32] Donaghey's hard work, his legislative success, his appointments, and his ability to present Arkansas in a more favorable light must have had an impact on the voters too. Even though there was no emotional bond between him and the Arkansas voters as there had been with Davis, there must have been some respect and admiration. The *Arkansas Gazette* stated about Donaghey's landslide that "Mr. Kavanaugh could not move mountains; nor do we believe that any other man could have moved them."[33]

State Conventions and the State General Election

As he had done in 1908, Donaghey, with the help of his advisors, picked a slate of candidates for all offices to be selected at the state Democratic Convention which was to be held on June 7 and 8. Not much opposition to the Donaghey slate was expected given his huge margin of reelection,[34] but there was speculation that O. C. Ludwig, secretary of state until January 1911 and a former ally but now a steadfast foe of the governor, would try to break the slate.[35] Ludwig did try to run for the position of permanent secretary against the Donaghey-supported candidate but was defeated by a vote of 485 to 124.[36] No more opposition surfaced at the Democratic Convention despite the presence of Davis as a member of the Pulaski County delegation.[37]

The Democratic Convention began on June 7. Donaghey was praised by a variety of speakers and made a short acceptance speech of about thirty minutes in which he talked about progress on the state capitol and the four agricultural schools.[38] A platform, prepared in just four hours, praised Donaghey in general and endorsed his administration "unreservedly and unqualifiedly"[39] and more specifically commended him for his appointment of the commission to study school laws and for his action on the railroad rates. The platform also applauded the action of the Little Rock and Fort Smith bankers who lent money for the state to begin construction of the tuberculosis sanitarium and backed initiative and referendum, pointing out that it would enable the people to put their views on record on the matter of prohibition. The platform took a backward step on convict labor. It deplored the practice but would allow it "where extraordinary conditions arise which shall make it actually necessary for their [the convicts'] maintenance."[40] The platform was passed without dissent on June 8, the final day of the convention, and R. F. Millwee and Bruce Bullion were reelected as party chair and party secretary.[41]

There was more drama to the state Republican Convention that convened on June 9, one day after the Democrats went home. There were rumors in April of 1910 that the Republicans would not nominate a candidate against Donaghey in recognition of his appointment of Remmel to the State Capitol Commission and the issue that this had become in the 1910 Democratic primary.[42] Remmel and some Little Rock Republicans argued that Donaghey should be given a clear field, but Powell Clayton, the Republican national committeeman and unofficial leader of the party, returned from Washington, D.C., and took the opposite view that a full ticket should be chosen, if only to maintain the party organization.[43] By the time the Republicans met, Clayton's position had prevailed and a full ticket was nominated.

Andrew Roland, the county judge in Hot Spring County, normally a Democratic county, was selected to be the gubernatorial candidate, and a full slate of state constitutional officers was also nominated. Remmel, who was chosen to be the chair of the party, seconded Roland's nomination along with Powell Clayton.[44] The platform condemned the Democrats for fiscal mismanagement and the legislature for meeting too long. Donaghey was complimented for "having taken a moderate step"[45] toward the principle that state boards should be representative of both parties. Abolishment of the convict lease system was endorsed again, and a resolution from the floor was passed to support initiative and referendum.[46] The platform was adopted, and the convention adjourned on the afternoon of June 10.

The next step in the political process was the September general election between the Democrats and the Republicans. In 1910, the races for state offices were overshadowed by another issue, the proposed initiative and referendum amendment (Amendment 10) to the state constitution whose fate had to be decided in the same September general election. It captured the attention of the voters to the exclusion of everything else. Two factors contributed greatly to this single focus. One was that Arkansas was the only state in 1910 where the choice for initiative and referendum was put before the voters.[47] The other was the requirement that a state constitutional amendment had to be adopted by a constitutional majority, that is, the amendment had to have not just a majority of the vote on the amendment itself, but a majority equal to the majority of the total vote for the state constitutional office for which the highest number of votes had been cast, normally the office of governor.[48] This unusual condition put more pressure on the proponents of the measure and increased both tension and interest.

The support for initiative and referendum was impressive. The State Federation of Labor, the Farmers' Union, and both the state Democratic and Republican parties backed the proposed amendment. Because of the national importance of the Arkansas campaign, George L. King, a representative of the National Initiative and Referendum League, was in Little

Rock to help launch the campaign and organize initiative and referendum leagues throughout the state.[49] The *Arkansas Democrat* was a strong advocate of Amendment 10 and said in an editorial that 90 percent of the newspapers in the state backed the proposal because it was "a weapon in the hands of the people to be used in compelling decency in public service and because it will curb the abuse of power."[50] Amendment partisans began the campaign to ratify the proposed state constitutional amendment on June 10, 1910.[51]

Opponents of initiative and referendum were equally vocal and had a powerful legal argument having nothing to do with the real merits of the proposal. As noted in an earlier chapter, the House Committee on Constitutional Amendments had added language to Amendment 10 to give to counties and cities the option of using initiative and referendum on local laws. Instead of accomplishing this, the language added was so badly drafted that, if taken literally, it would have allowed counties and cities to reject laws of the legislature and propose amendments to the state constitution. This poorly constructed and poorly placed part of Amendment 10 was referred to as "the joker." The best thing about the joker from the viewpoint of the opponents of initiative and referendum was that a voter could be very much in favor of the principle of initiative and referendum and still be against the amendment because of the joker.

Many lawyers opposed Amendment 10. U. M. Rose, who had been president of the American Bar Association from 1901 to 1902 and was one of Arkansas's most distinguished jurists, was especially outspoken. He felt that there "was only one way to deal with this spurious and bastard amendment. Vote it down!"[52] The *Arkansas Gazette* waged a passionate crusade against Amendment 10, running editorials against it on twenty-four out of twenty-five days from August 21 to September 14. Donaghey's crowd of enemies was also prominent in the ranks of the opponents. It included the three members of the penitentiary board (Ludwig, Norwood, Tucker) with whom he was always at odds, ex-Governor Jones, Murphy, Hinemon, and W. M. Kavanaugh. Ludwig, in a letter to the *Arkansas Gazette,* said he feared that Amendment 10 was an attempt to weaken the 1874 Arkansas Constitution. He listed in his letter all the delegates who had drafted the 1874 constitution and praised them to the skies.[53]

Donaghey worried about the opposition of so many lawyers, and fearful that the amendment would fail, he appealed to his good friend, William Jennings Bryan, "to come to Arkansas to help."[54] Donaghey and Bryan had been friends since the 1908 Democratic National Convention, and if Donaghey ever had a political model, it was Bryan. Most observers thought that Amendment 10 would receive a majority of the votes cast, but the question was whether it could get the "constitutional majority." In addition to asking Bryan to come to Arkansas, Donaghey arranged a special train, which he paid for himself, and arranged for substitutes to speak on his behalf in the general election campaign against the Republicans while he toured the state with Bryan.[55] Guy Tucker, one of Donaghey's opponents on the Penitentiary Board, wrote Bryan and asked him not to come, citing the objections of forty lawyers in Arkansas.[56] Bryan came anyway.

Bryan was recognized as the country's "most powerful champion . . . of initiative and referendum"[57] and must have been pleased to find his friend, George Donaghey, leading the fight in Arkansas for the same cause. Bryan spent five days in the state (September 6–10), opening in Fort Smith[58] and finishing in north Arkansas. He tried to deal with the problem of the joker and first said that it was just an excuse and that the courts would take care of it. Later, however, Bryan obtained a pledge from Donaghey; E. W. Hogan, president of the State Federation of Labor; and George Cole, president of the Farmer's Union to do everything possible to have the joker eliminated or corrected.[59] Since they were all traveling on the same train, this was easy to do, and Bryan mentioned the pledge frequently in later appearances.

At the many train stops, Bryan was introduced by Donaghey, whom he commended warmly for his leadership in the fight for initiative and referendum. Bryan usually spoke from ten minutes to an hour, using the same basic speech. His main theme was that the people can be trusted. As he once put it in a humorous aside, playing on the slogan of his 1896 presidential campaign for the unlimited coinage of silver at the legal ratio of 16 to 1, the odds are about 16 to 1 that "the people will come nearer to deciding what is right."[60] His biggest crowd was at Little Rock where fifteen thousand people heard him speak at the city park.[61] He was greeted officially at Little Rock by Harmon Remmel in his capacity as president of the Little Rock Board of Trade. Bryan said that he had no problem being welcomed by a Republican because "if you join a church, do you abandon it if a Republican joins?"[62]

Bryan's tour, which covered 1,750 miles and included fifty-five speeches,[63] had been a success, and even opponents conceded that

Amendment 10 would get more votes for than against. Donaghey forecast a 40,000 to 60,000 majority,[64] which would be more than enough to take care of the "constitutional majority." The amendment passed by a vote of 92,781 to 38,648,[65] a majority of 71 percent on the amendment itself and more than enough to meet the constitutional majority, which was 75,289.[66] It carried sixty-six counties, including most of the urban counties where the opposition was concentrated.

Donaghey paid glowing tribute to Bryan for passage of initiative and referendum against the opposition of most of the lawyers in the state and many of the state officials and said that he had "caused more laws to be passed than any man in the history of our country."[67] One final loose end was put into place when the Arkansas Supreme Court decided that the joker was a constitutional absurdity that would destroy the sovereignty of the people of the state as a whole, and therefore, it had no legal credence.[68] The provisions regarding statewide submission of constitutional amendments and referring legislative acts to the voters of the entire state were left intact. Another decision by the Arkansas Supreme Court[69] held that the passage of Amendment 10 did not change the total number of constitutional amendments that could be proposed in any two-year period. It was still limited to a total of three whether submitted by the legislature or by the people. Backers of Amendment 10 had assumed that the people could submit an unlimited number of constitutional amendments, and because of the decision and a need to clarify the language and procedures found in Amendment 10, another initiative and referendum amendment was drafted and passed in 1920. It replaced Amendment 10 in the Arkansas Constitution.

The election contest between the Democrats and Republicans was only a sideshow compared with the interest and drama surrounding the initiative and referendum amendment. Nevertheless, the Republicans opened their campaign at Ozark on August 4,[70] and the Democrats began theirs ten days later.[71] Before joining the Bryan train in early September, Donaghey made several speeches in Crawford County. Democrats were making a special effort there because Republicans had made some gains in 1908. The Republican candidate for governor, Andrew Roland, emphasized mismanagement by the Democrats. Remmel was active in the Republican effort and loyally supported Roland. He did, however, point out that both Taft and Roosevelt had appointed Democrats to their cabinets but when Donaghey attempted to appoint Republicans he was severely attacked. Remmel sensed a new spirit in Arkansas that said "come to Arkansas without regard to your politics."[72] Remmel clearly implied that notwithstanding his backing of Roland, a Donaghey victory was perfectly acceptable.

It was a very short general election campaign and one without lasting bitterness, much like 1908. Donaghey's appointments had disarmed the Republicans, and Amendment 10 had captured most of the political interest. Donaghey won easily, losing only Newton and Searcy counties as he had in 1908. Despite his vote total being below that of 1908,[73] this was probably the high point of Donaghey's political career. He had defeated Jeff Davis in his first campaign for state office, had had an enormously productive first legislative session, had obliterated with 69 percent of the vote a well-connected second-term candidate who had outspent him two to one, and, with the help of William Jennings Bryan, had brought initiative and referendum home with 71 percent of the vote.

Regular and Special Sessions of 1911

As the 1911 legislative session drew near, there was the problem of where the legislature was going to meet—the new state capitol or the old statehouse—and the accompanying intransigence of Ludwig, who was still the secretary of state, about the details of moving to the partially completed state capitol. This altercation between Donaghey and Ludwig has been described elsewhere, but it was settled by a vote of both houses[74] to move to the capitol building. A report from Auditor John Jobe was not encouraging about the condition of state revenues. Because of the cut in the millage rate for general revenues in 1905, appropriations in excess of revenues, and diminished collections from liquor licenses, another deficit was imminent.[75]

The usual pre-session battle for legislative leadership positions took place, and Donaghey, as he had done in 1909, proclaimed official neutrality in these contests, although Judge R. F. Millwee of Monroe County, who had skillfully managed Donaghey's 1908 and 1910 campaigns and was now the chair of the state Democratic party, was a candidate for speaker of the house of representatives. Millwee was elected speaker unanimously after his opponents withdrew.[76] The election in the senate was much closer, with Senator H. K. Toney of Pine Bluff becoming president of the Arkansas Senate by the margin of two votes.[77]

Senator Toney, along with Senator Webb Covington, had been indicted in the 1905 state capitol scandal on charges of bribery, conspiracy, and soliciting a bribe.[78]

Donaghey's second inaugural speech was about one-third shorter than his 1909 address. He spoke in the house chamber in the new state capitol, as he had promised, certainly a source of satisfaction for him. He repeated his belief that statecraft is "only an intensely practical matter."[79] Donaghey appeared to be somewhat more pessimistic than he had in 1909. He stated that he "had found many things to do, and, in most instances, but little to do them with."[80] He lamented the seemingly eternal fiscal crisis facing the state and blamed it on borrowing against future revenues and excessive expenditures. His agenda was less ambitious, only thirty items rather than forty-three as in 1909, but, of course, some of the 1909 recommendations were now law.

There were some new proposals in Donaghey's legislative agenda in 1911. Heading the list was a recommendation for an anti-lynching statute that would deprive any sheriff of his office if a prisoner were taken from him by a mob and lynched. Mild as this may seem, it contrasts sharply with the philosophy of Jeff Davis who once said in a speech in Eureka Springs that "in our country where we have no doubt about a negro's guilt, we do not give him a trial: we mob him, and that ends it."[81]

Other important recommendations not made previously included a new state health board with broad powers; a state constitutional amendment providing for recall of political officials; better legislative methods, such as introducing appropriations early in the session so that a better match between expenditures and revenues could be made; requiring public service corporations to give forty-eight hours' notice before discontinuing service; a workers' compensation law; and three educational bills recommended by the State Education Commission (creation of a state education board which was also proposed in 1909, a school consolidation bill, and a state high school board with an appropriation for its operations). He also included a state graduated income tax to support state government, although he had great reservations about ratification of the proposed income tax amendment to the federal constitution. Donaghey advised the legislature "to examine with the closest scrutiny this amendment to the Federal Constitution before you give it your sanction and approval."[82]

In the category of unfinished business, Donaghey again proposed such items as abolishing convict leasing; reorganizing the Penitentiary Board; doing away with the State Land Office; creating an office of deputy insurance commissioner to supervise insurance matters for the state auditor; strengthening the powers of the State Tax Commission and paying the salaries of the commissioners; discerning the will of the people on the sale of alcohol through initiative and referendum; allowing the minority party to have a greater voice in selecting election judges and clerks; and legislation to complete the capitol.

In the regular session of 1911, Donaghey was successful with some of his new ideas. A State Board of Health was supported by doctors throughout the state and passed easily. One had existed in the past, but it had had virtually no power and no money at all.[83] This new state board had power to regulate sanitation and inspect food and drugs. A modified workers' compensation law barred contributory negligence as a defense in a personal injury suit by an employee if the common carrier had violated any employee safety law.

The most sweeping and dramatic victories were in the field of education. The general assembly established a State Board of Education, and a State High School Board to assist high schools in the state, with fifty thousand dollars appropriated for this purpose. In addition, a school consolidation law was passed that set out procedures to encourage school districts to merge. This was a start toward solving the problem of 931 schools in the state with 35 or fewer students, 112 with 10 or fewer.[84] On the other hand, Donaghey had no luck with the anti-lynching or state income tax legislation, even though those measures were of considerable importance to him.

Donaghey drew a mixed verdict on the proposals carried over from 1909. Changing the Penitentiary Board received the same negative treatment as it had in 1909. On convict leasing, the house did pass a concurrent resolution stating the sense of the house to be that no convicts should be leased after July 1, 1911,[85] but this concurrent resolution was not adopted by the senate. The house greatly strengthened the State Tax Commission by giving it additional power to help in the search for more revenues. Assessment of property was to be at 100 percent of market value with a consequent lowering of the tax rate. Assessors faced heavy penalties if they put property on the books at less than full value, and appeal by taxpayers was to be to the circuit rather than the county court (county judge). This bill passed the house by a vote of seventy to seven,[86] but was killed in the senate.[87]

Donaghey had better luck on two other 1909 measures. One gave the state auditor authority to appoint a full-time deputy insurance commissioner, who would be in charge of the insurance department within the auditor's office relieving the auditor of that duty. Another perennial carry-over item was the state capitol. Donaghey asked for three bills that involved the capitol, two of which were passed with little opposition. One was the establishment of a Capitol Arts Commission to decide upon any work of art to be put in the building itself or on the grounds, and the other was a $75,000 deficiency appropriation to pay for the heating plant and other construction costs. The third capitol bill was an appropriation of $672,000 to cover furniture, terracing, and other construction expenses not included in the original contract. It was the most important of the three and passed the house on a close vote of forty-three to thirty-eight,[88] but Senator Covington, who had become Donaghey's chief legislative adversary, filibustered the appropriation to death in the senate on the last day of the 1911 regular session.[89]

Several other noteworthy incidents occurred during the 1911 legislative session. One bizarre event was Donaghey's veto of the legislative ratification of the federal income tax amendment, something a governor clearly has no power to do. Donaghey had expressed reservations about the proposed federal amendment in his second inaugural address and had sent a special message to the legislature,[90] again stating his position that this kind of tax should be left to the states. He also enclosed a letter from his friend, William Jennings Bryan, urging ratification. Bryan argued that there could be both state and federal income taxes and that thirty states had already ratified. This put the amendment so close to adoption that he wanted Arkansas to go on record in favor since it had "taken such an advanced position on other questions which concern the public welfare."[91]

The proposed amendment passed both houses by big margins but was vetoed by Governor Donaghey on June 1, 1911. Donaghey maintained that the state was in such deplorable financial shape that it should not surrender this tax resource to the national government. He said that to approve the federal amendment at this time would be "so erroneous in principle and so improvident in practice that it should meet with little consideration."[92] Both houses quickly overrode the veto and adopted a senate concurrent resolution that said the governor's veto was illegal and instructed the secretary of state to send approval notification to Washington, D.C.[93] Donaghey supporters such as Senator John Keel tried to make the best possible case for the governor, saying on the senate floor that it was not "a matter of merely romping on the Governor. It is simply a matter of the Senators doing their duty. The Governor has made a mistake and we should not be too hard on him."[94]

Donaghey's response to all this criticism was that the Arkansas Constitution gave him the right to approve or disapprove all bills and resolutions adopted by the general assembly.[95] Nobody agreed with him, and Secretary of State Earle Hodges, a Donaghey friend and ally, said that he would officially notify the Speaker of the U.S. House of Representatives and the U.S. secretary of state that Arkansas had ratified the income tax amendment. Hodges had also received a letter from Dr. David Thomas, a professor of history and political science at the University of Arkansas, in which he said the governor had no legal right to veto the action of the legislature in this situation and "that his veto is of no more legal weight than the objection of any good citizen."[96]

Congressman Joe T. Robinson, another Donaghey ally and friend at the time, introduced a resolution in the U.S. House of Representatives that the governor's veto was null and void and that the amendment had been properly ratified despite the attempted veto.[97] The income tax amendment became part of the U.S. Constitution on February 3, 1913, with Arkansas listed as a ratified state. Donaghey was still trying to explain this strange episode some twenty-eight years later when he said in his autobiography that he had vetoed the amendment in 1911 because the revenues from the federal income tax could be used for war purposes and war then looked probable in Europe.[98] The entire matter is still puzzling. It certainly did Donaghey no good, made him look stubborn and ill informed, and gave Joe T. Robinson a natural issue to use against him in their race in 1912.

Two other Donaghey actions worked against smooth legislative relations. One was his veto early in the session of the $200,000 appropriation bill for legislative expenses; Donaghey claimed it was $50,000 too much.[99] Although there had been attempts to reduce the amount prior to the veto, the veto hit the wrong note among legislators who argued that Donaghey should have used the line item veto instead of nullifying the entire appropriation. At any rate, within three hours after his veto message had been read, it was overridden by a vote of twenty-four to four in the senate[100] and fifty-seven to thirty-four in the house.[101] In the end, the actual cost of both the regular and special sessions was $192,000,[102] which made Donaghey look like a bad judge of events.

The other Donaghey action that led to more legislative discontent was the vetoing of three bills that were without doubt local legislation prohibited by the Arkansas Constitution. Nevertheless, a time-honored legislative tradition, sanctioned by the Arkansas Supreme Court, let the general assembly judge what was local legislation. The three cases involved school districts that were borrowing money and mortgaging property to pay for it. The sponsors argued that they could get a better interest rate if the transactions were approved by the general assembly. Donaghey thought that a general law allowing school districts to mortgage property would serve the same purpose and eliminate much local legislation.[103] These three vetoes were overridden by almost unanimous votes in both houses. Donaghey was probably right in the abstract, but he allowed his business instincts to overrule his political instincts, and he looked from a legislative point of view to be an intruder who didn't have to be taken too seriously.

Donaghey did take bold and decisive administrative action to meet the 1911 fiscal crisis. As in 1909, the state government was facing a deficit based upon the 1905 reduction in the millage rate for state general operations, borrowing in advance from state tax collections, and state expenditures exceeding state revenues. Donaghey estimated the deficit for 1911–1913 would be at least $650,000.[104] He again made the necessary hard cuts in the budgets of state agencies. In the 1911 fiscal surgery, thirty-one state agencies were affected, including the four agricultural schools.[105] His cutbacks would total about $575,000 over the next two years.[106]

Notwithstanding this reduction in state services and the sometimes rocky relations with the legislature, some comments about the regular session, particularly in the area of education, were very positive. Superintendent of Public Instruction George Cook was ecstatic and declared "that the Arkansas legislature had done more for education in Arkansas than any legislature in the Union has done for its state."[107] The *Arkansas Democrat* was a little more reserved but did call the session a great one for education since all the bills suggested by the Arkansas Education Commission were enacted.[108]

The death of the Tax Commission bill probably precipitated the special session. In vetoing $575,000 worth of appropriations, Donaghey emphasized that no permanent change could take place unless more revenues were found[109] and the Tax Commission was the way to accomplish this. Another factor may have influenced Donaghey's decision. Representative A. G. Little of Mississippi County resigned his seat on May 4, 1911,[110] in protest against the bribery and corruption that he claimed existed in the Arkansas legislature, especially in the senate. He characterized the senators "as unblushing a band of freebooters as ever scuttled a ship or looted the treasury"[111] and charged that liquor interests controlled the senate and made alliances with other groups when needed so that a governor was helpless when faced with this kind of power. Little also said that senators were being bribed to vote against the Tax Commission bill. Not much tangible came from Little's accusations, but it did serve to remind people of the unsavory legislative climate of 1905, when contractors, lobbyists, and legislators were indicted on charges of bribery. It also focused special scrutiny on those who might vote against the Tax Commission legislation in the special session and improved chances for passage, and thus may have helped persuade Donaghey to call a special session.

Thirty minutes after the regular session of 1911 adjourned on May 13, Donaghey had called a special session to begin on May 22.[112] Five items were in the call: raise sufficient revenue to meet the expenses of state government, abolish the convict lease system and reconstitute the Penitentiary Board, pass enabling legislation to implement the initiative and referendum amendment, pay court costs and accountant fees in the railroad rate case now appealed to the U. S. Supreme Court, and appropriate enough money to transfer the offices of the Arkansas Supreme Court and the state treasury to the new capitol building.[113] A special session of the legislature was rare; there had only been three since 1874.

Initially, Donaghey and the legislature argued over who should preside. Donaghey was greatly concerned that Senator Toney not preside, because of the bitterness between the two men. The senate had elected W. C. Rodgers as the president for the 1913 session, and Donaghey contended that the new officers should preside during the special session. If Toney presided, Donaghey said it would be an "act of usurpation."[114] Both houses, however, voted to have the old officers remain in their positions since a special session was merely a continuation of the regular session.[115] Donaghey then asked Attorney General Norwood to file a *quo warranto* proceeding against Toney to prevent him from presiding, but Norwood refused, saying that it was a matter for the senate to decide.[116]

A determined trio of senators was dedicated to causing the governor as much grief as possible. This bill-killing trio included Covington, who had been the president of the senate in 1905 and who had been indicted for bribery in connection with the 1905 appropriation bill (SB 370) for the state capitol that had been pushed by Caldwell and Drake; Toney, who had also been indicted for bribery and who had voted for SB 370 in 1905; and Senator E. F. Friedell. Covington had filibustered to death the 1911 state capitol appropriation that Donaghey had wanted so much. Toney had spoken for and supported the seventy-five-thousand-dollar deficiency appropriation for the heating plant early in the 1911 regular session, but his relations with Donaghey deteriorated after that. Friedell was the senator most responsible for submitting the tax commission measure passed in the special session to referendum. The influence of this trio alone may have been one of the reasons that Donaghey decided not to put in the call a request for a final appropriation to complete the state capitol. He also wanted to keep the session short and to avoid issues too closely identified with him personally.[117]

As might have been anticipated, relations between Toney and Donaghey reached new lows as the special session continued. Donaghey said that he would not have called a special session had he known that Toney would preside because Toney had "continuously called matters out of order and passed measures with the gavel."[118] Toney responded that Donaghey was incompetent and unfit to be governor.[119] Other senators also shared Donaghey's view that Toney had a quick gavel and selective eyesight. They almost ousted Toney from the chair over a particularly flagrant incident where he recognized Covington who moved to adjourn the senate. Despite twelve senators on the floor protesting these dilatory tactics and demanding a roll call, Toney declared the motion passed on a voice vote.[120] Toney survived this protest but it was a close call.

It was clear as the special session began that Covington, Toney, and Friedell were "the main opponents to the special session and to Governor Donaghey,"[121] who would try to adjourn the session, and if this failed, to delay everything so that the legislators would demand an end to the session. On the second day of the special session, Covington introduced a senate concurrent resolution that said there was no need for a special session and the legislature should adjourn the next day. It was defeated by a vote of eleven in favor and twenty against with three of the "yes" votes cast by Covington, Toney, and Friedell.[122] Covington tried the same tactic a week later,[123] but no action was taken on his second adjournment attempt.

Despite this opposition, much was accomplished. The expenses for the supreme court railroad case were funded as requested, as were the costs of transferring the offices of the Arkansas Supreme Court and the state treasurer to the new capitol building. Enabling legislation for the initiative and referendum amendment was passed. The only outright failure in the special session concerned convict leasing and the Penitentiary Board. The outlawing of convict leasing and three full-time penitentiary commissioners were both incorporated in a bill that passed the house by a vote of sixty-one to fifteen but was not acted upon in the senate.[124]

Without doubt, the most meaningful action of the special session was the passage of the "Turner-Jacobson" bill on assessment and taxation. This was almost the same bill that had been killed by a motion to postpone in the senate during the regular session. It incorporated assessment at 100 percent of market value and created an equalization board in each county consisting of three or five people depending upon population, with the county judge appointing one member and the governor the remainder. There were penalties if the assessor or the taxpayer failed to put property on the books at full value. A taxpayer who wished to appeal a decision of the equalization board had to take his case to the Arkansas Tax Commission or circuit court rather than the county court (county judge).

The tax rate would start at 6 3/4 mills but would decrease as the value of assessments increased. A tax table was provided that gave various tax rates geared to the level of assessed evaluation in the state. The measure passed the House by a very close vote of 33 to 30, with 37 absent and not voting[125] and, amazingly enough, the margin in the Senate was much higher, 18 to 8. As expected, Covington and Friedell voted no and Toney was paired against.[126] The Act was long and complicated, containing 128 sections and filling up 86 pages in the statute books.[127] It also did not have an emergency clause.

An emergency clause is a provision added to a piece of legislation adopted by the general assembly that says the bill is necessary for the preservation of public peace, safety, and health, and therefore takes effect immediately instead of taking effect the normal ninety days after the session has adjourned. The importance of this is that a bill with an emergency clause cannot be subjected to a referendum, but if the emergency clause is not present, it can. Senator Friedell took charge of the campaign to refer the Turner-Jacobson bill to referendum. He said that in an election, nine of ten would vote against Turner-Jacobson.[128] Only 7,573 names were necessary to submit an act to referendum and 17,000 signatures were gathered,[129] so the future of Turner-Jacobson would be decided in the state general election of 1912. Donaghey said many years later that Turner-Jacobson was passed with the express understanding that it would be referred to the voters,[130] which helps account for the surprisingly large favorable vote in the senate.

Donaghey was pleased with the results of the special session and felt that "the extra session did more for the state in the 15 days that it was held than the regular session did in 125 days."[131] The *Arkansas Gazette* agreed with Donaghey's verdict and pointed out that four out of five of Donaghey's recommendations had been approved and that the fifth (convict leasing and a reorganized penitentiary board) had at least been accepted by the house.[132] The *Arkansas Gazette* also noted that great enmity existed between Donaghey and certain members of the senate.[133] This made the outcome of the special session all the more remarkable considering the instantaneous opposition to anything Donaghey proposed by these three influential senators, one of whom was president of the senate and in control of the proceedings.

Administrative Events (1911–1912)

In his administrative role, Donaghey continued his distinctive pattern of appointments to state boards, trying to bring people with different backgrounds and skills to the boards and hoping to avoid choices based on "rewards for political service or favors of personal friendship."[134] To the new State Board of Health, he named seven doctors, and to the new State Board of Education, he nominated a history professor at the University of Arkansas and the professor of secondary education who worked jointly for the University of Arkansas and the State Department of Education.[135] Appointments to the Capitol Arts Commission included a newspaper editor, an art expert, and an architect.[136]

The State Board of Education, created in the 1911 legislative session, had authority over the public school system, including high schools, since the powers of the State High School Board had been transferred to the State Board of Education as soon as it was created. The State Board of Education was responsible for drafting regulations under which the fifty thousand dollars appropriated for the first time to non-specialized high schools would be distributed. The board picked ninety-five high schools for assistance, provided each enrolled at least twenty-five students, had a school term of eight months, and was willing to make some kind of matching contribution.[137] There was a 48 percent increase in high school enrollment (from 6,482 to 9,622) from 1911 to 1912,[138] much of which must have come from this new infusion of financial assistance. The State Board of Education in 1911 pushed efforts to organize school improvement districts and distributed 600,000 pieces of literature at the state fair in Hot Springs explaining how to consolidate schools, form school improvement districts, improve attendance, and in general, how to help the public schools.[139]

The 1911 legislature also created the State Department of Health and a new State Board of Health. The main concern of the new board in 1911 was hookworm, sometimes called "the great American murderer."[140] This disease was present in at least fifty counties. In these fifty counties, which were all visited, not a single rural school was found "with sanitary toilet facilities."[141] Since the Rockefeller funding to combat hookworm in the South was only for education about the disease, the State Board of Health had to rely on voluntary efforts. Physicians contributed their expertise, and some three thousand individuals were treated and many more examined. Municipalities were encouraged to pass ordinances to improve sanitary conditions. In addition, 287 public lectures were sponsored by the Board of Health.[142] The third annual conference of the Southern Association for the Eradication of Hookworm Disease was held in Little Rock in December of 1912. The conference was held in Little Rock at least in part to show recognition for the effort being made in Arkansas.

Donaghey continued his procedure of setting aside one day a month to work on pardons. He granted 236 in 1911, but 62 of these were simply to restore citizenship.[143] He also kept up his criticism of police courts for their excessive sentences.[144] One case that attracted national attention involved Earl Gilchrist, a black teenager who had been convicted of killing Will Longley, who was also black. Gilchrist was sentenced to be hanged, but there was a dispute about his age. The prosecutor introduced evidence at the trial to show that he was eighteen, but Gilchrist claimed that he was only fifteen. The national press picked up the story, and Donaghey received over ten thousand letters in August of 1911 protesting the hanging of a child. Many of the letter writers thought Gilchrist was only eleven or twelve years old.[145] After the Arkansas Supreme Court had denied a rehearing in the case, Donaghey, having satisfied himself that Gilchrist was fifteen or sixteen at the time of the killing, commuted his sentence to fifteen years in the penitentiary.[146]

In the matter of pardons and other administrative responsibilities where good staff work was required, Donaghey had already assembled a highly competent group of personal assistants with whom he had a very smooth working relationship.[147] One admiring though facetious comment about Bruce Bullion, Donaghey's chief of staff, was that he handled administrative matters and difficult questions with "characteristic aplomb and expressions of innocence which has caused friends to liken him to Socrates or to Julius Caesar."[148] At any rate, Donaghey had no trouble in getting the 1911 legislature to authorize two additional assistants for his personal staff.

The additions of State Auditor John Jobe and Secretary of State Earle Hodges to the penitentiary board helped, but it did not solve the problem of convict leasing. There was a contract in force covering two hundred convicts leased to W. L. Reaves. The terms of his contract were much more favorable to the state, in the sense that Reaves could take only convicts who could not be used on the state farm and the state could cancel upon thirty days' notice.[149] Nevertheless, the Reaves contract was renewed for one year with both Jobe and Hodges voting "yes," even though Donaghey opposed it. The contract brought in $1.00 per day per convict, and Jobe and Hodges probably thought the financial solvency of the penitentiary was at stake. More pleasing to Donaghey was the fact that three more counties were using the 1909 law that allowed counties to use convicts from the state penitentiary to work on roads in the same county from which the convicts had been tried and sentenced.[150]

Two more areas in which Donaghey found satisfaction were the State Tax Commission and outside funding for education. The State Tax Commission, since 1908, had added almost $100,000,000 in higher property assessments, both real and personal (from $326,985,096 to $426,413,893)[151] with $30,000,000 coming from higher railroad assessments.[152] During most of this period, the average assessment for an acre of land was $4.66, for a cow $8.18, and for a piano $41.80.[153] The State Department of Education in 1911 had three policy positions financed by Rockefeller aid: a professor of secondary education; a professor of elementary education, who also worked to consolidate rural schools; and a state organizer of school improvement associations.[154]

As regular as clockwork, the fiscal nightmare again appeared with no apparent solution, despite the work of the State Tax Commission and Donaghey's drastic reductions. The same factors causing the fiscal imbalances were present in both 1909 and 1911. The surplus in the state general operations fund had been exhausted; the tax rate for general operations had been cut one-half mill in 1905, costing the state $150,000 a year[155] or $900,000 in the six years since 1905; demand for services had increased, expenditures had exceeded revenues; and there were still outstanding warrants from state suppliers. The state had also been borrowing in advance on its tax collections. For example, 1911 taxes were due in July of 1912, but the county collectors were willing to forward their tax collections in January of 1912 rather than in July of 1912, thus allowing the state to borrow six months in advance. Even the $100 million in higher assessments levied by the State Tax Commission would only yield from $165,000 to $175,000 additional state revenues for general operations (only 26 percent of the state tax collections were devoted to state general operations). The state auditor in his report to Governor Donaghey[156] said he thought that revenues and expenditures were finally approaching balance, but because of past state borrowing from collections paid in advance, the state had to resort to scrip during parts of 1911 and 1912 and needed, in the auditor's estimation, an additional $500,000 to reach a sound financial basis.

Donaghey did take some time away from his official duties in 1911 and 1912. He went on a two-week hunting and fishing trip in Faulkner County in July of 1911[157] and a two-day bear hunt in November of 1912.[158] He was accompanied on the bear hunt by William Kirby, his former opponent in 1908 and now an associate justice of the Arkansas Supreme Court. Donaghey had been impressed with the graceful way in which Kirby had accepted his defeat in 1908,[159] and they had been close friends since that time. The governor continued his work with the Methodist church. He was elected chair of the Hendrix Board in 1912 to replace his close friend, W. W. Martin, who had died the year before.

There were also some humorous moments. Donaghey was not

allowed to ride the streetcar to the state capitol on one November day in 1911 because all he had was a five-dollar bill which the motorman could not change. The company policy was to furnish change only up to two dollars, and although Donaghey protested that he had received change in the past from even larger bills,[160] all this was to no avail, and the governor of the state of Arkansas had to walk to work. Governor Donaghey received the usual quota of letters from constituents seeking strange favors. Two women wanted him to get them divorces; one man wanted the state to finance a mineral rod for him so that he could find gold and other minerals, and, in return, he would share his discoveries with the state 50-50; and another man wanted the governor to find him a wife, one who was under sixteen years of age and who was "no social butterfly and a girl willing to work."[161]

During 1912 Donaghey spent some time with Woodrow Wilson, the third president he had met in his four years as governor, and the one about whom he had mixed emotions. In his capacity as a Democratic governor, Donaghey attended the ceremony in which Wilson, at his New Jersey summer home in Seagirt, received official notification that he was the Democratic nominee for president in 1912.[162] While at Seagirt, he went to a reception held by Wilson and met his wife and children.[163] Donaghey seemed to enjoy himself and when asked how Arkansas would vote in the 1912 presidential election, he said "We have already voted."[164] When Wilson for President clubs were organized in Arkansas, he joined one headed by his friend, James Harrod, and later joined still another Wilson club formed by the college men of Arkansas and headed by President John C. Futrall of the University of Arkansas.[165]

The negative side of the Wilson relationship is shown by Donaghey's comment that Wilson was a "Democrat in theory, an imperialist in thought, and a Czar in action."[166] He also sided with Bryan when he resigned from the Wilson cabinet over the *Lusitania* incident in 1915. Donaghey said "Bryan did not want war. Wilson did, and he gave the order for the United States to join in it."[167] As mentioned earlier, Donaghey later said he vetoed Arkansas's ratification of the federal income tax amendment because it might be used for war purposes. Donaghey said in his autobiography that Wilson was displeased with him because of this.[168] At any rate, Donaghey did not give the same uncritical acclaim to Wilson that he gave to Taft and Teddy Roosevelt.

With the approach of the Democratic primary in 1912, it seemed a certainty that Donaghey would try to run for the U.S. Senate against Davis, his bitter and unforgiving enemy. After all, he had defeated him once, and two potential rivals, Hal Norwood and Joe T. Robinson had both finally announced for governor by 1912.[169] Instead, Donaghey, in probably the worst political decision of his career, decided to run for a third term as governor.

SIX

Third Term Defeat and Vindication (1912–1913)

The question still is unresolved. Why did Donaghey decide to run for a third term for governor in 1912 instead of running against Jeff Davis for the U.S. Senate? Since the 1908 campaign, Davis had been unrelenting in his opposition to Donaghey, and although it was not Donaghey's custom to carry a grudge, he probably made an exception in the case of Davis. Senator James P. Clarke, the other Arkansas senator at the time, had broken with Davis and sent an emissary to Donaghey urging him to challenge Davis.[1]

Joe T. Robinson, who had supported Donaghey in 1908 and 1910 and who had severed ties with Davis in 1904,[2] would most likely have supported Donaghey for the Senate because Robinson was planning to run for governor in 1912. State Senator Charles Jacobson wrote to Robinson in early September of 1911 and said he had talked to Donaghey and informed him that ex-Congressman Stephen Brundidge, who was planning to take on Davis, would withdraw if Donaghey chose to enter the contest.[3] This left Donaghey a clear field. He could assume with reasonable certainty that he would be Davis's main, and possibly only, opponent. A senatorial election also would defuse issues like the Turner-Jacobson bill, prohibition, and the state capitol since they would not have the same impact that they would in a race for governor.

Nevertheless, despite the guaranteed difficulties of another gubernatorial race,[4] and his own weariness with the stress of being governor, he decided to seek a third term as governor. The main reason he gave was his fear that progress already made on the state capitol would be reversed.[5] He mentioned another aspect of the state capitol matter in a memorandum that he wrote years later. "No other public man," he said, "knew all the technique of the capitol construction as I did."[6] Joe T. Robinson saw another motivation for the third term, he suspected that Donaghey wanted to run against Senator Clarke in 1914. Robinson was unkind enough to write in a letter that this is "the real motive that underlies his candidacy now."[7]

Robinson, a ten-year congressman from the Sixth Congressional District (twelve counties in south central Arkansas) had originally intended to run for the Senate against Davis. He officially announced on June 2, 1910.[8] A tour of thirty counties showed little support for his candidacy. In addition, Brundidge, who also wanted to run against Davis, would not withdraw, which meant that the anti-Davis forces would be split.[9] Robinson had also heard that Donaghey would not seek a third term.[10] For all these reasons, Robinson decided to switch choices and announced for governor on September 15, 1910. People were surprised but began to speculate about a Robinson-Donaghey combination with Robinson for governor and Donaghey for senator.[11] Robinson was only thirty-nine years old, a relative newcomer to statewide politics but looked to be on his way up. Donaghey called him the "greatest orator in the State."[12] Robinson was "a dynamic and forceful speaker, with a style often compared to that of William Jennings Bryan."[13] He was so good at public speaking that in 1913 he could command fees of from $250 to $500 per speech.[14]

Another gubernatorial candidate was Hal L. Norwood, the attorney general of Arkansas in 1912. He had been a state representative, state senator, and prosecuting attorney before becoming attorney general. He announced on May 4, 1910,[15] that he was running for governor no matter who else ran. He did say in a later news release that he would not start campaigning until December 1, 1911.[16] This late start was undoubtedly to counter charges of doing too much campaigning while drawing a state salary. Norwood's decision was not much affected by what Donaghey did since the two men had clashed repeatedly on the penitentiary board and elsewhere. He may have also assumed that Donaghey would honor the two terms for governor tradition in Arkansas that had only recently been broken by Davis.

Robinson opened his campaign at Osceola on July 4, before a crowd of 3,500.[17] The issues raised in his speech sounded much like those George Donaghey or any other good Progressive would have raised: a corrupt practices law, direct popular election of senators, the abolition of convict leasing, recall except for judges, penitentiary commissioners, laws to limit campaign expenditures, and state expenditures limited to the revenues available. An early July start was an advantage because it usually took four months to cover all seventy-five counties, based on two speeches a day and a five-day week. That meant an average of ten speeches per week, although many counties would require more than one speech due to large populations or large geographical areas.[18] It was assumed that a good campaign would cover all seventy-five counties.

After Robinson and Norwood had officially announced but before Donaghey's entry into the race, which did not come until late October, one clear issue developed. It was the Turner-Jacobson bill on property assessment which had already been referred to a vote of the people in the September 1912 general election. Both Norwood and Robinson attacked Turner-Jacobson, claiming that it would centralize power, increase taxes, and make the right of appeal harder.[19] It was an easy target because it was complicated and contained 128 sections that required 86 pages in the statute books. It did require assessment of property at 100 percent and would without a doubt raise the taxes of some people. Donaghey, even though not officially a candidate at the time, rose to the defense of the Turner-Jacobson bill and was willing to stake his political future on it.[20] Beginning on Labor Day in a series of speeches, he championed the measure by pointing out that $300 million in untaxed property in Arkansas was not on the tax rolls, and the only person who could possibly be harmed by Turner-Jacobson was the freeloader who was escaping taxation.[21] Donaghey thought that Turner-Jacobson was the only way to put the state on a sound fiscal basis without a tax increase.

Governor Donaghey announced for a third term and officially began his primary campaign on October 22, 1911.[22] As was traditional on such occasions, he defended his record and called attention to the reduction in railroad rates, the employers' liability act, the agricultural schools, initiative and referendum, his vetoes of $1.2 million in state appropriations and $200,000 for legislative expenses, his appointments, and the progress on the state capitol. He advocated, as he had before, an end to convict leasing, reorganizing the state Penitentiary Board, a state income tax, and Turner-Jacobson. He said that he was standing again for governor not to satisfy personal ambitions of his own but because of the "evil conditions"[23] that paralyzed state government.

The unusual feature of this campaign opening was that Donaghey chose to pitch his reelection attempt not on his record or against Robinson, Norwood, or even Davis, but rather against the Arkansas Senate and the "evil conditions" that it caused. He blamed the senate, or more specifically the six to eight members who controlled that body, for frequent defeats of bills to outlaw convict leasing, for filibustering to death appropriations for the state capitol, and for failing to act on the Tax Commission bill during the regular session and submitting it to referendum after the special session of 1911. He went beyond this, however, and accused the whiskey lobby of controlling the senate and running the state. Donaghey said that they took care not only of legislation involving liquor but were also involved in other matters and deliberately promoted disputes over other issues so that attention would be diverted from whiskey. "They are strangling the life out of the state . . . the wheels of government are now almost locked."[24] Donaghey then traced his own evolution on prohibition stating that he was originally neutral, but due to the deliberate interference of the whiskey lobby in the proper functioning of state government, he was now going to support statewide prohibition as a device to rid the state of the liquor people and to help cure the "evil conditions" they brought.

It was a tough, slashing attack that showed promise. Many senators had been indicted, and one convicted, in the state capitol scandal, and there had been an almost successful revolt against the leadership of Covington and Toney in the 1911 special session. The image projected by the Arkansas Senate and senators must have dismayed the public, and running against them might have offset the downward pull on Donaghey of the Turner-Jacobson bill. This, however, was an emotional issue that had to be dramatized, which was hard for Donaghey, "a plain facts" man who always looked for rationality and logical solutions. Nevertheless, this speech was a good beginning for his anti-legislative theme, especially when he said in one of his opening statements that in the Arkansas House of Representatives there were "more good men than bad but in the Senate more bad men than good." He closed his talk with this peroration, "I appeal to the people of the state to stop sending men to become members of the General Assembly of Arkansas who ought to be sent to the penitentiary instead."[25]

Norwood, who had already been on the stump for some time, made his presence official on November 5, 1911. He came out against Turner-Jacobson, wanted to consolidate the Tax Commission and the Railroad Commission, and favored limiting legislative pay to the first sixty days of a session. He wanted to keep the Penitentiary Board as it was, and he was for a statutory enactment prohibiting the sale of alcohol rather than a constitutional amendment.[26] Both Norwood and Robinson tried to get Donaghey to debate, but he again refused.

About this time, the state's fiscal situation worsened. State employees in October were left, at least temporarily, with state warrants that could be redeemed at full value only when state money was available or could be cashed for a slight discount right away.[27] This undoubtedly hurt Donaghey. He responded by blaming most of the problem on the 1905 legislature that had cut the millage for general operations of the state by a half a mill, costing the state $150,000 a year in lost revenues. He declared that the state was still in the hole where "the 1905 Legislature put us."[28] Donaghey also emphasized his two budget cuts that totaled $1.2 million.

Other Arkansas politicians were also working hard for one candidate or another. John Hinemon, Donaghey's opponent in 1908, supported Norwood and, after he withdrew, Robinson. William Kirby, a former Donaghey adversary in 1908 and an associate justice of the Arkansas Supreme Court, backed Donaghey, but Kirby's strongest advocate in 1908, Jeff Davis, remained consistently opposed to Donaghey. Even though Davis was involved in a serious reelection contest himself, he attacked Turner-Jacobson repeatedly[29] and Donaghey even more often. Davis did, however, say on one occasion that he thought he was no longer in the business of picking governors: "I made such a mess of it when I attempted to elect Kirby, and you made such a mess of it when you refused to accept my advice, that I have quit attempting to elect governors."[30]

In the first part of January, the candidates were averaging about two speeches per day,[31] with the two most important issues still being Turner-Jacobson and prohibition. Donaghey was in favor of Turner-Jacobson while Robinson and Norwood were opposed; Donaghey supported statewide prohibition by a constitutional amendment, Norwood wanted statutory prohibition, and Robinson was for local option. Relations between Norwood and Robinson were surprisingly good judging by a letter Norwood sent to Robinson in early November thanking

him for some quail that Robinson had sent to him and his family.
Norwood wrote that his family had "all joined in a discussion of your
good qualities and refrained from thinking up any schemes that would
be to your detriment."[32] Some months later in a speech at the state
Democratic Convention, Norwood said that neither he nor Robinson
had said anything during the campaign "to destroy the most pleasant
personal friendship that has existed between us for years."[33]

The same was not true of Donaghey whose relations with both men
were strained. Robinson, for example, spoke in Donaghey's home town
of Conway, which no other opponent had done, and blasted Donaghey
for an hour and a half. Robinson accused Donaghey of dodging taxes in
Conway, removing good material from the state capitol and replacing it
with bad material, and looking ridiculous when he tried to veto the federal income tax amendment.[34]

On January 14, 1912, Norwood withdrew from the race declaring
that it was too expensive and that to continue he would have to go too
much into debt.[35] He had hoped to spend a reasonable amount of money,
but it could not be done "without resulting in an unequal contest between
at least one of my opponents and myself."[36] Ignoring this implied criticism, Donaghey said that Norwood had been a strong contender and that
he would rather run against Robinson than Norwood.[37] Robinson commented that he was glad that Norwood had withdrawn and he wished
that "Donaghey would do likewise."[38] Needless to say, Norwood did
endorse Robinson[39] thus solidifying the anti-Donaghey vote.

Robinson's advisors cautioned him about being too confident after
Norwood's withdrawal. Senator Clarke was unusually pessimistic and
wrote Robinson that he had not seen any great surge of support coming
after Norwood's withdrawal. He was also worried about the prohibition
issue, which he thought Donaghey might exploit since he "is no mean
artist when it comes to playing the demagogue successfully."[40] Robinson
was beginning to hear that Donaghey was counting on the eastern
Arkansas machine counties and the St. Francis Levee Board—a major
political power in the Delta—to make up for any weaknesses elsewhere
in the state.[41] There was also the frightening factor of Donaghey's
wealth. Robinson's biographer, Nevin Neal, estimated that Donaghey
"could put from $40,000 to $60,000 into the campaign while Robinson
would have to borrow from his friends."[42]

During the next two months after Norwood's departure, the race accelerated. In addition to the clear differences on Turner-Jacobson and prohibition, Donaghey was attacked for failing to debate, not finishing the state capitol on time, granting too many pardons, spending too much money on the election, allowing the state's finances to deteriorate, and violating the two-terms-for-governor tradition. Donaghey continued his assault on the state senate, declaring that "the majority of the members of the last Senate were the greatest set of political tyrants that ever cut a throat or scuttled a ship."[43]

Donaghey stated in a memorandum many years later that he knew about forty days before the end of the campaign that he was going to be defeated.[44] He also mentioned some unfavorable omens, such as the burning of his home in Conway and a near accident on the Black River, when he was trying to cross the flood-swollen river in a skiff. Donaghey barely managed to jump to the shore before the skiff sank.[45] To Donaghey, with his highly developed sense of superstition, these two incidents pointed to defeat.

Another more tangible indication that things were going wrong was Donaghey's campaign staff. Donaghey had expected Frank Milwee to manage his campaign, as he had done so successfully in 1908 and 1910. Milwee, the speaker of the house of representatives in 1911, was a candidate for the state senate from Arkansas and Monroe counties. At first it was thought that he would have no opposition,[46] but another candidate did file, and Donaghey supporters speculated that this was a move by Robinson to keep Milwee busy with his own campaign rather than "coming to Little Rock to take charge of Donaghey's campaign."[47] Milwee decided to stay at home but was defeated anyway.

Turning elsewhere for his staff, Donaghey selected Eugene Williams of Forrest City to take charge of his third campaign.[48] Williams had been active in eastern Arkansas politics for many years and was the treasurer of the St. Francis Levee Board. Donaghey headquarters was filled with people from eastern Arkansas:[49] John I. Moore of Helena, former president of the Arkansas Senate; A. C. Battle from Blytheville, the representative who had accused some members of the Arkansas Senate in 1911 of taking bribes to vote against the Tax Commission bill; and Senator O. N. Killough, president of the St. Francis Levee Board. The strong eastern Arkansas flavor in Donaghey's command center indicated a last desperate gamble to carry eastern Arkansas by a large enough margin to compensate for losses elsewhere. Another major problem was that Williams had joined the campaign on March 7, only three weeks before the March 27 primary, which meant a very late start.

During the last two weeks of the Democratic primary, Donaghey undertook a whirlwind campaign to salvage what appeared to be a losing effort. Speaking engagements were increased, and the issues of prohibition and Davis's support for Robinson were stressed. Donaghey's advertisements made the points that he was a prohibitionist who would do everything in his power "to put the saloons of Arkansas out of business"[50] and that the liquor interests were against him and in favor of Robinson. Robinson countered with advertisements signed by John Hinemon, a trusted prohibitionist, who endorsed Robinson and said that he would sign a statewide prohibition bill if it was passed by the legislature.[51] The other issue of Jeff Davis and his backing of Robinson was featured in a number of advertisements with some captioned "Jeff Davis Dictator."[52]

In a full-page advertisement on March 24, Eugene Williams, Donaghey's campaign manager, predicted that he would carry fifty-seven counties and gave the anticipated majorities in each of those counties. A 1,400 majority was predicted for Faulkner and 500 for Pulaski. Donaghey closed the campaign with a speech in Argenta (North Little Rock) in which he once again defended Turner-Jacobson and assailed "the whiskey ring and its grip on the Arkansas Senate."[53] Robinson closed in Little Rock saying that he would sign a statewide prohibition bill and that he did not know of any liquor support for his candidacy. He condemned excessive spending on the election, saying that he had heard that Donaghey's personal income was sixty thousand dollars a year and that he would spend twice that for a third term.[54]

The results were a great triumph for Robinson. His majority was 43,819 out of a total vote of 137,221.[55] He received 66 percent of the vote, which was very close to Donaghey's winning percentage over C. C. Kavanaugh. Donaghey carried only six counties, three of which were in eastern Arkansas (Cross, Poinsett, and St. Francis by only fifty votes). The strategy of concentrating on eastern Arkansas had obviously failed. He won his home county of Faulkner by only 85 votes and lost Pulaski County by more than 2,000.[56] Donaghey was philosophical about his defeat, which lends some credence to his later claim that he knew forty days before the vote that he was going to lose. He promised to support Robinson and accepted the results "without complaint."[57] Robinson returned to Lonoke, his home town, to celebrate his great victory and was greeted there by his supporters, some of whom, such as O. C. Ludwig, John Hinemon, and W. M. Kavanaugh, were also the state's most dedicated Donaghey opponents.[58]

Donaghey was not able to sell the "save the state from the corrupt senators bought by the whiskey lobby" theme. It required drama and emotion, not his strong points. In addition, Donaghey had to shoulder the massive weight of Turner-Jacobson, a much needed reform, but one that lent itself to the charge of raising taxes, because of its long and complicated nature and because it required property assessment at 100 percent. One political observer, writing to Robinson as early as September 1911, said that Donaghey "is trying to duplicate the feat of Senator Davis without the ability to do it. The Turner-Jacobson bill has ruined him."[59] A similar analysis in Conway's *Log Cabin Democrat* mentioned the impact of the state resorting to scrip, which was blamed on Donaghey, who was accused at the same time of being heartless when he vetoed appropriations. These issues put Donaghey on the defensive from the beginning and forced him finally to make prohibition the key to his campaign.[60] Robinson was a fresh face, at least on a statewide basis, a young man on his way up, and a gifted speaker. He skillfully portrayed himself as progressive enough to satisfy the reformers but not so progressive that the conservatives were turned away.

Donaghey supporters throughout the state lost election bets, including one in Rison where two Donaghey men had to push two Robinson men in wheelbarrows from the courthouse to the railroad station while a Donaghey partisan walked between the wheelbarrows playing a fiddle.[61] J. N. Heiskell, editor of the *Arkansas Gazette,* pointed out the immediate decline in Donaghey's influence, noting that before his defeat Donaghey could not walk the distance from the Gleason Hotel to the state capitol in less than an hour because of people who wanted to shake his hand and wish him well. After his defeat, he could cover the same area in five minutes.[62] Donaghey himself described what it was like to lose by remarking that a defeated candidate "starts out sure of victory, and, as the campaign wages strong and hot, he sees his friends rallying to his support and his majority mounts by leaps and bounds (in his imagination). And when the vote is counted, he finds, like Gideon of old, his army has deserted him."[63]

There was one encouraging development after this devastating and total defeat. The *Arkansas Gazette* wrote a sympathetic editorial the day after Donaghey's defeat declaring that "George W. Donaghey can well be content with the honors of two terms as Governor; the more because he was privileged to leave in the new capitol, stone upon stone, a memorial to the work of his hands while in public service. And the state will have to come to some measure of revenue reform like the one for which he stands sponsor and that did its part in bringing about his defeat."[64] The editorial continued, saying that Donaghey would surely be vindicated "and his policies of government shown in better light when the mist and clouds of politics have cleared away."[65] Donaghey said that this editorial written by J. N. Heiskell gave him a badly needed lift in his spirits.

The 1912 primary was the second in which expenses had to be listed. Robinson had gone deeply into debt to finance his campaign. He spent his own money, borrowed from banks, and received a loan of $7,000 from A. B. Banks of Fordyce.[66] His campaign expenses report showed a total of $11,870.37 spent with the three big categories being newspaper advertising ($3,256.44), postage ($3,665.10), and printing ($2,443.10).[67] Robinson said that it would require years of hard work to pay off his debts.[68] Donaghey's expenses were $11,668.50, with his three largest items being printing ($2,675), postage ($4,250), and headquarters expenses ($2,500).[69] This preliminary report put Donaghey's expenses below those of Robinson, but Donaghey said in the same report there were additional bills in the amount of $6,290 that had not yet been audited. Much of this probably involved newspaper costs since Donaghey had advertised extensively,[70] even though his preliminary report showed only $754 for newspaper expenses. The additional $6,290 should therefore be included. Thus, Donaghey in all likelihood spent a total of $17,958.50, about $6,000 more than Robinson.

The state Democratic Convention, as was the custom of the time, would be under the control of the new Democratic nominee for governor. The convention met from June 5 to June 7, and the Robinson people were in charge. In his keynote address, Robinson devoted much of his speech to the state's fiscal crisis, saying that expenses must be limited to revenues and that the state will either have to borrow to pay off the debt or increase taxes. He took at least one dig at Donaghey by stating that the state's financial system did not appear to have been "wisely administered at all times in the immediate past."[71] But he did say also that "gratifying progress had been made in education in Arkansas during recent years."[72]

A preliminary platform drafted by the Robinson forces included such issues as reorganization of the Penitentiary Board, reform in the revenue system, and short legislative sessions (no pay after sixty days).[73] It also endorsed a proposed constitutional amendment that would have limited suffrage to those who could read and write and interpret the Arkansas Constitution. A grandfather clause waived these requirements if the individual could have voted prior to January 1, 1866, or was descended from people who could have voted at that time or prior to that time. It was designed to reduce drastically the black vote. The full convention, however, refused to endorse the constitutional amendment, and the grandfather clause was defeated by a margin of 324 against and 242 in favor, with most of the opposition coming from eastern Arkansas where the black population was the heaviest.[74]

The platform, when finally adopted, did embody such Progressive measures as the popular election of U.S. senators, reorganization of the Penitentiary Board, and a corrupt practices act. "There was no reference in the platform to the liquor question, and no attempt was made in the convention to secure the adoption of any plank on this subject."[75] There was no mention of the state capitol or Turner-Jacobson either. The *Arkansas Democrat* editorialized that "the people of the state are now given notice that they will not be expected to be the receptive victims of this or that experiment in government," and Robinson has shown himself "to be in perfect accord with those ideas which, while vigorously progressive, are not radical or unsettling."[76]

State General Election

Turner-Jacobson had been handled roughly in the March Democratic primary, but prohibition was more viable. In either event, under the provisions of initiative and referendum, both would have to be voted upon in the September general election since Turner-Jacobson had been subjected to a referendum and prohibition was an initiated act. There would be a total of nine measures, five proposed constitutional amendments, three initiated acts, and one act referred to a vote by referendum the fate of which would be decided in September. The ballot for this first election under initiative and referendum was eight inches wide and twenty-two inches long, and there were so many items on the ballot that candidates were to be in one column and the constitutional amendments and initiated acts in another.[77]

Prior to July of 1912, the prohibitionists were working to put an initiated act on the ballot that would mandate statewide prohibition. The Anti-Saloon League decided that Donaghey's defeat in the Democratic primary had no bearing on their new efforts for prohibition.[78] They were trying to get Bryan to tour the state in the interests of prohibition and wanted to raise twenty-five thousand dollars for the September campaign.[79] The Anti-Saloon League was eventually successful in placing the prohibition measure on the ballot as an initiated act.

The campaigns for the proposed initiated acts and constitutional amendments began to be more visible during July and August of 1912. Donaghey was still fighting for Turner-Jacobson and prohibition, and Arkansas had the unusual political spectacle of the Democratic governor of the state and the Democratic nominee for governor traveling the state and speaking on opposite sides of both these issues.[80] Senator Jacobson officially opened the campaign for Turner-Jacobson on July 4 in Bigelow. He declared that Davis was responsible for the state's deficit because of his one-half mill tax cut in 1905, and that the only recourse was Turner-Jacobson.[81] With the exception of Donaghey, the Arkansas Farmers' Union, and the *Arkansas Gazette,* there was little vocal support for Turner-Jacobson. Even the *Arkansas Gazette* conceded that it would probably lose, because most people assessed their property at 30 to 50 percent and might feel that to assess at 100 percent meant a doubling of taxes.[82] Sensing the inevitability of defeat, supporters and opponents began to concentrate on other issues.

Donaghey played a prominent role in the prohibition effort. He went all out in his fight against the saloons, even offering to pay $500 a year for five years in addition to his regular taxes to Pulaski County to make up for the revenues lost from saloon licenses. In the same speech, he alluded to his father, saying that he had "tasted the bitter conditions caused by whiskey in my own family."[83] The opponents of prohibition conducted a vigorous campaign for local option, a choice that Robinson endorsed. They bought twenty-nine advertisements in the *Arkansas Gazette* and *Arkansas Democrat;* only two advertisements were run for the prohibition cause. Toward the end of the campaign, Donaghey began to talk about an alliance between black voters and the liquor interests to defeat both prohibition and the constitutional amendment embodying a grandfather clause.[84]

Surprisingly enough, Donaghey enthusiastically championed the grandfather cause and plunged wholeheartedly into the ratification campaign. It is hard to explain this distressing episode in his political career. As election day neared, he began to drop Turner-Jacobson and focus his energies on prohibition and the grandfather clause. He may have wanted the grandfather clause because he was irritated when he saw an unofficial alliance between blacks and the liquor interests. It could have been the typical Progressive attitude that well-informed voters were needed since he declared on one occasion that the grandfather clause did not prevent blacks from voting if they knew what they were voting for,[85] or perhaps he thought blacks were too easily intimidated and lent themselves to fraudulent elections.[86] Donaghey may simply have shared the prevalent attitudes in the state among whites that they should control the state.[87] It was certainly not an edifying occasion for Donaghey, particularly when Norwood, his former opponent, attacked the grandfather clause with the telling comment that it was "a reflection upon the white citizenship of Arkansas to endeavor to give them an advantage over the Negro."[88]

Donaghey supported, except for judges, a constitutional amendment to allow recall of all elected state, county, and local officials once they had been in office for at least six months.[89] The main instigator of recall was the Arkansas State Federation of Labor. However, the recall amendment attracted little attention. A newspaper article found this lack of attention applied to most of the initiated acts and constitutional amendments and predicted that the entire election would be a terribly confusing one since people were voting for so many issues at once.[90]

Conflicting victory claims were made by proponents and opponents of prohibition with the opponents predicting that prohibition would lose by forty to fifty thousand while supporters estimated a twenty to twenty-five thousand victory margin.[91] The great imponderable was the black vote and how large it would be. There were forecasts of a large black turnout[92] to vote against prohibition and the grandfather clause. Prohibition did seem to be the main issue, however, and vote totals for and against prohibition exceeded those for all other initiated acts and constitutional amendments.

Prohibition was defeated by a vote of 69,390 (45 percent) for and 85,350 (55 percent) against.[93] The news was even more discouraging for the prohibitionists because there was an unforeseen switch of sixteen counties from dry to wet, and only three from wet to dry.[94] This was remarkable given the campaign waged for prohibition. Even more remarkable was that within six months the general assembly passed a law[95] that made all counties officially dry but with the option to petition to change to wet. Only two years later in 1915, Arkansas was officially dry statewide.

Turner-Jacobson went down by an even larger margin, 57,176 to 79,899, or 42 percent in favor and 58 percent against.[96] The defeat, big as it was, may have been lessened somewhat by the language on the ballot explaining the act, which stated that Turner-Jacobson was "an act to reduce the rate of taxation and to revise and amend the revenue laws of Arkansas."[97] The grandfather clause suffered the worst defeat of the five rejected measures in the state general election of 1912. It was defeated by a vote of 51,334 to 74,950 or 41 percent to 59 percent.[98] Most black counties voted heavily against the grandfather clause as well as prohibition.[99] The recall constitutional amendment received a majority of votes on the issue, 71,234 to 57,860, but not a constitutional majority, which in 1912 was 84,805 since the total vote for governor was 169,610.[100]

The November general election of 1912 was a formality with Robinson becoming governor, and Woodrow Wilson, the Democratic presidential nominee, winning the state easily. Donaghey, as has already been discussed, found Wilson to be lacking in warmth and did not like him as well as he liked Taft or Theodore Roosevelt.[101] Nevertheless, he visited with Wilson in the governor's office in 1912 when Wilson was still seeking the nomination and later joined Wilson for President clubs and worked for him in the November general election. Donaghey's role, however, was minor since he was a defeated candidate. W. M. Kavanaugh was in charge of the Wilson campaign in Arkansas, and Donaghey was not even a member of the Arkansas Finance Committee for the national Democratic ticket which had been chosen by Kavanaugh.[102] Donaghey was also not a member of the speakers' bureau for the national ticket, but he did give one hundred dollars to the Arkansas Finance Committee.[103]

Convict Pardons and Vindication

In the closing days of his administration, Donaghey took dramatic action on a matter that had worried him for years. This decisive act caused more comment than anything else he did in all his years in public life. On December 17, 1912, Donaghey pardoned 360 convicts, and this action killed the convict lease system. There had certainly been past indi-cations that Donaghey intended to do something about the problem. He had consistently opposed the leasing of convicts, and in the 1912 cam-paign, he had said on several occasions[104] that if the legislature failed to act, he would pardon every convict in the penitentiary. He gave as one of his reasons the duty "of a governor to protect the unfortunate citizens of the state."[105] Donaghey had been part of a determined and losing minor-ity on the penitentiary board for four years, always voting against the leasing of convicts to private contractors.

Donaghey had regretted the tight time constraints on the peniten-tiary board and their membership on other state boards, which made it difficult to visit railroad or county convict camps. He criticized at vari-ous times the unfairness of the state furnishing food, shelter, guards, and clothing for convicts leased to private contractors and the inhumane conditions at the camps. In the railroad camps, the convicts were housed in cattle cars, with no beds, no medicine, and no physicians. The worst offenders had a ball and chain fastened to their ankles every night.[106] He had also denounced unfair sentencing by police courts, which lacked uniformity and sent people to the penitentiary to serve long sentences for minor crimes, as when a black man was sentenced to 180 days for disturbing the peace in Mississippi County and three other black males in Jefferson County for similar minor offenses were sentenced to 1,244, 741, and 319 days.[107]

Another precipitating factor was Donaghey's attendance at the Governors Conference at Richmond, Virginia, the first week in December.[108] At that conference, he attended a panel on prison reform, a major topic at the conference.[109] He heard Governor Cole Blease of South Carolina tell of the mass pardoning he had used to rescue convicts from the unsanitary and unsafe conditions under which they worked. Blease had pardoned 400 convicts in two years and "hoped to make the record 800" before his second term expired.[110] Ten days later, when informed of Donaghey's mass pardoning on one day, Blease said, "He has laid me in the shade."[111] After hearing other governors talk about "how prison reforms were being carried out in their states, Donaghey left the impression that probably something of the same nature could be expected of him when he returned to his home state."[112]

Donaghey sent Bruce Bullion to see the superintendent of the peni-tentiary, Jim Pitcock, and to inform him that in order to shut down the convict camps, Donaghey was going to pardon all surplus convicts not needed for cultivating the state farm. The penitentiary was also now out of debt for the first time in years. Bullion was to get convict records, which showed sentence, length of sentence served, age, and other details.[113] Hamilton Moses, another member of Donaghey's staff, was sent to report on conditions at the convict camps where convicts were worked under lease. He reported that they were fed pork and beans, slept twenty-five to a cattle car under filthy conditions, and were subject to being lashed at the contractor's request if the work was deemed unsatisfactory.[114] These reports reinforced Donaghey's belief that convicts were entitled to protection "and to their lives after they had served their sentence. But, under the convict lease system, they were often returned to society ruined in health and filled with hatred."[115]

On December 17, 1912, Donaghey issued 360 pardons, covering about 37 percent of the convicts in the state penitentiary.[116] The volume of paper work was so heavy that extra clerks had to be hired to process the forms. According to Donaghey, those pardoned were serving comparatively short sentences for minor crimes and most of them had already served one-half or more of their sentences.[117] Donaghey also said that the pardons were conditional and that if pardoned individuals violated state law again, they would be returned to the penitentiary to serve the remainder of their terms.[118] Three county convict camps in Desha, Mississippi, and Jefferson counties were wiped out. Just enough convicts were left to work the state farm with no surplus left to be leased. Donaghey estimated that it would take at least two years before the convict population was back to its prepardoning level.[119] The pardoning was so complete that no cooks were left at the penitentiary. Almost twice as many black convicts as white were pardoned.[120] Donaghey stated that his principal reason for the mass pardoning was "for the purpose of forever breaking up the convict lease system in the state," and he called convict leasing "a repudiation of the principles of civilization."[121]

Local and national reaction to Donaghey's act was extraordinary in its intensity. Most of it was favorable, but some in Arkansas was harshly negative. The Arkansas State Association of Prosecuting Attorneys called Donaghey's action "an insult to the courts, the juries, the officers, as well as the citizens of the state who believe in law enforcement"[122] and recommended that the pardoning power be removed from the governor and placed in a board. Joe T. Robinson wired the *Arkansas Democrat* from

Washington[123] that Donaghey's wholesale pardons "were a blow at the judges and juries of the state, an insult to those who stand for law and order" and "an impeachment of his [Donaghey's] own intelligence."[124] Senator Jacobson of Turner-Jacobson fame and Donaghey's ally in the fight for fiscal fairness, called Donaghey's deed inexcusable.[125]

Some newspaper comment was equally unrestrained. The *Arkansas Democrat* had six editorials in six days, all critical of what Donaghey had done. In one quite bitter editorial, the *Democrat* declared that "Governor George Donaghey, who is soon to retire to private life, with a desire to go to the United States Senate has made another bid for personal popularity" and has set "his individual judgment against those of men sworn in court to return verdicts according to the evidence in trials."[126] The *Democrat* also supported taking the pardoning power away from the governor to ensure that "no future governor should even be given an opportunity to do what Governor Donaghey has done."[127] In a more stately manner, even the *New York Times* found fault with Donaghey, declaring that he had "passed, if not beyond the letter of the law, certainly beyond its spirit, for he has misused the power of Executive Clemency with which he was entrusted."[128]

The praise for Donaghey was equally as passionate and much more widespread. Within the state, he was commended by the Little Rock Trades and Labor Council for removing this blot from state government.[129] The *Arkansas Gazette,* even though believing that the lease system would have been abolished eventually, still felt that Donaghey's "pardoning, by its effect on public opinion, will make sure the abolition of the lease system."[130] Other Arkansas comments were highly laudatory. A typical example came from the Rev. C. S. Mason of Cotter who called Donaghey's pardoning of the convicts "an act of justice requiring courage of a rare type."[131] Donaghey must have been especially pleased by the statement of T. C. Monroe of Magnolia, who was the state auditor from 1901–1905 and who had some first-hand knowledge of this issue. He said, "I think it is the most humane and patriotic official act that has occurred in this or any other state for forty years."[132]

Out-of-state reaction was overwhelmingly positive. It included such famous people as Theodore Roosevelt, Eugene V. Debs,[133] and Walter Rauschenbusch, father of the Social Gospel. Rauschenbusch wrote to Donaghey that he was profoundly grateful that "your human and official conscience has led you to so signal an act which will be productive of new conscience far beyond your state."[134] The *New York Times* achieved balance and compensated for earlier mildly critical remarks by some mildly favorable remarks which were found in a feature article about pardoning actions throughout the country that had been prompted by Donaghey's act of December 17. This article said: "Governor Donaghey's action has been generally regarded by the press of the country as a startling way of dealing with an intolerable condition of penal servitude, in which convicts were serving unwarrantable long terms at the same time that they were forced to endure the most horrible abuses at the hands of contractors."[135]

There were also letters from less famous people and institutions, from British Columbia in the west to Massachusetts in the east. One letter from South Carolina thanked Donaghey for "striking a blow for free labor and to uplift fallen humanity."[136] This letter was from the John R. Queen Barber Shop in Spartanburg, South Carolina, and was signed by "John Queen and six laboring men of Spartanburg." In addition, there were numerous out-of-state newspaper editorials, including two from Canada.[137]

Even more heartening to Donaghey than these supportive letters and editorials was the passage by the Arkansas General Assembly of Act 69 of 1913, less than two months after his dramatic proclamation. This law created a new Penitentiary Commission to be composed of three full-time salaried commissioners, a significant victory for Donaghey in itself. Section 9 of Act 69 provided, "The said commission should not hire out or lease, or permit any person to hire out or lease any of the convicts of this State to any person or persons whomsoever." The death of convict leasing followed the pardons by only fifty-six days. In his *Autobiography* Donaghey wrote, "I had been denied the opportunity of signing the measure for which I had fought, but the satisfaction was mine."[138]

The last month of Donaghey's second term was crowded with historical events. On January 3, 1913, Senator Jeff Davis died unexpectedly while Donaghey was still governor. The law at the time provided that the governor could appoint a successor who would hold office until the legislature elected a new senator on the second Tuesday after its organization.[139] In this case the date was January 28 because the anti-Robinson forces had managed to postpone the formal organizational meeting of the legislature until that date. This offered the possibility of three terms to be filled: an interim term from early January to the end of January, a short term from the end of January to March 4, when senatorial terms normally began, and a long or regular term of six years after March 4. Donaghey could have left the whole matter to the legislature, but he chose not to do so. One additional complicating factor was that in the event that Governor-elect Robinson won the regular senate term, and this looked very likely, a special election for governor would have to be called.[140]

Four prominent politicians were mentioned almost immediately for the long or regular term. These were Governor-elect Robinson, Governor Donaghey, Attorney General Hal Norwood, and ex-Congressman Stephen Brundidge, Davis's opponent in his reelection campaign.[141] On January 6, Donaghey declined to be a candidate for the U. S. Senate for the Davis seat but reiterated his plans to oppose Senator Clarke in 1914 in the Democratic primary.[142] There were rumors at this time that Judge William Kirby would run for the Davis seat, and he eventually did. Given the close friendship between the two men, there is likely a close connection between Donaghey's withdrawal and the Kirby rumors. Incidentally, Donaghey did not run against Clarke in 1914, but Kirby did.

On the same day that Donaghey announced he would not enter the senatorial contest, he appointed J. N. Heiskell, editor of the *Arkansas Gazette,* to the interim term, January 9 to January 31.[143] This was another one of Donaghey's unexpected choices that seemed to suit almost everyone. The *Arkansas Democrat* reported on January 6 that Donaghey had offered the position first to Judge Kirby out of gratitude for his help in the 1912 primary, but Kirby had declined.[144] Kirby would have been a logical choice, but Donaghey certainly enjoyed the surprise of the Heiskell selection. Officially, the reason given for Heiskell's appointment was that Donaghey wanted to honor the press of the state,[145] but he said later that he had picked Heiskell out of gratitude for Heiskell's editorial on March 29, 1912, which did so much to restore his spirit after his political annihilation by Robinson.[146] Shortly after his appointment, Heiskell said that he thought, in general, Donaghey deserved praise because he was a "builder . . . and what an undeveloped state like Arkansas needed in its governor's office, as well as its legislature, is more constructive work and less politics."[147]

W. M. Kavanaugh of Little Rock, a strong Robinson supporter in 1912, was chosen by the legislature to fill the "short" term from January 31 to March 4. Then the legislature elected Governor Robinson to fill the "long" or regular term from March 4, 1913, to March 4, 1919.[148]

This was the last selection of a senator by a state legislature because the Seventeenth Amendment requiring the popular election of senators was ratified on April 8, 1913.

Robinson remained as governor until March 10, when he took his senate seat. A special election to fill the vacancy caused by Robinson's resignation was held in July of 1913. Donaghey announced that he would not run for the vacancy.[149] The eventual winner was George W. Hays.

Donaghey delivered his farewell speech on January 15, 1913. It was shorter than most of his addresses and was only about twenty-two thousand words long. His last public statement is in some ways a philosophical essay that indicates what he believed and what he saw as his most important achievements.

In the address, Donaghey reviewed the fiscal situation in Arkansas. Upon assuming office, Donaghey found that the $500,000 surplus available in 1904 had been spent, the state was $135,000 in debt, mostly for penitentiary expenses, and was already drawing on future revenues. During his four years in office, state assessments were raised $130 million, but offsetting this, state expenditures had increased $900,000 (the two biggest items were the agricultural schools and the tuberculosis sanitarium) because of increasing demand for state services. Donaghey also mentioned his veto of $1.2 million during four years and took pride in the expenditures of over $4 million in four years without raising taxes.

Donaghey was also proud of the State Tax Commission and its work during his administration raising assessments by 1913 from $325 million to $455 million. He felt that the Tax Commission "had done more for the revenue department of the State than all other forces combined since the Civil War."[150] Donaghey regretted the defeat of the Turner-Jacobson attempt at tax equalization and thought that this nullified the whole purpose of government because the expense of government was "for the express purpose of protecting the poor and weak; and if this principle is not in some measure observed in applying the laws of taxation, what do governments exist for?"[151]

The reasons for the mass pardoning of the convicts in December were explained in some detail, particularly the abuses in the railroad convict camps. Donaghey hoped such practices "will not fail to cause you [the legislature] to give it some consideration."[152] The state capitol fund would be more than $400,000 by July of 1913, which he hoped would take care of the grounds and interior decoration. The most important item was that the structure itself had been paid for and the new state capitol was "doing more to redeem the State from the erroneous impression abroad that our people are non-progressive than any other tangible object to which the attention of the visitor may be directed."[153] Donaghey was elated that one thousand students were attending the agricultural schools and pleased with the new interest in scientific farming. He stressed again that he favored allowing blacks to vote only when they were "fully prepared by both education and intimate knowledge of the conditions or subjects under consideration."[154]

Some of Donaghey's final exhortation was philosophical in nature, such as the section entitled "Causes of Crime." In this section, he condemned society for failing to attach enough importance to the protection of human life, pointing out that if someone stole a horse, he would invariably be sent to the penitentiary, while if he killed a fellow human being, the laws of self-defense were so broad that three times out of five he would go free. Lynching fell in the same category; he recommended that the official in charge forfeit his office if he failed to give due diligence to the protection of human life. He attributed most crime in Arkansas to three causes: allowing deadly weapons to be brought into the state, the carrying of concealed weapons by those with criminal tendencies, and most important, the operation of saloons, which he thought responsible for about 75 percent of the crimes because most were committed by people who were drunk. In keeping with the Progressive emphasis on the importance of environment, he believed that the criminal in many instances "is the product of conditions for which society is responsible,"[155] and that it was the duty of the state to "remove those conditions which are admitted to be sources and causes of crime."[156] In Donaghey's judgment, the best way to make society safe from crime was to eliminate the liquor trade, which he saw as the cause of most of the crimes.

Donaghey was also very thoughtful about the role of the governor of a state as well as the role of the state itself. A governor in Arkansas, he felt, had little time or power to bring about the reforms demanded of him by the people. The Arkansas Constitution intended that the governor should be the "Chief Executive of the State, in all that the term implies, but through legislative action the Governor has been overburdened with so much drudgery that should be done in clerical departments that no man's mental or physical structure is strong enough to meet the requirements."[157] The governor had been put on twelve to fifteen boards, one of which required him to know the price of hay, another to keep in touch with the mule market.[158] Donaghey made no specific suggestions except to say that the office needed some relief from the imposed ministerial duties.

At the end of his last message to the general assembly, Donaghey listed eleven of his most important accomplishments. The list included the state capitol (number one on the list), agricultural schools, tuberculosis sanitarium, State Tax Commission, initiative and referendum, lower freight rates, appointments to state boards, and his vetoes of $1.2 million in expenditures.[159] Surprisingly enough, it did not contain the hookworm campaign or the creation of the new State Board of Health with the authority to enforce sanitary regulations, nor did it mention the State Board of Education and the state's assumption of responsibility for high schools. Another significant omission was the transformation of Arkansas's image to such an extent that sizable outside money was available for both education and health.

Because Donaghey was a lame duck, there was very little press commentary about his concluding remarks. The *Arkansas Democrat,* however, possibly still angry about the releasing of the convicts, editorialized that much of what Donaghey said in his last address had been said before and that he could retire to private life "with the consolation that he is the greatest prison liberator Arkansas ever elected to its highest office."[160] The editorial continued, "Governor Donaghey came into office a popular man. This can hardly be said of him now. He had a political future, but blighted it."[161] Donaghey still had the satisfaction of the famous *Arkansas Gazette* editorial of March 29, 1912, written by Heiskell immediately after Robinson's victory, and among other complimentary observations about the retiring governor, the editor of the *Gazette* stated that "Governor Donaghey has been a builder and a man who has done things. In his years to come, and we hope they may be long, he can have the gratification of knowing that he did his duty as he saw his duty."[162] Donaghey's last official acts on January 16, 1913, were to sign two pardons and the legislative appropriation bill of seventy thousand dollars for expenses of the 1913 session.[163]

Donaghey escorted Governor-elect Robinson into the house chamber where he gave his inaugural address on January 16, 1913. Robinson's main concern was the state deficit, which he blamed on the tax cut in 1905, and on the increase in state institutions and state services.

Robinson advocated a strict matching of expenditures to revenues received, no anticipation of revenues, and a bond issue to pay off the current state fund shortage. He recommended a tougher penalty for non-assessment of personal property, a reorganization of the Penitentiary Board, and an investigation of Donaghey's charges about the treatment of convicts. He thought the prohibition question had been settled by the state general election of 1912, at least for a reasonable period of time.

The 1913 general assembly could have been expected, in the light of Robinson's impressive landslide, to repudiate many of Donaghey's policies. In fact the reverse occurred, and the 1913 general assembly gave a clear and convincing vote of confidence to Donaghey's program, and indirectly, to Donaghey himself. An article, published in March of 1912 and entitled "New Conditions Seen in Politics," stated that "the legislature, although elected as a pro-Robinson and anti-Donaghey body, lost little time in adopting the policy that Governor Donaghey has been advocating for four years. It passed a law abolishing the convict lease or contract system and placing the management of the penitentiary in the hands of three commissioners who will devote their entire time to their duties."[164] In the opinion of this author, that legislative action was a stamp of approval for Donaghey's pardon of the 360 convicts.

In addition to reorganizing the Penitentiary Board and abolishing the convict lease system, the 1913 legislature appropriated $452,000 to finish the state capitol. It was finally completed in 1915, and in one of history's justified rewards, Donaghey was a member of the State Capitol Commission at the time and could see the end of his long and beloved enterprise. Other Donaghey measures approved in 1913 included a strengthened tax commission,[165] which was granted power to assess and tax the real and personal property of public utility corporations (gas and electric, water, streetcar and other similar corporations). Lastly and most unanticipated, there was an abrupt change in sentiment toward prohibition. The 1913 legislature tightened procedures for local option elections so that all of Arkansas became officially dry unless a majority of white adults in a county petitioned for local option and it was approved in an election. Individuals circulating local option petitions had to certify that the names of the petitioners were signed in their presence with appropriate penalties for perjury if anything was false.[166] In February of 1915, Arkansas enacted statewide prohibition.

A Model Ex-Governor (1913–1937)

Business and Service Activities

When George Donaghey left the governor's office in 1913, he was fifty-six years old and still had a quarter of century of activity before him. There are no written rules or guidebooks to tell ex-governors, or ex-presidents for that matter, how to behave or what to do when the aura of office has ceased. History and contemporaries do render a verdict as to whether an ex-governor has enhanced, simply maintained, or even eroded his gubernatorial image. Ex-governors still need to earn a living, and Donaghey worked in a variety of business enterprises after his political retirement. In addition, he devoted himself to many civic, charitable, and public-service projects. Eight years before his death, he left his entire fortune to a struggling junior college in Little Rock, an act, in its own way, as dramatic as the defeat of the Davis machine in 1908 and the pardoning of the convicts in 1912. When Donaghey died in 1937, his estate was valued at only $53,715,[1] and from 1929, the time of the bequest to Little Rock Junior College, to his death in 1937, he worked as a salaried employee of the Donaghey Foundation at $1,000 a month. His focus on public service and returning to the community much of what he had obtained through his own efforts is a useful primer for future ex-governors to follow.

Donaghey became involved in banking soon after the end of his term as governor. He was one of the vice-presidents of Bankers Trust Company from 1913 to 1925. The bank at Second and Main in Little Rock had been organized by Harmon Remmel, who served as board chair while Donaghey was a vice-president. Sam Frauenthal was legal counsel[2] for the Bankers Trust Company. He had moved to Little Rock after his service on the Arkansas Supreme Court, and with both Remmel and Frauenthal active in the Bankers Trust, Donaghey was among friends. Donaghey later became president of the First National Bank in North Little Rock, which he established in 1923. Remmel was a stockholder and helped Donaghey get a national charter.[3] The bank was located at 200 Main in North Little Rock, and Donaghey said that while he would not give up his Little Rock interests, he would have an office in the new bank and would give it close supervision.[4] He was president from 1923 to 1926.

Another banking venture was the Federal Bank and Trust Company of Little Rock, which had its office in the lower floor of the Donaghey Trust Building at 112 East Seventh Street. The five-story building had been constructed by Donaghey, and as time went on, it was often called the Federal Bank and Trust Building. It was renamed the Waldron Building in 1946.[5] Donaghey was the founder and president of the Federal Bank and Trust Company, which went into voluntary liquidation in 1931 during the Great Depression but paid off its depositors.[6]

Donaghey also expanded into savings and loan and life insurance but only in a small way. He was the president of the National Savings and Loan Association of Arkansas, vice-president of the National Savings and Loan Association of Texas, and vice-president of the National Savings Life Insurance Company of Arkansas, Kansas, Missouri, and Texas. Not much information is available about these companies, except that two of them, National Savings and Loan of Arkansas and the National Savings Life Insurance Company of Arkansas, Kansas, Missouri, and Texas, were located in offices next to each other in the Donaghey Building at 701 Main, and that the same William M. Glass was listed as agency director for the life insurance company[7] and secretary-treasurer of the Arkansas savings and loan company.[8]

Construction, Donaghey's first love, was not overlooked. In Little Rock, he built the Bankers' Trust Building at Second and Main; the Beal-Burrow Dry Goods Company Building, a seven-floor structure at

107–111 East Markham; the Exchange National Bank building at Main and Capitol, now called the Exchange Building; the Aviation Warehouse in 1917 located southeast of Little Rock, which stored airplane engines and cost $1 million;[9] and the Wallace Building in 1928, a nine-story structure at the southeast corner of Markham and Main named for his wife's family. He also built in 1917 the Old Main Building at what is now the University of Central Arkansas.

His most publicized construction project at that time was the Donaghey Building or the New Donaghey Building at Seventh and Main. It was built in 1926 at a cost of more than $1 million and was fourteen stories tall, the tallest building in the state at the time. The Donaghey Building was dedicated on April 1, 1926. About five thousand people went through the building at night when all fourteen stories were flooded with light.[10] Donaghey conducted tours through the building himself and gave a short talk in which he said that he wanted to leave something behind that would aid his fellow citizens of Little Rock and he thought a building appropriate for that purpose, because even though the Donaghey Building might change ownership, still "it will stand until there is no longer any need for it."[11] He was unusually pleased with a telegram from Jo Frauenthal, president of the Conway Chamber of Commerce, congratulating him on his new building and declaring that they were proud of the fact that Conway had "contributed to the state such a distinguished governor and to Little Rock such a progressive citizen."[12]

The erection of the Donaghey Building and the Wallace Building along with the Federal Bank and Trust Building gave Donaghey twenty-eight floors to rent. In connection with the management of these three buildings, he began publishing the *Donaghey News*. It was a small pamphlet that contained news of interest to tenants and an editor's page on which Donaghey usually set forth his philosophy on a variety of issues. The *News* was published once a month for ten years, was distributed to all tenants in the three buildings, and eventually had a circulation of three thousand.[13] Donaghey's essays in the *News* were collected and published in book form (*Homespun Philosophy*) by his wife. One of his tenants in the Donaghey Building thought that Donaghey did regard his tenants, in some sense, as an extended family and that the newsletter reflected that.[14]

Other business-related interests included the Beal-Burrow Dry Goods Co., in which he invested fifty thousand dollars[15] profitably and became a vice-president and a member of the board for ten years, and the Donaghey Real Estate and Construction Company organized in 1915 to deal in real estate.[16] The state of Oklahoma employed Donaghey to appraise the value of railroad buildings on the lines of three or four railroads in the state,[17] an easy job since Donaghey had constructed many of the original structures himself. He managed to appraise one thousand buildings in three months. He was also a promoter and stockholder in the Albert Pike Hotel in Little Rock.[18]

Throughout his thirty years in Little Rock, Donaghey retained his ties to the land. As he once said, "I have never been without a farm. It has always been a consoling thought for me that in the event of everything else failing, I would have a piece of land which not only would make a home but a living for me as well."[19] Donaghey had spent from 1907 to 1916, almost ten years, reclaiming some swamp land southwest of Conway. He had reclaimed over 700 acres at the time of its sale in 1916.

His last love, however, was a plantation of three thousand acres near McGehee in Desha County. With some others, Donaghey incorporated the Chickasaw Land Company in 1919[20] to buy and sell real estate, build houses, and sell merchandise and livestock. The land was mostly swamp and cutover timber, but each year more acres were brought into cultivation. In 1931 Donaghey bought out his partners and became sole owner of the Chickasaw plantation on which he raised cotton, sold timber, and rented land to other farmers. He was so attached to this land in Desha County that he tried to visit it at least once or twice a week, even though it was 108 miles from Little Rock and took 2 hours and 15 minutes driving time to get there. In a letter in 1937 when he was eighty-one years old, he said that in spite of the long drive, he still had five or six hours to get on a horse and supervise the cultivation of his plantation.[21] His wife, Louvenia, was not impressed with this heroic feat and felt that a man his age had no business burdening himself "with a plantation of almost three thousand acres, more than a hundred miles from Little Rock, in the Mississippi bottoms,"[22] but Donaghey declared that these weekly visits to the Chickasaw plantation gave him great pleasure.[23]

Donaghey's nonprofit work was equally impressive. Probably most rewarding for Donaghey in the area of public service was his appointment to the State Capitol Commission from 1913 to 1917 when the state capitol was finally completed. He was also a member of the Capitol Arts Commission for many years. Largely due to appointments by

Governor Tom McRae and Governor J. M. Futrell, Donaghey was president of the Board of Control of the State Charitable Institutions for four years, president of the State Board of Education for two years, chair of the State Board of Charities and Corrections for two years, and chair of the State Planning Board at the time of his death. His service on honorary state commissions was also worth noting. He was a member of the Honorary Educational Commission created by Governor McRae to survey local school conditions in the state, the Honorary Board for the Management and Operation of the State Hospital for Nervous Diseases and the Hospital Dairy Farm, the Capitol Grounds Commission, and the Arkansas Centennial Commission.

The Donagheys continued to be active members of the Methodist church. Donaghey was on the Hendrix board from 1906 to 1937, and when his good friend W. W. Martin died, he was selected as chair to succeed Martin. He served in this capacity from 1912 to 1914.[24] Earlier in his career, he had helped persuade the General Education Board to make a $75,000 donation to the Hendrix endowment fund on the condition that Hendrix secure an additional $225,000.[25] Donaghey also made sizeable personal financial contributions to Hendrix during his thirty years on the board. He was a member of the National Board of Finance of the Methodist church.[26] Both he and his wife joined the First Methodist Church in Little Rock, where he served on the Board of Trustees from 1916 to 1937 and was chair of the board from 1927 to 1937.[27]

Other religious and charitable work included the Arkansas Tuberculosis Association where he was chair for eight years. He also carried his share of volunteer work during World War I and was praised by the Treasury Department for his participation in the third and fourth Liberty Loan campaigns. He received a "War Medal Certificate" for his efforts, which entitled him to a war medal made from the metal of captured German guns.[28] Donaghey's charitable and religious commitment extended to predominantly black institutions. He was chair of the Board of Trustees of Philander Smith College for a number of years[29] and served on the advisory board of the Haygood Industrial Institution in Pine Bluff for eighteen years.[30] C. C. Neal, who was president of the Haygood Industrial Institute at Donaghey's death, wrote that Donaghey had been very generous with his money even though he had wanted the Institute to merge with Philander Smith. When this did not occur, Donaghey still renewed his contributions to both institutions, and Neal concluded that Donaghey "was always ready to speak for understandable race relations and wished to see the Negro rise in the scale of good citizenship."[31] By the time of his death in 1937, Donaghey had resigned from all but three of his volunteer activities: Hendrix College, the State Planning Board, and the Arkansas Tuberculosis Association.[32]

One of the best examples of Donaghey's community spirit that had an enduring impact in Little Rock for many years was the construction of the Broadway and Main Street bridges across the Arkansas River between Little Rock and North Little Rock. They were a good combination of Donaghey's civic spirit and his building skills. The old Main Street bridge, made of iron, had been used for about twenty-five years, but it was fast reaching its capacity.[33] The attempt to build a new bridge started in 1913 but bogged down over the question of whether the new bridge should cross the river at Main or Broadway. The Main Street faction was led by Donaghey, and the Broadway faction was led by Justin Matthews. The deadlock was broken in 1919 when the legislature passed a bill that established a Broadway–Main Street Improvement District with Donaghey as chair and Matthews as secretary. The solution, of course, was to erect two bridges, one at Main and one at Broadway, and a bond issue of $2,225,000 was authorized.[34] Construction began in January of 1921.

The Broadway Bridge was completed in a little more than two years and was officially opened on March 14, 1923. It was dedicated to the Arkansans who had died in World War I and was celebrated by the greatest parade in Little Rock history with two and one-half miles of marching civic and military organizations.[35] Senator Joe T. Robinson was the main speaker, but Donaghey also spoke in his role as the chair of the Broadway–Main Street district that had built the bridge. In his talk, Donaghey spoke on behalf of the 350 construction workers who had built the bridge, the 150,000 taxpayers who had financed it, and the bridge commissioners who had worked on it for ten years.[36] It cost $971,000.[37]

The Main Street Bridge was finished a year later, on May 22, 1924. In this case, Donaghey gave the dedicatory address in his official capacity as the chair of the Broadway–Main Street Bridge District Commission. The completion of the Main Street bridge generated a three-day celebration in Little Rock and a big parade, which took forty-eight minutes to pass a given point.[38] In his dedicatory address, Donaghey mentioned that forty thousand dollars of the money available had been saved.[39] The bridge was dedicated to sailors, marines, and nurses of World War I. Admiral E. W. Kittelle acknowledged the dedication on behalf of the navy. He later wrote to Donaghey that "If you never did anything else in your life . . . there is nothing that would shine more clearly in the future than the construction of this splendid viaduct across the Arkansas River."[40]

Donaghey was active in several civic organizations including the Masons. He belonged to the Green Grove Lodge 107 in Conway where he was secretary from 1884 to 1886.[41] He took minutes in his own handwriting and also kept the dues list, which showed that he had paid his $2.00 dues for both 1897 and 1899. Many Conway friends were also Masons, such as James Harrod, J. A. Pence, and Sam and Jo Frauenthal. In his autobiography,[42] Donaghey expresses his gratitude to Dr. George Douglas Dickerson who was his instructor in Masonic studies that lead to the first three degrees in Masonry. Donaghey passed these first three degrees and later became a thirty-second degree Mason in 1904.

The Little Rock Junior College Bequest

Donaghey reached the age of seventy the same year that he constructed the fourteen-story Donaghey Building, and he began searching for an appropriate and beneficial way to devote the profits from the building to worthy causes, since he and Louvenia had no children.[43] It was apparently a joint decision to leave the Donaghey estate to some Arkansas school. Donaghey had a strong belief in the value of education. This was reinforced by the incident, related in his autobiography, in which he met an elderly man at the University of Chicago who had bequeathed his fortune to that university and appeared to be very happy with his decision.[44] Donaghey was so impressed with the man and his peace of mind that he was certain that that contact was the "springboard from which soared my ambition to endow a college for Arkansas."[45]

Another factor that may have contributed to the decision was a pamphlet found in Donaghey's 1903 scrapbook, entitled "Great College Memorials." It was a sophisticated appeal for money from Hendrix College and presumably came into Donaghey's possession because he was a trustee. It started with a quotation from Calvin Coolidge about the benefits of endowing universities and then gave some famous examples of universities started with private fortunes, such as Harvard, Duke, Vanderbilt, Brown, and Stanford. The appeal was especially aimed at businessmen and stressed that a bequest was an investment and not a gift or charity. It closed with the thought that endowing colleges had been overlooked as a field for investment, and because Arkansas educational institutions are so poor, Arkansas "offers a rare opportunity for the development of one or more great colleges through which to channel the course of history, such an opportunity as only a state with underdeveloped institutions can offer." What role this pamphlet played in Donaghey's decision is pure conjecture, but he did think enough of the pamphlet to save it for his scrapbook.

Once the decision had been made to leave the Donaghey estate to a school or college, the next question was which school was to be the beneficiary. Donaghey spent three years studying all the schools in Arkansas[46] and finally chose Little Rock Junior College. He had thought earlier about endowing a School of Technology in Little Rock with the understanding that maintenance would still be a state responsibility, but abandoned this idea because there were so many communities competing for state-supported schools.[47]

Little Rock Junior College (LRJC) had been founded in 1927 and was the youngest college in the state. It was occupying space on the north end of the new Little Rock Senior High School building (later Little Rock Central). John Larson, the principal of Little Rock Senior High School, had started the junior college with the approval of the Little Rock School Board under whose authority and control the junior college initially operated. One condition of approval by the Little Rock School Board was that the board assume no financial responsibility. That meant LRJC would have to finance itself through tuition, because no public funds would be allowed as long as it operated under the authority of the school board.[48] This made the financial case for LRJC even more appealing to Donaghey. Other reasons for his choice were the presence of 100,000 people within five miles of the center of the state, the inability of most people to leave home to go to college,[49] and the fact that "Little Rock was the commercial center of the State . . . and more advantages would accrue to the greatest number of Arkansas citizens."[50] Or to put it another way, LRJC was young, poor, and centrally located.

The actual bequest was timed to coincide with Donaghey's seventy-third birthday on July 1, 1929. The trust deed itself conveyed the

Donaghey Building and the Federal Bank and Trust Building (Waldron Building) to the George W. Donaghey Foundation to be held in trust for the benefit of Little Rock Junior College. Payments on existing mortgages of about $800,000 had to be made first at a rate of $40,000 a year. Donaghey was still to manage the property under the direction of the trustees, with a salary of $1,000 a month as long as he lived.[51] Local realtors estimated the value of the gift as being between $1.5 million and $2 million. The *Arkansas Democrat* said, "Never before has so generous a gift been made for a Little Rock or Arkansas institution, public or private."[52] An unselfish tribute came from Hendrix College. This tribute was in a Hendrix pamphlet entitled, "Dividends of Giving," and declared "Ex-Governor Donaghey has also helped a great senior college. In addition to contributions to Hendrix, the Governor has served for a quarter of a century on its Board, indeed one of its most faithful members. Captain W. W. Martin of Conway did for Hendrix College largely what Governor Donaghey has done for the Junior College, namely, founded it."[53]

Donaghey made a second bequest of Main Street property to the Donaghey Foundation in October of 1937. It included property on the southwest corner of Eighth and Main and at 117 Main.[54] The two properties together were valued at $100,000, and the Donaghey Foundation now held in trust four pieces of Main Street property. It was also announced at the time of the second bequest that the original debt had been reduced from $800,000 to $500,000.[55]

Things, however, had not been as rosy as originally predicted for LRJC during the period between the first bequest and the second bequest, because the stock market crashed within four months of Donaghey's gift and the Donaghey Foundation met weekly to deal with the heavy debt and financial crisis brought on by the Great Depression.[56] During the first ten years, LRJC averaged less than three thousand dollars a year,[57] and this was only because Donaghey at various times during this ten-year period donated at least ten thousand and possibly fifteen thousand dollars of his salary payments to LRJC.[58] By 1938 the Depression had lifted somewhat, the mortgages had been refinanced, and professional clients, such as doctors and dentists, began moving into the Donaghey Building. Consequently, payments increased to about ten thousand dollars during the 1940s.

The mortgages were paid off in the early 1950s, and contributions to LRJC were raised to seventy-five thousand dollars annually, which was 32 percent of the operating budget from 1953 to 1954. This percentage declined, however, as enrollment increased, private donations grew, and federal programs started, so that in the late 1950s the Donaghey percentage was in the range of 20 to 25 percent.[59]

Times were prosperous enough for a change to a four-year college to be considered, and the Ottenheimer Committee recommended to the Little Rock School Board in May of 1956 that a four-year college be established by 1961 to be called the "George W. Donaghey College of Little Rock."[60] Incidentally, Donaghey himself had favored a four-year institution and said in one of his speeches, "We have set our hearts upon a University for Little Rock and we are going to have it."[61] In one of his last interviews before his death, he told a reporter from the *Little Rock Junior College Chatter,* the school newspaper, that he hoped "that someday Little Rock Junior College would become a four-year university."[62]

Little Rock Junior College did become a four-year college on June 1, 1957, but it was not called the Donaghey College. Dr. Carey B. Stabler, the first president of the new four-year college thought that "Little Rock University" would carry a broader appeal and was able to persuade the board to make the change.[63] With the advent of a four-year institution, the Donaghey Foundation raised its contributions to $90,000 annually and it stayed at that level throughout the 1960s.[64] When Little Rock University became a state-supported institution as part of the new University of Arkansas system in 1969, Donaghey Foundation money was switched from maintenance to special projects or enrichment. Although Donaghey money is no longer a major factor in the operating budget of the University of Arkansas at Little Rock (budget from 1989 to 1990 = $45 million; Donaghey contribution = $312,000),[65] it was certainly crucial in the 1940s and 1950s and still serves as a source for innovative programs and needed assistance for faculty and curriculum. Since 1929, the Donaghey Foundation has made $4 million available to Little Rock Junior College, Little Rock University, and the University of Arkansas at Little Rock.[66]

Little Rock Junior College expressed its gratitude to Donaghey in numerous ways. Initially, a Donaghey week was held in honor of both Donagheys during which a special assembly and a banquet were held. Later, the time was shortened and was called Donaghey Day, involving a luncheon at noon and a reception at night.[67] In 1963 the event was renamed "Founders Day,"[68] and eventually, through lack of interest, even this ceased. This would have mattered little to Donaghey, who was so ecstatic about his gift even ten years after it had been made that he said on the occasion of the second bequest (two months before his death) that the estate bequests to LRJC were so important to him and his wife that their lives had "been somewhat extended. We are both now enjoying years beyond that of our allotted time."[69] In 1987 the Student Union building at University of Arkansas at Little Rock was officially named the Donaghey Student Union.

Death and Commemoration

At the time of his death, most of Donaghey's business relationships as well as many of his personal ties were in Little Rock, although he still made monthly visits to see his friends and relatives in Conway.[70] His death was unexpected and quick. He suffered a heart attack on Monday night, December 13, 1937, and lost consciousness within an hour of the attack.[71] There appeared to be little hope after he was stricken, and a medical bulletin issued four hours after he lost consciousness mentioned that Donaghey's situation was so serious that he could not be removed to a hospital.[72] He died on Wednesday, December 15, at 4:30 A.M., at the age of eighty-one.

The body lay in state in the capitol rotunda from noon to 2:00 P.M. on December 16. The casket was banked with blankets of chrysanthemums, and Arkansas National Guardsmen formed a ceremonial guard. A crowd of several hundred people came by to pay their last respects, despite a steady downpour.[73] Flags at the capitol were flown at half-mast, and the Arkansas State Capitol, Little Rock City Hall, the Pulaski County Courthouse, and Little Rock Junior College were all closed at noon.

Donaghey's body was taken to the First Methodist Church in Little Rock for the funeral, the same church at which Joe T. Robinson's funeral had been held only six months earlier. In spite of a drenching rain, which was somewhat reminiscent of the atrocious weather in Morrilton when Donaghey officially opened his first campaign for governor in 1907, the church was filled. There were 200 honorary pallbearers, including the judges of the Arkansas Supreme Court, ex-governors J. M. Futrell and Tom Terral, and a representative of Governor Carl Bailey, who was ill at the time.[74] A section was reserved for the faculty and students of Little Rock Junior College, and a portion of the balcony was set aside for blacks.

There were many eulogies, including one from Dr. A. C. Millar, the former president of Hendrix College and editor of the *Arkansas Methodist,* who had known Donaghey for forty-seven years and said of his friend that "he made enemies, but he was kindly, he never held a grudge."[75] One of the most insightful testimonials was given by Dr. J. H. Reynolds, president of Hendrix College when Donaghey died, who thought that Donaghey "represented a blending of two men in one—a rugged pioneer individualist and a great socially-minded citizen. The dominance of the individualistic element in him was during the first fifty years, and the ascendancy of social mindedness during the last quarter of a century of his career."[76] Reynolds saw a definite transformation from the first self-centered period in his life in which he had built his private fortune to the second or socially-centered period, a time during which he devoted his money and skills to community concerns. This transformation, according to Reynolds, was similar to what had taken place in the lives and careers of Andrew Carnegie, John D. Rockefeller, James B. Duke, and others. He seemed to suggest that Donaghey in a way was the Arkansas equivalent of some of these financial giants who later became philanthropists.

Donaghey was buried in Roselawn Memorial Park in Little Rock where former governors Robinson, Brough, Martineau, and Parnell also have their burial plots. Donaghey and the other four former governors of the state all died within two years of each other, between 1935 and 1937, and are resting "within a stone's throw"[77] of each other at Roselawn. Louvenia Donaghey died on July 28, 1947, at the family home on Gaines Street. She was eighty-four at the time of her death and is buried beside Donaghey at Roselawn.[78]

Tributes to Donaghey poured in from across the state. Former governor J. M. Futrell said that "Governor Donaghey was firm. Once convinced that he was right there was no power that could swerve him from his planned course of action."[79] Chief Justice Griffin Smith felt "He was a moral force in every venture to which he lent his splendid abilities and untiring will."[80] Fred W. Allsopp, the business manager of the *Arkansas Gazette,* described Donaghey "as plain as an old shoe, he had a heart of gold and was a friend of everybody."[81] Lieutenant Governor Robert L. Bailey declared that "the state has lost its greatest governor."[82]

Letters of condolence came from people in all walks of life. Secretary of State Earl Hodges, who had fallen out politically with Donaghey just before his death, still said that "he was one of the best men I ever knew."[83] Three waitresses from the Greystone Coffee Shop in McGehee sent a sympathy card, signed "The three waitresses who waited on Governor Donaghey."[84] Several other expressions of admiration came from two valued Conway friends, not at the time of death but still appropriate to the occasion. Jo Frauenthal wrote to Mrs. Donaghey in 1940 to thank her for sending him *Homespun Philosophy* and said in his letter that "this collection together with the former book, reveals the life of a courageous, unselfish, great man."[85] Bruce Bullion, on Donaghey's eightieth birthday, wrote, "Let me say that you are the one man in my life with whom close association has done nothing but kindle an increased love and respect . . . and I do believe that when the future history of Arkansas is written, your name will appear there as having been, both in business and politics, the State's most useful citizen of your period."[86]

Newspaper comments were equally complimentary. The *Arkansas Gazette* said that just as his private life was spent in building useful structures, "so as Governor of Arkansas he sought to build useful institutions and agencies for public service."[87] The *McGehee Times* editorialized that "probably some of the happiest hours of his lifetime were spent on the large farm which he owned on the western outskirts of McGehee, the Chickasaw Plantation. The governor's keen mind and ready Irish wit gained the admiration and friendship of many local citizens."[88] The *Arkansas Democrat,* which had not always been an admirer of Donaghey, declared that "in the death of George Donaghey, the state has not only lost a fine citizen, but a man who at all times believed that he owed more to his fellow man than to himself."[89] A popular local column in the *Arkansas Democrat* called "Run of the News" and signed M.S., said "in five years of newspaper work in Little Rock we have never heard one intelligent adverse criticism of him."[90]

Several memorials have been erected to Donaghey to commemorate his life. One has already been mentioned in the preface, the Donaghey State Park in Union County, located on the border between Louisiana and Arkansas. The idea for the park came to Donaghey one day as he was reading "100 Years Ago" in the *Arkansas Gazette* and noticed that an engineer who had surveyed the Arkansas-Louisiana boundary line had just returned home.[91] This suggested to Donaghey that it might be appropriate to mark the spot "where the states meet between the place of his birth and the scene of his early childhood."[92] He then approached his architect to design a suitable monument, paying him three thousand dollars for the project. The next step was to buy some land in the general vicinity. Donaghey talked to one of the lumber companies in the area about selling him one acre and was told that they would make a forty-acre gift if the whole undertaking could be converted into a state park.[93]

This was done, the forty-acre donation (half in Louisiana and half in Arkansas) was made, the monument erected, the park dedicated in 1933 in the presence of at least 700 people,[94] and commissioners were appointed by Governor Harvey Parnell of Arkansas and Governor Huey Long of Louisiana to take charge of the park.[95] Notwithstanding the innovative nature of a state park shared and maintained by two states, it rapidly fell into disuse and neglect. As early as 1941, Mrs. Donaghey complained about the difficulty in reaching the Donaghey Park,[96] which today is still inaccessible and unknown to most people.

Another monument to Donaghey was placed on the outskirts of the town of Strong in Union County, on Highway 82. Strong is six miles from Donaghey's birthplace, and again as with Donaghey State Park, Donaghey was active in planning and building the marker.[97] This, however, was a much smaller endeavor and simply involved placement of a centennial marker by the Arkansas Centennial Commission to celebrate the 100th anniversary of Arkansas statehood.[98] The monument or marker at Strong says that Donaghey was born six miles south of the structure and that he was the former governor of Arkansas who built the state capitol and started the Donaghey Foundation for education. The centennial marker was dedicated on May 15, 1937. The main speaker was C. Hamilton Moses, former aide to Donaghey, who later became president of the Arkansas Power and Light Company. Moses said that the Little Rock Junior College was Donaghey's greatest accomplishment with the state capitol being next.[99] The mayor officially accepted the marker on behalf of the city of Strong, and the entire event was part of the Union County centennial celebration.[100]

A visit to Strong, a city of 785 people, in 1988 showed little awareness of the existence of the Centennial marker in honor of Donaghey. The marker was located next to a furniture store and across the street from a gasoline service station. A year later, a telephone call to the mayor of Strong revealed that the marker had been removed from Highway 82, because of fear that the highway might be relocated, to the Strong City Park.[101] Despite the efforts of the officials at Strong and the Donaghey Foundation to salvage what they could from the move, it is still another reduction in the visibility and memory of Donaghey. Not much is left of the two attempts to leave some fitting state memorials to Donaghey.

Personality and Political Style

Donaghey's physical appearance was not particularly impressive. At the age of twenty-three, he weighed 150 pounds and had a head of thick black hair.[102] In later years, he was usually described as stocky since he weighed about 175 pounds[103] and was only five-foot ten or eleven. He was grey-haired, with a receding forehead, wore small gold-rimmed glasses, and was slightly stooped, at least when he was in his seventies. Donaghey was seldom without a coat and often wore a seersucker suit with a bow tie. The consensus seemed to be that he was a natty dresser.

As mentioned earlier, Donaghey's personality is hard to decipher because there is a distinct difference between the way he was regarded in Conway and the way he was viewed in Little Rock. In Conway where his family roots were, he was looked upon as kindly, friendly, and approachable. In Little Rock, some saw him as more austere and aloof, with an urgent need to conserve his time and finish whatever business was at hand very quickly. Even so, most of the individuals interviewed found Donaghey to be closer to the warm and friendly personality associated with Conway than the reserved and detached governor as seen by some in the capital city.

Donaghey was something of a social loner and probably quite shy. When courting Louvenia Wallace[104] he acknowledged being shy, a condition that was possibly made more acute by what he saw as his educational deficiencies. There was not much social entertaining while he was governor, and one tenant of the Donaghey Building never saw him at lunch and assumed that he ate in his office.[105] He did like to be noticed and must have overcome some of his shyness, but it was still a characteristic noted by many people who were interviewed both in Little Rock and Conway.

Donaghey had a low-key sense of humor and a strict sense of courtesy. However, there were some occasions when his temper took over. There was a fist fight in Conway where Donaghey lost the election for mayor and knocked to the ground one of his persistent election critics and was sued for five thousand dollars. On another occasion there was a shoving match with Speaker of the House Allen Hamiter over some unkind words about Donaghey's intensive lobbying in the house of representatives. A third fight involved Donaghey and Sam W. Reyburn, president of the Union Trust Company in 1913. Donaghey was constructing a building for the Bankers Trust Company at Second and Main, and Reyburn was the agent for the building next door. The argument was over the fire wall separating the two structures, and Reyburn knocked Donaghey to the ground, and then Donaghey knocked Reyburn to his knees and "they clinched and rolled over and hammered each other like a couple of school boys."[106] They both were ordered to appear in police court, but apparently because of the embarrassment of having two prominent members of the Little Rock power structure flailing away at each other, neither Little Rock paper covered the fight, although it has been verified by three separate sources.[107]

Donaghey's only recreation was hunting. He did not play golf and could not drive a car. He had a chauffeur, Percy Ware, who drove him and worked in his home for twenty years. Donaghey's principal diversion was reading, and he would read from three to four hours a day. At one time he subscribed to as many as twenty periodicals.[108] Although he was carefully prepared for important occasions such as his inaugural addresses to the legislature and talks to civic groups, he was occasionally absent-minded and would write telephone numbers on the sweatband of his hat.[109] He was not charismatic, but he did have a kind of quiet authority.[110]

Donaghey's political style was a product of his personality, his working background, and his political campaigns. He was a business Progressive who saw his main role to be that of problem solver, and he ran the government as much as possible like a business with an emphasis on careful preparation, efficiency, and rationality. Donaghey preferred administration to campaigning, was suspicious of the spoken word, favored pamphlets rather than speeches, and refused to debate, except on special and isolated occasions, during his entire political career. He usually avoided posturing and heeded the warning of Alexander Hamilton that "there are certain seasons in every country where noise and bluster pass current for facts."[111] Donaghey lived by the Progressive faith that facts would make people free.

Conclusion

George Washington Donaghey is best known for building the state capitol. Recognition of that accomplishment would please him since the project was so interwoven with his political life and with his chosen career as a builder. Certainly, the state capitol was important, and without it Donaghey probably would not have been governor. Nevertheless, he left his mark on the Progressive movement in the state and on the state itself, and what he left behind in Arkansas was much more than just the state capitol.

His defeat of William Kirby, the Davis-backed candidate for governor, and the Davis machine in 1908 gave a new direction to the reform movement in Arkansas. Reform leadership passed to Donaghey placing a businessman in charge who appealed to an urban middle-class constituency, who saw an active role for the governor beyond that of just guarding the treasury, and who viewed the state not only as a regulator but as a source of needed services. Progressivism under Donaghey, and later Brough, did not dramatize rural-urban differences or class conflicts. It attempted to end the cultural and political isolation of the state caused by the policies and personality of Jeff Davis.

In addition to giving the reform movement in Arkansas a different outlook and a change in emphasis, Donaghey had an extraordinary impact on the state that is still evident today. The state capitol was pushed to completion by Donaghey's fierce determination and unlimited energy. Arkansas today possesses a beautiful state capitol building which is both a popular and artistic success. It cost $2,205,779.42 to build, and is now insured for $300,000,000.[1]

The state capitol is not the only visible reminder of Donaghey and his administration. There are also nine public-supported universities in Arkansas that offer at least four years of college and usually degrees beyond the baccalaureate level. Six of these nine institutions owe their existence to George Donaghey. These six Donaghey-founded or supported universities had a total enrollment in the fall of 1990 of 37,086 students.[2]

There was also important legislation enacted at Donaghey's behest that still has a significant effect some eighty years after passage. The initiative and referendum amendment to the state constitution sponsored by Donaghey, and helped to passage by William Jennings Bryan, has been used, with some changes and modifications, seventy-three times since 1912[3] for initiated constitutional amendments. Arkansas is still the only southern state with both initiative and referendum. If public accountability is to be the wave of the future, Arkansas, thanks to Donaghey and Bryan, has a mechanism already in place to assist with this.

Other legislation of lasting value that originated with Donaghey includes the Board of Education created during Donaghey's second term; the State Board of Health, with authority to regulate sanitation and inspect food and drugs; and the tuberculosis sanitarium, which was built in Booneville in 1910 and offered treatment for sixty years. Another action that Donaghey took, the pardoning of 360 convicts, led to the elimination of the convict-leasing system within two months, "a reform which humanitarians had been seeking for forty years."[4]

More intangible, but still important, were the public-service and philanthropic model he provided for future ex-governors to follow and the improved image of Arkansas. During Donaghey's administration, and due to conscious effort on his part, the General Education Board, the Peabody Fund, and the Southern Education Board, practically the only sources of outside funding to which a state could turn, began to find Arkansas worthy of financial attention. This would have been unthinkable during the Jeff Davis era when the image of the state was interchangeable with Davis himself and his rough, rambunctious style. Harmon Remmel in the 1910 general election spoke of a "new spirit in Arkansas where people would be welcome without regard to their politics."[5]

There are several other incidents in Donaghey's administration where he showed unusual political courage and demonstrated that he was not afraid on occasions to swim against the tide and speak against the silence. One magnificent failure on Donaghey's part was the State Tax Commission which had the potential to cut the Gordian knot of Arkansas politics—tax assessment. After passage by the legislature, the State Tax Commission was submitted to referendum and defeated. It was a staggering burden for Donaghey to carry in his third term campaign, since it smacked of possible higher taxes, but he did his best. The state tax problems would have been much less formidable had he succeeded. Another example of unrewarded courage was the veto of $1.2 million in state appropriations over a four-year period. The veto subjected Donaghey to harsh criticism, but it averted a financial collapse of the state.

Donaghey shared a similar philosophical outlook with two other governors of his era, Charles H. Brough and Tom McRae. His hard battles for Progressive causes laid a foundation upon which both Brough and McRae could build. In addition, Donaghey was a close personal and political friend of both men.

The closest modern parallel to George Donaghey was probably Winthrop Rockefeller. Both were wealthy, shy businessmen interested in applying administrative efficiency and business techniques to state government. Both took dramatic action where the prisons were concerned: Donaghey pardoned 360 inmates to destroy convict leasing; Rockefeller commuted the sentences of fifteen men on death row because of his opposition to capital punishment. They shared an interest in penal and tax reform, helped to improve the state image, and took great pride in the caliber of their appointments to state offices. They were both poor public speakers, and both were soundly defeated in ill-advised third-term campaigns after having said previously that two terms were enough. They became model ex-governors who contributed to their state in political retirement much of their valuable time and fortunes.

Donaghey certainly had his political weaknesses. Along with Jeff Davis, he shamefully exploited Mann's 5 percent architectural fee as being too high when he must have known as a contractor that it was a standard fee. Some of his attacks on Caldwell and Drake were groundless, although some hit the mark. He would sometimes needlessly antagonize the legislature and never seemed to understand the legislative way of looking at politics. His unconstitutional veto of the federal income tax amendment and his later rationalization that it was done so that the money would not be used for war purposes was an example of his stubborn refusal to listen to advice in the first place and dissembling in the second place.

His support of the grandfather clause that would have disfranchised thousands of black voters is hardest to excuse from a current perspective. It did seem to be an aberration rather than a pattern in his political life. One mitigating factor was that Donaghey served on the boards of black institutions and helped them financially which was a way to work for better race relations in his era.

Despite some political failures, Donaghey still stands as one of the state's best governors, if not the best. He was an activist governor who increased the service role of the state to meet human needs. This was done with a minimum of posturing, and his campaigns were conducted with little resort to character assassination.

There are two phrases that epitomize George Donaghey. One is found in a campaign speech that he made in Fort Smith in 1909 in which he said, "Set your watch ten minutes fast and keep up with it,"[6] and the other is inscribed over his grave in Little Rock and reads, "He left the world better than he found it." The first statement symbolizes Donaghey's determined and energetic approach to any issue or problem. The second stands for what he finally accomplished, and both match the reality of Donaghey's life.

Appendix

Building the State Capitol: Beginnings

1899–1901

The building of the state capitol is difficult to place chronologically in a biography of George Donaghey. It was his constant professional and political companion from 1899 to 1917 and was the main issue that made him governor. He had almost an obsessive interest in the capitol, both because he was a builder and saw it from that point of view, and also because he was a politician and saw its symbolic and practical importance to the state. Because Donaghey was involved for eighteen years with the capitol, spanning virtually his entire political career, it is examined here as a separate entity with a history of its own.

In its long history, the state capitol was haunted by three intractable problems that were present from the beginning. The first and most important was Jeff Davis's unremitting and sometimes irrational hostility toward the project when Davis was at the height of his power and his influence was pervasive throughout the state. A second problem was the limitation of $1 million initially placed on construction costs, which would cause great cutting and trimming as well as mass confusion as time went on. The third problem was the decision to finance the state capitol on a "pay as you go" basis. That made sense given Arkansas's public debt, but it had the unfortunate consequence of holding the construction of the state capitol hostage to the vagaries of economic conditions and their impact on state tax collections.

The old state capitol was built in the late 1830s, and "despite a major renovation in 1885, by the late 1890s the old building had deteriorated almost beyond repair."[1] What apparently stopped any serious consideration of a new capitol in 1895 was the lack of a suitable site. The grounds of the old state capitol on Markham Street in Little Rock were too small, and the cost of building was too great, especially when the effects of the depression that began in 1893 were still present.

This attitude began to change as the depression faded and as working conditions in the old state capitol worsened. At the time the 1899 legislative session convened, heavy rains had aggravated the leaky condition of the roof of the old state house. Large chunks of plaster fell from the ceiling in the senate chamber to the desks below. Only one or two senators were present, and fortunately no one was hurt.

Official recognition of the problem came from Governor Dan Jones when he addressed a joint session of the house and senate on January 18, 1899. He recommended that the penitentiary be removed from its present location on Fifth Street, the highest point within the city limits at the time, since the land was too valuable to be used for a prison.[2] Governor Jones suggested further that if a decision was reached to build a new state capitol, it should be located on the penitentiary land, part of which could be sold to help pay for the new statehouse. He estimated the cost at "something near $600,000 a little more or less, and that it would take from six to seven years to complete such a structure."[3]

On January 12, 1899, Senate Concurrent Resolution I (SCR I) was introduced by Senator Jerry C. South. It stated that it was the sense of the legislature that a new state capitol be built, that the state was financially able to erect the building, and that a joint committee of both houses be appointed to consider the question of constructing a new capitol building and to report by bill or otherwise their ideas on the matter.[4] It was passed by the Senate on the same day it was introduced.[5] When SCR I went to the House, opposition arose. The original clause providing that the state was financially able to erect a new building was struck and a new clause added that required a thorough investigation to see whether the state was actually able to make the expenditure necessary for the building.[6] SCR I as amended passed the house fifty-five to thirty-four.[7] The senate concurred in the house amendment on February 1, and the governor signed SCR I on February 13, 1899.[8]

There were two bills introduced in the joint committee created by SCR I. One, by Senator South (SB 214), provided for a bond issue of $4 million, $700,000 of which would be used to build the new statehouse, and the remainder would be used to refund the state's undisputed indebtedness.[9] The other, by Senator J. D. Kimbell (SB 202), contained no bond issue and included an appropriation of only $50,000 to meet all beginning expenses for the capitol, including the employment of an architect. Kimbell's proposal was substituted for South's,[10] with some amendments added. The most important amendment required that the new state capitol be located on the present penitentiary grounds. This amendment barely passed by a vote of sixteen to fourteen.[11] This was, however, a significant victory since the opponents of the new state capitol had insisted on the Markham Street location as their main argument to block the entire process. Kimbell's bill (SB 202) as amended passed the senate on March 20, 1899, by a vote of nineteen to eight.[12] The *Arkansas Democrat* editorialized the next day that if the house would also pass the bill, "the thirty-second general assembly will cover itself with glory and go down in history as having accomplished great things for the state."[13]

The house did pass the bill. It was signed by Governor Jones and became Act 128 of 1899. The act created a board of state capitol commissioners to be composed of the governor and six qualified electors to hold office until the capitol was completed and accepted by the state. The commission was to secure a set of plans and specifications for the new building which was not to exceed $1 million in construction costs. Two hundred convicts were made available for construction work, and fifty thousand dollars was appropriated from the sale of state lands to employ an architect and to meet the preliminary construction expenses. Act 128 also required the new state capitol to be located on the present penitentiary grounds on Fifth Street and authorized the board of penitentiary commissioners to move the penitentiary to a new location in Pulaski County.

The *Arkansas Gazette* was upset that only fifty thousand dollars had been appropriated but concluded that the amount would do to start with.[14] The reason for such a minimal appropriation was probably the fear of an adverse public reaction if a higher amount had been specified, and the expectation that future legislatures would appropriate enough money to build a suitable capitol. This approach, however, put a premium on starting quickly and getting good value for the fifty thousand dollars because the initial work would be the key to future legislative appropriations.

Governor Jones quickly appointed six members to the State Capitol Commission, including three legislators: Representative Thomas Herrn of Sharp County, Speaker of the House A. F. Vandeventer, and Senator Jerry South, author of SCR 1. The other three included George Donaghey, already a prominent builder in Conway. Something happened before the confirmation vote or Governor Jones changed his mind, because all three legislators were rejected by two to one margins in the Arkansas Senate.[15] Although Donaghey and the other two non-legislative nominees were confirmed, the legislators were replaced by three individuals who were not members of the legislature. The best known member of the commission was George Murphy of Little Rock, a prominent criminal lawyer. The other members were Charles G. Newman, editor of the *Pine Bluff Commercial;* Judge Alfred E. Carrigan of Hope, a former state senator; R. M. Hancock, former sheriff and clerk of Baxter County; and J. M. Levesque, an attorney and former county clerk of Cross County for twenty years.

The first meeting of the new State Capitol Commission lasted for seven days.[16] Governor Jones convened the commissioners in his office on May 11, 1899, and presided over the organizational meeting.[17] The most important decision taken was to employ George R. Mann as the architect for the state capitol. Mann was from St. Joseph, Missouri, and had designed the city hall in St. Louis. Before the legislature convened in 1899, Mann placed a four-foot by six-foot watercolor drawing of a capitol building in the governor's office and estimated that such a building could be built for $650,000 to $1 million.[18] He also had a complete set of plans for the building that had originally been designed for the Montana State Capitol. These drawings "had been on hand while the Capitol bill was before the legislature. Their attractiveness not only eased its passage, but also drew attention to Mann."[19]

There was controversy over the hiring of Mann because of the decision not to have competitive bidding in the selection of an architect. This was probably done in the interests of saving time. The commission's decision was that it was "more advisable to employ an architect outright rather than to submit to the delays and annoyances of a competition."[20] The amount of Mann's fee was also controversial. He had asked for fifty thousand dollars—5 percent of the building cost—but the commission had taken no action and simply passed a resolution "that the compensation for the architect shall be what is usual and customary in these cases."[21] Donaghey opposed the lack of competitive bidding and tried to delay the selection of Mann. When this failed, he voted against the hiring of Mann along with one other commissioner.[22] This was, undoubtedly, the beginning of bad feeling between Mann and Donaghey.

Other decisions reached at that first commission meeting were to sell none of the penitentiary land and to reserve six acres for the capitol building. Resolutions were passed authorizing Donaghey to work with the architect to develop plans for the capitol and authorizing Donaghey to represent the board and remain in continuous charge of the work on the state capitol proposed site. Donaghey worked with Mann to prepare the excavation work for the capitol as well as the plans, and decisions were quickly made to place the capitol at the end of Fifth Street where it would run 500 feet from north to south,[23] with a basement 17 feet deep.[24]

One of Donaghey's first acts as construction foreman was to lay the foundation of the building so that the east-west axis would be the center line of Fifth Street, while the north-south axis would be at right angles to the center line of Fifth Street. He drove a center stake at what appeared to be the center line of Fifth Street and then marked off the foundation on true east-west and north-south lines.[25] Donaghey was handicapped in this task because his view to the east down Fifth Street was impeded by a number of penitentiary buildings, which were surrounded by masonry walls twenty feet high.[26] Another problem was that Little Rock's east-west streets had been laid out parallel to the Arkansas River rather than on true east-west lines. The result was that the state capitol was not aligned at right angles with Fifth Street and other intersecting streets but was slightly off center. This mistake was not discovered until later, after the penitentiary walls were torn down. It was not an auspicious start, even though there was no real functional damage because of the mistake.

Actual work did not begin until July of 1899 when Donaghey took six mule teams and ten convicts and began the excavation for the foundation.[27] In spite of the difficulty of obtaining enough skilled convicts for the job, the excavation work was completed in about three months.[28] However, the mule-driven shovels cut through grave sites on the old penitentiary grounds. It was either a cemetery for Confederate soldiers captured during the Civil War, or a burying area for convicts. In either case, the incident was looked upon as a bad omen.

After some delays caused by the soft slate and quicksand, the concrete foundations were laid, and some foundation walls were over thirty feet in height.[29] Donaghey had another altercation with Mann during this time. He felt that Mann should not have been allowed a fee for "detailed" plans since they were, in Donaghey's view, included in the fee for "general" plans. When the State Capitol Commission decided in favor of Mann, Donaghey submitted his resignation, but Governor Jones persuaded him to reconsider.[30] At any rate, progress on the foundation was made, and by October of 1900, the foundation was almost ready. This had been done within eighteen months of the passage of the state capitol bill, despite some predictions that it would take five years.[31] The first annual report of the capitol commission estimated that $84,459.70 of construction work[32] had been done for an expenditure of only $43,252.53, when free convict labor and materials from the penitentiary walls were considered. The commissioners were "elated with the work thus far . . . ,"[33] and Donaghey's fear that "if we did not make a good showing with the resources which had been placed at our command, the next legislature would abandon the erecting of a capitol, at least for a time"[34] was seemingly laid to rest.

One person not sharing in the euphoria over the successful beginning of the capitol construction was Jeff Davis, who was the state attorney general when the construction bill was approved. He was asked then to give an opinion in his capacity as attorney general as to whether the bill had legally passed. The question was whether the fifty-thousand-dollar appropriation for the state house was "a necessary expense" of government under Article 5, Section 31, of the Arkansas Constitution which needed only a majority vote or another kind of expense that required a two-thirds vote. The attorney general issued an opinion that two-thirds was constitutionally mandated and stated that he was "thoroughly wedded to a strict interpretation of the constitution."[35] Governor Jones signed the state capitol bill anyway.

Davis was never one to be discouraged by setbacks, and during the months of May and June, he "stalked the Capitol Commission"[36] with whatever legal ammunition he could find. He filed numerous suits against the Capitol Commission, one of which went to the Arkansas Supreme Court where the main issue, the question of the two-thirds vote, was decided against him. The Arkansas Supreme Court ruled that what was a necessary expense of government was up to the legislature to decide and that when both presiding officers had signed the bill as a validly passed piece of legislation, this was, in effect, a legislative judgment that it was a "necessary expense."[37] Although Davis lost all the suits he filed, he certainly harassed the commission and put himself unmistakenly on record as being opposed to the building of the new state capitol.

Jeff Davis's annoying legal attacks had not kept the State Capitol

Commission from celebrating the beginning of construction with a groundbreaking ceremony on July 4, 1899. The only departure from the generally optimistic tone of the speakers on that occasion came when Senator Kimbell said that Jeff Davis had "entered upon a public crusade against the enactment of a new state capitol, and well may the friends of the measure tremble for its fate."[38]

At the same time the groundbreaking ceremony was taking place in Little Rock, Jeff Davis was announcing his candidacy for governor in a speech before a large crowd at Hardy. One theme of Jeff Davis's campaign for governor was to be the statehouse scandal. He talked about the groundbreaking in Little Rock and said, "They are breaking dirt for what they claim to be a million dollar state house, but it will cost three million dollars and prove to be the most infamous steal ever perpetuated against the people of Arkansas."[39]

Meanwhile, work continued on the new capitol whose completed foundation was 440 feet long and 165 feet wide.[40] People could now begin to visualize the series of columns in front, three and one-half feet in diameter and thirty-two feet high and extending up through the first and second stories. The laying of the cornerstone and the accompanying ceremony were held on November 27, 1900, some seventeen months after the official groundbreaking had taken place.

The cornerstone celebrations started with a parade of forty-four different organizations and about four to five thousand people. Speeches were given by Governor Jones, Senator Kimbell, Senator G. Quarles, and others. Senator Quarles seemed to grasp the spirit of the occasion when he said to the commissioners in the course of his speech, "You have accomplished more than any of us thought possible with the means placed at your disposal."[41] Everyone seemed pleased with the fast work and the low cost.

1901–1903

The first State Capitol Commission had to face a new and potentially volatile situation in January of 1901 because Jeff Davis, who had been elected governor in the fall of 1900, would now become the ex officio chair of the commission. His distaste for the building of a new state capitol became a never-ending nightmare for capitol supporters. The commission met on January 2, 1901, before Jeff Davis had been sworn in as governor, and completed a report requested by the legislature. The report showed actual expenditures of $43,252.53,[42] including $9,750 for the architect. This left $6,747.47 out of the original $50,000 appropriation. In addition, construction work completed, counting convict labor, was valued at $84,459.70.[43] Donaghey received for 1899 and 1900 payments totaling $1,031.80 for mileage, per diem, and work as construction foreman.[44] The commission at the same meeting approved a requested payment schedule from George Mann calling for an additional $21,517.21 to be paid to him for preliminary plans, general drawings, detailed drawings, and general work supervision. He had been paid $14,750 to date.[45] It was also agreed that Mann's compensation "should be such as is usual and customary in such cases."[46] Mann had asked for $50,000—5 percent of the estimated $1 million cost.

According to Donaghey, the commission believed that the work already done on the capitol, which included most of the foundation in place, was worth $84,480.70, and this, plus the cost already incurred of removing the penitentiary and its buildings, would persuade Governor Davis to finish the capitol.[47] This assumption was totally mistaken. Davis immediately attacked Mann's fee as excessive when nothing but the foundation had been finished. Mann's fee schedule was probably a normal fee schedule for an architect, but, at least on the surface, a large amount of money was being spent for problematical results.

By the January 31 meeting of the commission, Davis had been sworn in as governor and was participating as ex officio chair of the commission. Davis immediately moved that the approval of Mann's fee schedule be rescinded and that the amount be left to the discretion of the commission. This motion was defeated. A substitute motion was finally adopted the next day for a committee to be appointed to report at the next meeting the amounts to be paid the architect and the time of the payments. Davis appointed to the committee Judge A. E. Carrigan; T. M. Mehaffy, who had replaced George Murphy on the commission when Murphy had resigned upon being elected attorney general; and Donaghey

At the next commission meeting on February 12, a majority report and a minority report were presented. The majority report from Carrigan and Mehaffy said that the commission had never determined what the "usual and customary fee" was and recommended that the commission determine this after hearing witnesses. Donaghey gave a minority report in which he admitted that 5 percent was the fee recommended by the American Institute of Architects but that many architects worked for less. He gave several examples of architects who had offered to bid on the statehouse at smaller fees than Mann.[48] Donaghey, who seemed irritated that no competition had been held for architectural plans, concluded that the $14,750 already paid to Mann was fair compensation and that the action of the commission in approving Mann's request for another $21,517.21 should be revoked. Donaghey's minority report was not adopted even though it was "in line with the views of Governor Davis on the subject."[49] The majority report was approved, and Davis again appointed Donaghey to a three-person committee, with J. M. Levesque and C. G. Newman, to ascertain what fee was usual and customary and what was owed Mann.

This new committee reported on February 27 that it had determined by correspondence and personal inquiry that 5 percent was the usual and customary fee for architects and that Mr. Mann's financial accounts to date were "just and correct."[50] This report was later amended to read that Mann's fee should not exceed 5 percent of the cost of the building and that the unpaid amount of his fee should be paid by the commission as the work progressed. This was adopted. Donaghey again dissented and referred the commission to his earlier minority report. Davis said that the claim approved by a majority of the commission was "unconscionable, unjust, and exorbitant."[51]

It is hard to understand the intensity of Donaghey's opposition to the fee to be paid to Mann. It caused him to disagree with Governor Jones who backed Mann and who had appointed Donaghey to the commission. It put him on the side of Jeff Davis who opposed the whole capitol project, which Donaghey supported. It also placed him at variance with most architects and professional people, because the 5 percent fee was the normal and accepted amount. Donaghey considered resigning over the issue, but decided not to because of his consuming desire to be connected with the building of the capitol. He used the analogy of a lawyer wanting to be on the U.S. Supreme Court to show that one of the highest ambitions of a builder was "a seat on a Commission to build a State Capitol."[52] It may have been that Donaghey was still angered by the refusal of the commission to use competitive bidding to select an architect, which was the way in which Donaghey had always obtained his own contracts. He obviously preferred Charles Thompson, a prominent Little Rock architect, to Mann and had voted for him instead of

Mann.[53] It may also have been that Donaghey personally disliked Mann. Or he may simply have seen a popular issue with which to identify.

The setting of Mann's fee was the last significant act of the first State Capitol Commission. Its final meeting was held on April 11, 1901.[54]

The 1901 legislative session met with the future of the state capitol clouded by the hostility of a new governor with a large popular majority behind him. Relations between Governor Jones and Governor-elect Jeff Davis were so strained that Jones broke long-established custom and refused to participate in Davis's inauguration.[55] In his farewell address, Jones recommended that a three-fourths of a mill tax be enacted to complete the capitol and that the present board of the state capitol commissioners be retained until the building was completed.[56] He strongly opposed any attempt to replace the commission with a new commission consisting of state constitutional officers.

In his inaugural address to the legislature on January 18, Governor Davis said that he had never opposed the building of a new statehouse as long as it was "built upon the proper site and under proper and business-like management."[57] He was, however, of the opinion that "it would be better for the state to abandon the entire work as a bad investment rather than continue the same under the present plan of operation."[58] More specifically, "he recommended the abolition of the present Capitol Commission, the firing of the architect hired by the commission, the creation of a new commission made up of state officials, and the use of competitive bidding and convict labor."[59] Finishing his remarks on the state capitol, Davis said that if the legislature chose to proceed with the building of the capitol, he would accept that as long as the construction was placed on a "safe and business-like basis."[60] He repeated this same offer in a special message to the legislature on April 2, 1901.[61]

On February 13, 1901, Senator Robert J. Wilson from Washington County, the new president pro tem of the Arkansas Senate elected with the support of Governor Davis, introduced a bill (SB 122)[62] to repeal the 1889 legislation authorizing the building of the state capitol. He said at the time that he agreed with Governor Davis that the whole scheme was a failure "and ought to be abandoned."[63] No further action was taken on his proposal. A compromise was suggested by the select committee on the state capitol. The elements of the compromise were to continue the project as originally funded with the same $1 million appropriation limit, to retain the architect at 4 percent, to require that Mann's plans be checked by an outside architect, to let Davis appoint members of a new commission, and to provide a funding source of one-half of a mill on each dollar of taxable property.

The compromise (HB 491) was introduced by the select committee on the state capitol consisting of two senators and three members of the house of representatives. It passed both houses easily. Governor Davis signed the bill on April 29,[64] and it became Act 132 of 1901. The *Arkansas Gazette,* no great friend of Davis, praised him and said "for the approval of this measure Governor Davis will receive the plaudits of every progressive citizen in Arkansas."[65]

The new legislation, while keeping the state capitol project alive, did contain some harsh provisions reflecting misgivings about the capitol plan and its architect. It retained Mann but dealt him a slap in the face by reducing his fee from 5 percent to 4 percent. An outside architect was to be hired to examine Mann's plan for defects and deficiencies. If the visiting architect found the plans "complete and perfect"[66] and found that the building could be erected on its present foundation for $1 million, then Mann should be kept. If the plans were incomplete, or if the estimated cost exceeded $1 million, then Mann was obligated to redraft the plans so that the construction expenses were held to $1 million. If Mann failed to comply with the provisions of the new act, he was to be replaced.

There was one forward-looking provision in the act that must have eluded Davis's attention. It provided for a tax of one-half of a mill on each dollar of taxable property in the state to be collected in 1901 and annually thereafter until the building was completed. Though subject to the uncertainties of the economy and state tax collections, it still provided a permanent source of funding.

On May 2, 1901,[67] Governor Davis appointed the second State Capitol Commission. This time George Donaghey was not included. The agreement between Davis and Donaghey on Mann's fee was presumably not enough to offset Donaghey's support of ex-governor Dan Jones in his campaign for the U.S. Senate in 1900 against the incumbent senator, James Berry. Donaghey helped to carry Faulkner County for Jones,[68] but Jones withdrew after failing to win any other county primaries. Jones and Davis were bitter enemies, and Davis campaigned actively for Senator Berry. This political difference and Donaghey's independence must have been factors in Davis's decision not to reappoint him.

The two most important members of the second state capitol commission were James P. Eagle who was an ex-governor of Arkansas, former speaker of the house, and a prominent Baptist layman, and Thomas Cox of Dardanelle, a lumber dealer who also had done some construction work.[69] According to Davis's biographer, Raymond Arsenault, the members of the second commission were "all Davis stalwarts."[70] The first priority of the second commission was to select an expert visiting architect, and at its July 10 meeting, the commission wrote to a number of architects designated by the supervising architect of the United States Treasury Department. They finally settled on Frank Day, an architect from Philadelphia, who agreed to examine and report on the plans for $750 plus expenses.[71] At about the same time, Mann was quoted as saying that with the use of convict labor the capitol could be kept within estimates.[72]

Day's report was given to the commission on September 9. In general, it was a very favorable report. The general design called for a centrally located great rotunda, with a dome that dominated the entire building and then wing buildings for the house and senate each with a smaller dome. Day praised the concept as "well suited to the needs of the state . . ." and "distinctly superior to that of the average state capitol."[73]

There were some negatives, however. Day felt that the corridors were too wide and there was too much space for circulation, that the specifications were not detailed and specific enough in some cases, and that the cost would probably approach $1.5 million, but certainly, "the building as planned cannot be constructed for such a sum [$1 million]."[74] Day did feel that savings could be made by remodeling and the use of convict labor, although he had reservations about the convicts handling some of the difficult construction. He also felt that the 4 percent to be paid to Mann rather than what was usual and proper was insulting.

At the commission meeting on September 9, Governor Davis again suggested that a new statehouse be built on the foundation of the old one.[75] The commission rejected this and adopted a resolution that the "specifications of George R. Mann are not in all things complete; and further, that, as planned, the capitol building cannot be constructed at a cost of one million dollars."[76] It also voted to refer the report of Frank Day to Mann so that he could begin remodeling. While Mann was revising his plans in St. Louis, he was astounded when Governor Davis, also in St. Louis, asked him to come over to the governor's hotel room. Once Mann had arrived, Davis told him that he did not want a building built, but if one had to be erected, it should be only one-half the size of the capitol now planned. Mann replied that that would be inadequate, and Davis then asked him to resign, saying that he would arrange for a ten-thousand-dollar payment. Mann, as he reports the incident, refused and left the room.[77]

Mann submitted two amended plans to the October meeting of the commission[78] to bring the cost under $1 million. One plan was to reduce the size of the building, using only part of the present foundation; the other was to use concrete instead of granite for the second story for a savings of $250,000.[79] Both plans were referred to Thomas Cox, a commissioner with some building knowledge, who was to make a detailed examination and report back to his fellow commissioners. At the November meeting, Cox recommended against both plans. According to Cox, the plan to reduce the size of the building was impracticable because the foundation was already complete, and the second plan to change to cheaper materials would result in a shoddy product.[80]

After Cox's report had been discussed, the commission decided to ask Attorney General George Murphy, a former commissioner, whether the new state capitol had to be built upon the existing foundation. Murphy's opinion was that the proposed statehouse did have to be erected upon the present foundation, could not be built at any other location, and must be constructed for $1 million.[81] Once Murphy's opinion had been received, the commission adopted a resolution stating that the capitol building could not be completed upon the present foundation for $1 million and that to use inferior materials would be unsuitable. The resolution continued that the "board can proceed no further at the present time because of the prohibitory terms of the act of April 29, 1901."[82] This meant work would have to stop until the 1903 session of the legislature. A writer on this subject felt that the second commission had done exactly what Governor Davis wanted, that is, to "strangle the capitol with the very laws that gave it life."[83]

The seventh and last meeting of the second commission was held on December 17, 1901. The most important matter before them was the conditional resignation of George Mann. The capitol architect agreed to resign if he were paid the major portion of the amount allowed by the first commission for his plans. Specifically he asked for $17,000 which when added to the $14,000 he had already been paid would have meant a total fee of $31,000. Mann also said that his plans were so complete that they could be carried out by a local superintendent.[84] After consultation with Attorney General Murphy, the commission decided to refuse Mann's offer. The commission pointed out that very little work had been done since the passage of Act 132 on April 29, 1901, and they would not make any additional payments until further work had been done on the building.[85] The *Arkansas Gazette* deplored the two-year delay in construction in an editorial entitled "Very Disappointing."[86]

Governor Davis, on the other hand, found this two-year delay to be liveable and probably was overjoyed by what had occurred. Davis was campaigning for a second term in 1902 and again used the word "steal" in reference to the state capitol. His opponent in the Democratic primary, Elias Rector, author of the Rector Anti-Trust Act, said that he had voted for the capitol bill while he was a member of the Arkansas House of Representatives and was proud of the vote. He wanted Davis to identify the thieves.[87]

Davis won the Democratic primary on March 29, 1902, by an overwhelming margin against Rector. It is impossible to know the impact of the state capitol issue on the election, but it did not discourage Harry H. Myers, Davis's Republican opponent in the state general election in September of 1902, from using the issue. In a joint debate at Brinkley, Myers said that Davis did not want a new state capitol because he was not progressive and "the old owl roost, where the bats and moths run wild, is in perfect keeping with Governor Davis himself. That's the reason he likes it. Both are about thirty years behind the times."[88] The general election result was another sweeping victory for Davis as was to be expected.

On March 30, the day after the Democratic primary, Davis asked former Governor James P. Eagle to resign from the State Capitol Commission because he had supported U.S. Senator James K. Jones, the incumbent, while Davis was backing James P. Clarke, the challenger. Eagle refused to resign, saying that his duty was to serve the state and that the governor could not remove him just for political reasons.[89] Reaction to the requested resignation of Eagle, who was greatly respected in the state, was so negative that a few days later Davis pulled back and said that if Eagle wished to stay on the commission he was at "liberty to do so and I wash my hands of the entire affair."[90]

The whole incident was further complicated by the Baptist affiliation of both men. Eagle had been president of the Arkansas Baptist Convention since 1880 and would become president of the Southern

Baptist Convention in 1902.[91] Davis was the vice-president of the Arkansas Baptist Convention at the same time Eagle was president. On April 7, 1902, Davis resigned as vice-president because "those in high authority in the denomination have taken no occasion to deny the vile slanders that have been made against me,"[92] and to remain might reflect upon the Baptist cause. The slanders related to Davis being drunk in public on numerous occasions. Eagle, as president of the convention, accepted Davis's resignation.

About ten days after his resignation, Davis changed his mind about allowing Eagle to stay on the state capitol commission. On April 19, he wrote Eagle "you are removed"[93] since there was so much tension between them. The firing of Eagle infuriated legislators and the Baptist establishment and gave Davis's vendetta against the state capitol much less credibility.

Another interesting meeting took place during 1902 between Donaghey and Davis. Donaghey dropped in to see Davis at his office in the old statehouse on Saturday, October 18, 1902.[94] According to Donaghey, it was just a casual meeting (this can be taken with a grain of salt). The conversation turned to the new state capitol.[95] Donaghey then offered to build the new capitol for $1 million and give a performance board to guarantee it. He felt this could be done with the use of convict labor and also believed that architect Day's estimates were too high since they were in some cases based on Eastern rather than Arkansas prices. Davis was not interested, and some bad feeling developed because Davis believed that Donaghey had leaked the affair to the press. Donaghey placed the blame on several other people also present[96] who knew how interested the newspapers would be in the meeting.

The Donaghey offer showed a basic disagreement between the two men because "Donaghey wanted to have a new capitol; Davis did not."[97] Donaghey in a later interview with the *Arkansas Democrat*[98] said that he did not leak the story but the newspaper accounts were accurate. He repeated this same offer in February of 1903 to the joint senate and house committee set up to devise ways to complete the new capitol.[99]

This meeting with Davis was a bonanza for Donaghey. It clearly delineated an issue about which he and Davis disagreed. He got much favorable publicity from the state newspapers, which portrayed him as a person willing to risk much for his state as contrasted with Davis the obstructionist. A comment from the *Arkansas Democrat* is typical: "The truth is that George

Donaghey can complete this building according to the plans of Architect Mann for a million dollars and make money. He is willing to risk the savings of a lifetime on that proposition."[100] Donaghey even received a letter from Mann prompted by the newspaper articles. Although Mann alluded to their differences, he offered to help in any possible way should Donaghey obtain a contract to build the new state capitol.[101]

As the 1903 legislative session approached, sentiment for completing the state capitol was on the upswing. The brutal firing of Eagle, the two-year delay in construction, and increasing doubt about what Davis was trying to do all contributed to the "complete the capitol" sentiment. Maybe the most important factor was that plaster was again falling in the old statehouse, putting legislators' lives and limbs in jeopardy.

1903–1905

The year 1903 was not a good one for Governor Davis. Not only was plaster falling from the ceiling in the old statehouse, but the legislature attempted to impeach him, and failing this, quickly overrode his veto of the 1903 state capitol bill. It also found that his firing of ex-Governor Eagle was illegal.

In his inaugural address to the 1903 general assembly, Davis was not playing the peacemaker. He recommended that Mann be fired and that the old statehouse be modernized and another story added, so that it would last the "state of Arkansas for one hundred years to come."[102]

Davis's suggestions fell on infertile soil. The atmosphere in the general assembly toward Governor Davis got chillier as time went on. The governor had included in his inaugural address an explanation of why he had dismissed Eagle. He cited tensions between them and said he had full authority under Act 132 of 1901 to discharge Eagle. The act stated that commissioners could be removed for cause by the governor who would then have to certify such cause to the Arkansas Senate. A resolution was passed in the Arkansas Senate asking the committee on public buildings and grounds to report on the legality of Eagle's removal.

The majority report of the Committee on Public Buildings and Grounds on February 10 concluded that the action of Governor Davis in discharging Eagle was "arbitrary, irregular, unwarranted by the facts, and without authority of law,"[103] and that Eagle was still a member of the commission. A minority report held for the governor on the grounds that he was the sole judge of what constituted cause for removal.[104] The *Arkansas Democrat* probably reflected the opinion of many when it commented that "it was simply a case of acting without authority and no other man would have done it."[105]

Representative Edward M. Merriman of Pulaski County introduced a bill (HB 400) on March 2, 1903,[106] that provided for the completion of the new state capitol on its partially completed foundation at the penitentiary site. An amendment was added to his bill to allow the architect a 5 percent fee. The bill as amended passed the house on March 25 by a vote of seventy-six to four.[107] Representative Tillman Parks of Lafayette County spoke for the bill, saying that he "was in favor of a new capitol and so are ninety-nine out of every one hundred persons in Arkansas."[108] Donaghey also testified several times before the Special Committee on the State Capitol in February and March of 1903, offering again to complete the capitol for $1 million according to Mann's plans and with the free labor of two hundred convicts.

Opposition in the Arkansas Senate was stronger but still not significant. House Bill 400 was passed in the senate on April 8 by a vote of seventeen to twelve.[109] This new state capitol bill was not designed to please Governor Davis since it called for completion of the capitol on its present foundation; a possible 5 percent fee for the architect, and retention of Mann in that capacity; and the selection of a new state capitol commission by a joint session of the house and senate rather than the governor.

Davis vetoed the state capitol bill on April 15 in a lengthy message covering seven pages in the *House Journal.*[110] The main argument was that placing the appointing power in the Arkansas General Assembly was contrary to the Arkansas Constitution and a violation of separation of powers. On the same day, his veto was overridden by a vote of seventy-one to ten[111] in the house. After the override was announced, there was prolonged cheering.[112] The vote to override in the senate came the next day and was twenty-four to eight.[113] No one spoke against the override.[114]

On the same day (April 16) that the senate overrode the governor's veto, Governor Davis appointed his own state capitol commission of five members, on the grounds that the legislature had unconstitutionally usurped his executive power of appointment.[115] The *Arkansas Democrat* in an editorial asked the people appointed by the governor to resign so that they could not be used as "pawns on the political checkerboard."[116] The legislative response to this bold move by Governor Davis was to elect their own commissioners in a joint session on April 21,[117] and, needless to say, those commissioners were all strongly anti-Davis.[118] The senate by resolution (SR 20) also asked the attorney general to institute proceedings against the governor's commissioners and to oust them from the positions they sought to fill.

Attorney General George Murphy was happy to oblige. He had already issued an opinion saying that the commissioners could be appointed by the legislature.[119] The case went to the Arkansas Supreme Court in early January of 1904.[120] It ruled that the legislature could appoint in certain situations and concluded that "the appointment by the governor of these defendants to serve as members of that board was without any authority in law to support it."[121]

The act, Act 146 of 1903, that generated so much controversy provided for a five-person commission of "successful businessmen" to be selected by the legislature, a possible 5 percent fee for the architect and retention of Mann in that capacity, completion of the new state capitol on its partially completed foundation at a cost not to exceed $1 million, and continuation of the one-half of one mill tax on each dollar of taxable property until the capitol building was completed. There was one new provision, however, that would cause trouble. One section of the 1903 act said, "as far as may be practicable, the Board of State Capitol Commissioners shall contract for Arkansas materials in the construction of the building."[122] Despite the permissive nature of the language, it was given an almost mandatory interpretation.

The 1903 commission quickly went to work and decided to advertise for bids on the building above the foundation.[123] They hired Donaghey as the foreman to complete the foundation, which was still 25 percent incomplete and had suffered some weather damage during the two years of inactivity.[124] In June of 1903, a subcommittee of the commission went to visit the new state capitol of Mississippi that was nearing completion. Donaghey accompanied the group, presumably in his role as foreman. Donaghey was impressed with the Bedford stone used for the outside facing of the upper stories in the Mississippi capitol. It was cheap, easily available, and quite satisfactory for the job. The people in charge of the Mississippi project, especially George Dugan, the stone contractor, assured him that if the state of Arkansas expected its capitol to be completed within four or five years, it must use Bedford stone and not consider using other more expensive stone from an undeveloped quarry.[125]

The warning from the Mississippi builders referred to the large deposits of stone in the state located near Batesville and often called "Arkansas marble." Donaghey was aware of these deposits and the strong "Arkansas materials preference" clause in the 1903 legislation, but he was convinced that the use of Arkansas marble would be too costly and would take too long.[126] He had assumed that the subcommittee had drawn the same conclusions and would recommend that bids require Bedford stone for the superstructure. Such was not completely the case.

Donaghey resigned his job as foreman, which he had held for about two months, on July 16[127] so that he would be eligible to bid on the statehouse contract which was to be let on August 12. Every prospective builder was asked to make a bid in two parts; one using Batesville stone, and the other using Bedford stone. The commission was aware that the Batesville stone would cost more since it was nearly as dense as granite and the cost of cutting it was much greater than the cost of cutting Bedford stone, which was soft limestone.[128] Still, it preferred the Batesville marble. J. M. McCaleb, the chair of the commission, said that "it was superior to any stone in the United States."[129] One of the bidders at the August meeting called it "the finest building stone he ever saw."[130] These complimentary judgments were reinforced by the Arkansas materials preference clause.

There were five bidders on the contract, with Donaghey being the only Arkansas bidder. Donaghey did not use the forms furnished by the commission[131] and did not make a bid using Batesville marble. His bid was for $937,450 using Bedford stone only. The winning contractor, Caldwell and Drake of Columbus, Indiana, bid $947,846 if Arkansas marble were used and $898,658 if Bedford stone were used. The commission debated several hours before awarding the bid, apparently, at least according to George Mann, wanting Donaghey to make a bid containing his estimates if Batesville marble were used rather than Bedford stone. Again, according to Mann, "all the Board, as well as myself, wished for Donaghey to have the contract."[132] Nevertheless, Donaghey did not make a bid using Batesville marble, and the contract was awarded to Caldwell and Drake who had the lowest bid using Arkansas materials. Caldwell and Drake, who had built the state capitol in West Virginia, also contracted to finish the capitol by December 23, 1905.[133]

Donaghey's judgement and his strong personal convictions cost him the bid when, as Mann indicated, it was almost his for the asking if he had only used Arkansas marble. The temptation must have been strong, but by sticking to his guns he showed how firmly he trusted his own building judgment, which he was not willing to sacrifice even though building the state capitol had been his highest aim in life. He was not disposed to depend upon an undeveloped stone quarry at Batesville, and subsequent events showed how right he was. It was one of Donaghey's most courageous acts in the long and sometimes uninspiring history of the state capitol.

After failing to obtain the contract to build the statehouse, Donaghey went back to his railroad work in Oklahoma with some intermittent work in Arkansas at Morrilton and at Fayetteville,[134] where he built the county courthouse in 1904–1905. For about two years he had little contact with the state capitol project.

Even after Caldwell and Drake received the statehouse contract, it was necessary to complete the foundation and repair any weather damage before major work on the superstructure could begin. This was done by March of 1904,[135] and extensive work on the superstructure began at that time. As early as May, there began to be complaints about the delay in receiving stone or marble from the Batesville quarry.[136] By September, an entire force of stonecutters had been laid off because of further delays in marble delivery. There had been machinery breakdowns at the Batesville quarry because of the hard quality of the stone and a flood that depleted the deposits of sand used to help cut the marble.

Donaghey had little sympathy for Caldwell and Drake in their misfortune. In a letter to the *Arkansas Democrat* from Fort Smith, dated September 10, he expressed disbelief at all the commotion. Caldwell and Drake had agreed to use Arkansas marble and should be held responsible and penalized for any contract failures due to the use of Arkansas materials.[137] Some unintentional support for Donaghey came from a comment by C. T. Caldwell, brother of G. W. Caldwell and superintendent of construction, that the only way to complete the contract on time was to use Bedford stone,[138] just as Donaghey had originally recommended.

Things seemed to get a little better in October and November, and the first story was completed.[139] This improvement did not last long. Work stoppages due to infrequent deliveries began again in December, when a drought in the northern part of the state caused a shortage of water that made it difficult to cut the marble. The final blow came when it was realized that no work had been done since December 15 and that sufficient stone would not be available from Batesville until March 10.[140] This discontent on the eve of the 1905 legislative session was best summed up in a comment by Governor Davis, who said in his address to the general assembly on January 11, 1905, that Arkansas did not have "enough State House to create a suspicion."[141]

1905–1907

In his third inaugural address, Davis reiterated his usual themes that it was a mistake to build the new state capitol at its present site and to take control of the construction away from the governor's office. He ended by warning the legislature that if the new capitol was to be built as planned, "it will cost you five million dollars and at the same time a very inferior building will be erected."[142] This was the same message in which Governor Davis recommended a cut in the state millage rate.[143] Even though the final cut was not as large as he recommended, the rate was still reduced by one-half of a mill. This reduction would have ruinous effects during Donaghey's first term as governor.

Senator T. W. Milan, a Davis supporter, introduced a resolution (SR 12) on February 15 on behalf of the Senate Committee on the State Capitol. The resolution requested permission to employ experts, to send for people and documents, to examine witnesses to see what had been constructed, and "what kind of material was being put into the building."[144] This resolution spoke to the concerns of many legislators and passed the senate by a voice vote with only three or four dissents.[145] The *Arkansas Gazette* editorialized that "an investigation can do no harm and it may do much good."[146]

The Senate Committee on the State Capitol decided to employ Frank M. Day of Philadelphia, who had made the first report on the state capitol in September of 1901, to make a second report since no one on the committee was an architect or builder. Day found several major problems, none of which aroused "any suspicion of the good faith or integrity of the architect or the Commission."[147] He did say that errors of judgement may have been made in dealing with these major problems.

Day's first major concern was the quality of stone that was being taken from quarry "B" in Batesville. The original stone used in the ground floor was taken from quarry A in Batesville, about six miles from quarry B. Quarry B was opened because of the difficulty of obtaining stone quickly from quarry A, and Day felt that the new stone from quarry B was not as hard as the stone from quarry A, looked like limestone, and did not have the peculiar beauty of quarry A stone.[148] Day did not seem terribly distressed, but was worried that this was a change that had been made without any formal action of the commissioners. Day's use of the limestone comparison and the unfortunate confusion between quarry B stone and the language in the original bidding procedure on the capitol, which mandated all bidders to make two bids—one using marble designated "A" stone and one using limestone designated "B" stone—led many, including Donaghey, to say that Caldwell and Drake were substituting limestone for marble.

Day's other findings seemed to be of much greater concern. The specifications concerning fireproofing required a specific spacing of reinforced iron rods in the floor spans no less than one foot apart and large quantities of steel in the floor construction when the beams were more than eight feet apart.[149] There was an "alternative fireproofing" provision that allowed alternate systems of fireproofing as long as they were acceptable to the architect and conformed in quality to the original specifications.[150] Most bidders on the capitol contract had elected to use an alternate system of fireproofing, including Caldwell and Drake. Day was worried about the system used by Caldwell and Drake, called long-span reinforced concrete construction, that placed floor beams some fifteen feet apart and spanned the distance between the beams with cinder concrete reinforced with some metal and with round iron rods placed two feet apart, as opposed to steel floor framing with beams not placed so far apart and more closely spaced iron rods. Day felt that an error in judgement might have been made when Caldwell and Drake were allowed to adopt their alternate system. Day was also uneasy that none of the iron or steel used had been tested.[151]

In a later report to Senator John Logan, chair of the Senate Committee on the State Capitol, Day expressed even stronger reservations. In a letter, dated April 19, 1905, from Philadelphia, Day asked Logan not to quote him because he wanted to mention some things he did not deem advisable to include in his official report.[152] Day then expressed strong reservations about the floor spans being more than six feet apart, iron and steel being too light for the assigned job, and, in general, floor construction being inadequate to support the densely packed crowds that would congregate there on special occasions. Day's letter to Logan did not become public until two years later, in April of 1907.[153]

At about the same time Day made his report to the Senate Committee on the State Capitol, Senator John Hinkle introduced for the State Capitol Commission a bill (SB 370) that appropriated $800,000 more to finish the capitol and levied a tax of one and one-half mills for that purpose. The $800,000 new appropriation plus the original $1 million would be enough to finish the capitol down to its last detail. It was estimated that the new mill and one-half tax would generate $400,000 a year and raise $800,000 in two years, at which time it would cease.

Hinkle's bill was passed by the full senate twenty-one to nine.[154] One of the strong supporters of the bill was the president of the senate, Webb Covington, who had opposed the 1903 state capitol bill, but now supported the new bill and its increase in taxes because "if a mill and half was levied, the people would not protest."[155] John Logan, chair of the Senate Committee on the State Capitol, voted no.

Shortly after senate passage of SB 370, George Donaghey released to both the *Arkansas Democrat* and the *Arkansas Gazette* a letter that accused Caldwell and Drake of substituting limestone for marble, of not carrying out the fire-proofing specifications, and of failing to use the energy and diligence required of contractors. He also felt that it would be pointless for the state to appropriate another $800,000 since the contract required Caldwell and Drake to finish the state capitol by December 23, 1905. Donaghey also condensed his letter and portions of Day's report and had this statement placed on the desk of each member of the house of representatives.[156] It urged them to vote against the $800,000 appropriation.

The Senate Committee on the State Capitol, which had hired Day, issued its report on April 27[157] and included with it Day's full report. The senate committee majority was critical of the lack of testing of iron and steel, worried about the strength of the floors, and felt that the commission needed to do a better job of supervising the architect and contractors. There were two additional reports filed in the senate: a minority report from Logan and Milan suggested that the architect be fired if possible and the State Capitol Commission abolished; a report from a group including Hinkle defended the Capitol Commission.

The death blow to the new appropriation was administered by the House State Capitol Committee report released on April 25. The report criticized commission members because of their lack of knowledge about architecture and practical building but did not question their integrity. The House State Capitol Committee concluded that the building should be completed, as far as possible, under the existing contract and that it was "inadvisable to appropriate any sums of money . . . at this time and until the necessity for the same can be more closely demonstrated."[158] The bill was tabled on April 27 by a vote of fifty-four to thirty-eight.[159] This action in the house of representatives was greeted by cheers from the members.[160]

The *Arkansas Gazette* interviewed house members to try to ascertain the reasons for the defeat.[161] The consensus was that large sums of money were involved without adequate safeguards and that house members had been elected with the understanding that the capitol would only cost $1 million. "These arguments, together with a general feeling of distrust regarding the bill are said to have been responsible for the sudden death of the measure in the House."[162] The general feeling of distrust may have been caused by a suspicion of corruption since "the streets were full of rumors of bribery and boodling during the closing days of the session of the legislature."[163]

These rumors did have a basis in fact. By June 2, 1905, four senators and two representatives had been indicted for accepting bribes.[164] The most prominent person indicted was Senator A. W. Covington, the president of the senate. Covington had opposed the state capitol bill in 1903 but had voted for and spoken for the 1905 version.[165] Covington was accused of taking bribes in connection with two bills in the 1905 session, the most important of which was SB 370. Covington was accused along with senators F. O. Butt and R. R. Adams of taking money from Caldwell and Drake to help pass the $800,000 appropriation and to delay or keep the committee from employing architect Frank Day. Caldwell and Drake had hired two lobbyists, M. D. L. Cook and Thomas Cox, and the indictment charged that they gave Covington $6,000 to help with the state capitol bill.[166]

Cook, Cox, Adams, and George Caldwell all agreed to turn state's evidence and testified for the prosecution. Cox and Cook testified that George Caldwell had given them $17,500 to prevent the legislature from sending for Frank Day and to secure the passage of the state capitol appropriation.[167] Caldwell did not deny that he had given money to the lobbyists but said it was only to protect the interests of Caldwell and Drake. He said he did not know what they had done with the money.[168] Both Cox and Cook testified that they had given the money to Covington to ensure passage of the state capitol bill and to prevent Day from coming, or failing that, to secure a report from Day that would not prevent the passage of the bill. Both Cook and Cox testified that Caldwell knew for what purpose the money would be used.[169] Covington denied all the accusations, and his defense was that Cook and Cox simply pocketed the money.

Covington was acquitted on July 5, 1905, after the jury had deliberated for seventy-two hours.[170] Senator Butt, on the other hand, was indicted and charged with paying Adams one hundred dollars to support the appropriation bill and four hundred dollars later, once his vote had been cast.[171] Senator Adams testified against Butt at the trial saying that in the end he returned the one hundred dollars and voted his conscience. Adams is recorded as voting for SB 370. Butt was convicted, sentenced to two years in the penitentiary, and fined two hundred dollars.

The Arkansas Supreme Court, in upholding Butt's conviction, said that the evidence showed that "there was a conspiracy between Covington and Butt and others to pass Bill 370 through the Senate by bribery."[172] The Arkansas Supreme Court was especially tough on Caldwell and Drake, saying they "were contractors of large means and rather lax ideas about the proper use of money,"[173] and, "Caldwell did not deal directly with these corrupt legislators but his desire to make money out of the expenditure for which this bill provided was the moving force that led to the crime."[174]

George Caldwell himself was indicted and charged with being an accessory to the crime of bribery on November 18, 1907.[175] The charge was that he had furnished money to Butt to bribe Adams in 1905. Caldwell was never brought to trial, and several years later, Prosecuting Attorney Roy Campbell decided not to prosecute Caldwell's case and others dating from 1905, 1906, and 1907. An article in the *Democrat* referred to these cases as "boodle" cases, and they included indictments against Senator Covington as well as indictments against Senator H. K. Toney for bribery during the same time.[176] The article indicated that the cases were dismissed for lack of evidence. It is interesting to note that while George Caldwell could already be counted as a relentless enemy of Donaghey, senators Covington and Toney would soon fall in this same category and become bitter and vindictive adversaries of Donaghey on most matters affecting the state capitol.

Despite the pessimism of the contractors who said at the conclusion of the 1905 legislative session that work on the capitol would have to be stopped within a year because the money would be exhausted, work progressed very satisfactorily during 1905 and 1906 as Caldwell and Drake were willing to work on credit. This gesture may have been prompted by the capitol corruption and their part in it. By the fall of 1905 the front of the building was three stories high.[177] Most of the stonecutting was finished by May of 1906, and the second story was also completed.[178]

Notwithstanding the building progress in 1905 and 1906, which even Donaghey conceded,[179] he continued his attacks on Caldwell and Drake in a speech to the Democratic State Convention in Hot Springs in June of 1906. According to Donaghey, his speech contained eighteen specific charges of irregularities against Caldwell and Drake, including the loss of money to the state because of contract changes.[180] He later had this speech put in pamphlet form and distributed to the members of the convention and still later statewide. The *Arkansas Gazette* asked that his charges be investigated fully and carefully by the next legislature in 1907.[181] Donaghey's success at the Democratic State Convention was more limited. A proposed plank in the state platform mentioned reports of irregularities in the construction of the state capitol and asked that the legislature investigate the matter. Despite Donaghey's vocal support for the plank, a motion to strike prevailed.[182]

Late in June of 1906, the State Capitol Commission had floor tests made on certain rooms in the state capitol to counter the accusations that the floors would not sustain the required weight.[183] The first tests were performed on the law library and a committee room on the second floor, more or less at opposite extremes, since the law library was supposed to carry a much heavier load. The floor of the law library was covered with brick to a height of two and one-half feet and fifty-seven men then stood on top of the bricks. The pressure averaged 350 pounds per square foot where the specifications called for only 300.[184] Gauges used to detect any sag showed none for the law library. The results for the committee room were even better, with an average pressure of 730 pounds per square foot with the specifications calling for only 150. There was a slight sag, the width of a pencil, in the committee-room floor, but this was deemed to be acceptable.[185]

A second series of tests was held in August with the same outcome. The law library and the same committee room were tested again. In addition, four other areas were tested, including the governor's reception room and another committee room on the north end of the building.[186] The state capitol commissioners, satisfied with the tests, officially accepted the results on August 8, 1906.

Donaghey wrote a letter to the *Arkansas Gazette* and *Arkansas Democrat* on August 7, 1906, protesting that the tests used on the floors were inadequate. His main point was that if reinforced concrete construction was used in the floor, the safety factor should be at least four times what the floor was designed to carry. He pointed out that there was no agreed formula for the testing of reinforced concrete and noted that the weight of the floor itself, any fixtures attached to the floor, and the distinct possibility of a large surging crowd stamping its feet were all additional factors that needed to be considered. He quoted the National Underwriters Association to the effect that concrete floor construction should have a safety factor of four, and a California architect who had said that if cinder block concrete was used, "the safety factor should always be large—never less than four, and better six."[187]

Donaghey also talked to the annual meeting of the Arkansas Farmers' Union in August, at the same time the floor tests were being made. He repeated some of the same charges: not enough iron was being used, the system of fireproofing was inadequate, and the floors should hold four times the weight provided for in the specification.[188] Donaghey was rebuffed by the Farmers' Union, whose delegates took streetcars to the state capitol to visit and inspect the building at the invitation of the State Capitol Commission and Caldwell and Drake. Lemonade and cigars were furnished.[189] At the conclusion of their visit to the state capitol, the delegates, full of lemonade, unanimously adopted a resolution stating that the floors were thoroughly safe and that the contractors were erecting the building "according to the plans and specifications so far as the floors are concerned."[190]

This rebuke to Donaghey had no lasting effect. By 1907 he had seized the state capitol issue as his own just when anyone connected with the construction of the building was, rightly or wrongly, under a cloud of suspicion because of the indictments and trials in 1905 and 1906. His charges against Caldwell and Drake would be the basis for a very thorough legislative investigation in 1907.

From this point on in the history of the state capitol, Donaghey played the paramount role, and his opinions and actions were decisive in the final outcome. He had an issue that would make him governor with great appeal to the Jeff Davis Populists because he had guarded the state treasury against the bribe-givers and the bribe-takers, and with equal appeal to the Progressives who knew that Donaghey wanted a new state capitol and would see that it was built.

Building the State Capitol: Completion

1907–1908

The State Capitol Commission, possibly to dampen or even pre-empt legislative investigation and criticism, hired architect Theo C. Link from St. Louis, who had built the Mississippi statehouse and the Union Depot at St. Louis.[191] After being hired rather quietly in November of 1906, he spent a month examining the new state capitol and made a report to the State Capitol Commission in December. Link strongly defended the use of cinder block concrete, saw no real difference in stone from quarries A and B in Batesville, found the floor tests to be satisfactory, and in general found things to be in good condition. He concluded that the State Capitol Commission and the state should be congratulated on the results and noted the "impressive architectural effect, judicious selection of materials, and good workmanship."[192]

Link was concerned, however, as Day had been before him, that the selection of materials was deteriorating compared with what had been done before[193] in an attempt to stay within the budget. He also worried about weather damage to the unfinished building and urged that it be speedily completed. Probably the most important part of his report recommended an additional $1 million to complete the building, including changing the dome from copper to stone, finishing the halls and corridors with marble, landscaping, furniture, lighting, and a power plant. Link was paid $500[194] for his report, which became a part of the 1906 report of the State Capitol Commission.

That 1906 report showed that $682,945.10 had been spent on capitol expenses through December 17, 1906, including $26,474.92 in payments to George Mann.[195] Not only were these figures hard for the legislature to swallow, but the 1906 report also contained Link's report asking for an additional $1 million to complete the capitol. The fact that Link had been hired quietly and had done his investigation with practically no visibility contributed to the already hostile and suspicious legislative atmosphere.

Outgoing governor Jeff Davis fanned the flames (probably with great glee) in his farewell address to the thirty-sixth general assembly in 1907. He recommended that authority over the capitol construction be returned to the governor and that no further appropriation be made. He advised the legislature to "shun any further appropriation . . . as you would shun a pestilence."[196] Davis regretted "that the real convicts, the real felons, who have attempted to bribe and debauch our legislature . . . are in the lobby today listening to the delivery of this message, when they ought to be wearing felon stripes."[197]

The new governor, John S. Little, although elected with the support of Jeff Davis, delivered a restrained and responsible message on the state capitol. He emphasized the need for a legislative investigation but also said that the new capitol had reached such a point in its construction that it needed to be finished. However, Little was soon incapacitated by a mental and physical collapse that precluded any active service as governor.

Senator Otis Wingo introduced a resolution (SCR 9) on January 24, 1907,[198] that gave broad authority to the Joint Committee on the State Capitol to investigate all charges against the architect and the contractors and to review the existing conditions at the new state capitol. One of its specific assignments was to report to the general assembly whether the contract with Caldwell and Drake could be canceled. An interesting "whereas" clause said that "one of the contractors is a self-confessed bribe-giver with reference to different appropriations in connection with the erection of said building."[199]

The resolution passed both houses unanimously,[200] and Senator John Simms probably expressed majority sentiment when he said that "the feeling is universal that the contractors should be jailed and not another cent spent until honest men were in charge."[201]

The Joint Committee consisted of the members of the State Capitol Committee in each house. Senator Kie Oldham, chair of the Senate Capitol Committee, was elected chair of the Joint Committee, and the report issued by the Joint Committee is often called the Oldham report. The Joint Committee was quickly divided into three subcommittees: one on the physical condition of the capitol and compliance with plans and specifications, one on the bonds of the architect and contractors and the legality of the contract with Caldwell and Drake and its possible abrogation, and one to look at the books of the State Capitol Commission. Hearings were to be secret with nothing released until the final report.

An engineer was to be hired (Gratz Strickler of St. Louis) to help with the technical details.

George Donaghey talked to an informal meeting of state legislators February 8, 1907, in the house of representatives and reiterated his charges that the specifications were not being followed, the contract had too many loopholes, and "the contractors should be fired and the work left to honest men."[202] Donaghey's charges against the contractors and Mann were the starting point for the investigation. The Joint Committee commended Donaghey "for pointing out to them the matters which should be thoroughly investigated,"[203] and further stated that they had used his deposition and pamphlets "as the principal basis upon which we have made our recommendations."[204] Donaghey testified before the Joint Committee off and on for eight days. He asked initially that the hearing in which he was to give his testimony be open to the public, but his request was denied.[205]

The Joint Committee met for a total of four months and heard testimony from all of the interested parties—Donaghey, Mann, Link, Caldwell, Strickler, and the state capitol commissioners—and written reports from Link, Strickler, and Frank Day. The most hostile questioning was directed at George Mann for changes he had made in the original specifications without notifying the commission, for not conducting tests on steel and concrete, and for siding with the contractors rather than with the commissioners on most disputed matters.[206] Mann defended his changes, believing they were necessary to keep the project within budget, since 250 convicts were not to be furnished as originally supposed. The delay and increased expenditures he attributed to the difficulty of getting stone. He did concede that the alternate fireproofing provision was added to cut costs and that tests on the cement, iron, and steel were made by a one-legged convict whose name he could not remember.[207]

Some of the major issues raised by Donaghey and others were decided in favor of the contractors, Mann, and the State Capitol Commission. The Joint Committee decided that the quality of stone in both stories was virtually identical. The committee also found the use of cinder concrete to be satisfactory. Donaghey had charged that the purchase of forty-seven thousand dollars worth of new brick was wasteful because old penitentiary brick was available, but the committee justified it on the grounds that much of the old brick was brittle and hard to clean.

Other issues were not so clearly resolved. The commission had paid the contractors $11,350 to construct the basement floor, and there was disagreement over whether the contract obligated the contractors to build the entire basement floor or just the steel beam support for it. Donaghey thought the contract included the entire basement floor. The Joint Committee was unable to agree on this item. Another area of some disagreement was whether the contractors should have been paid $27,246 extra for adding eight columns on the west front. The original plans called for sixteen columns, but eight were eliminated as a cost-saving measure. However, erasure of eight of the columns did not appear on all the sheets used by the contractors. Donaghey said that the contractors should have been responsible for building all sixteen and should receive nothing extra for the eight since some building sheets showed sixteen and some showed eight. The Joint Committee decided that the extra payment to the contractors was reasonable, but they had reservations about the whole process and pointed to the testimony of Link who thought the contractors deserved extra pay but found the whole matter confusing.[208]

Donaghey's concern about fireproofing was partially sustained, as the Joint Committee found that the bottom of the floors (ceilings) needed a coating of cement mortar about an inch thick and that the plaster being used would not protect the floor against intense heat. On the other hand, floor tests made by Strickler were satisfactory, and the committee accepted his judgment on the matter.

Surprisingly enough, the report turned out to be more a vindication of the contractors than many would have supposed, given the low public esteem in which they were held. The verdict on Donaghey was mixed. More of his charges were dismissed than sustained, but he still personified the nonpolitical businessman with no ax to grind who was trying to protect the state and bring some integrity to the construction of the state capitol, which had been fouled by corruption, delay, and controversy. The big loser, however, was Mann.

The first part of the Joint Committee report discussed some thirteen alleged deficiencies in the work of the contractors, most of which were found to be nonexistent or not serious. The second part, called "Independent Comments of the Committee," was devoted mostly to George Mann. He was taken to task for making significant changes in the original specifications (the alternate fireproofing provision, eliminating the eight columns on the west front, and removing marble from the interior walls) without getting board approval at the time. The Joint Committee recognized that changes in specifications were probably necessary to bring the cost under $1 million, but was bothered because when the changes were presented to the 1903 board, the board apparently thought they were part of the original specifications adopted in 1899. The Joint Committee blamed Mann for failing to have any of these major changes officially approved by the board. Another part of the "Independent Comments" dealt with the commissioners who were praised for their work, in general, although the committee felt some mistakes in judgment were made, mainly because the commissioners had to "rely for advice upon the architect selected by the legislature."[209]

The third part of the report recommended that Caldwell and Drake be required to complete the contract with the exception of the copper dome and the plaster wainscoting. While condemning "the conduct of the contractors before the last General Assembly,"[210] the Joint Committee still felt that the state would sustain a financial loss unless it kept the contractors. A new stone dome was to be substituted for the copper dome, and plaster for marble, but Caldwell and Drake were not to be allowed to bid on this. Another recommendation that did not mention Mann's name but was certainly directed at him suggested that a superintendent of construction be employed and required to remain continuously at the work site to see that the building was constructed in accordance with the plans and specifications.

Senator Wingo wrote a minority report in which he said that he agreed for the most part with the majority but was opposed to any additional appropriation, thought that there were sufficient grounds to abrogate the contract with Caldwell and Drake, and wanted Mann fired.

A report from Gratz Strickler, the civil engineer, was also included by the Joint Committee.[211] Strickler was generally satisfied with the work of the contractors. He concluded from his floor tests and general examination that the state capitol was safe as long as nothing radically different turned up in other investigations. He did mention a number of instances in which the original specifications were not being followed and was critical of the work on the attic because inferior materials had been used.[212]

Both the *Arkansas Gazette* and the *Arkansas Democrat* concluded that the report was mostly favorable to the contractors with "the only serious exception being the inadequate fire proofing."[213] George Donaghey apparently read the Joint Committee report the same way and wrote a letter on May 6 to both the *Arkansas Gazette* and the *Arkansas Democrat* from Conway. He reiterated many of his same accusations and recommended that no more work be authorized "until the present contract is completed."[214] Donaghey put his report in pamphlet form entitled "As White As Snow," the title satirizing a comment to the effect that some of the discolored marble in the second floor would soon be as "white as snow," and distributed it throughout the state.

An appropriation bill (HB 489) was introduced on May 3 by the State Capitol Committee for $325,000, including $150,00 for the stone dome, $75,000 for wainscoting with marble, and $75,000 for a terrace around the building. The money was to come from funds already appropriated and the sale of state lands until May 31, 1910.[215]

The appropriation bill was recommended by the Committee of the Whole on May 7 after some amendments were added.[216] However, an amendment to discharge Mann immediately was defeated on a tie vote of forty-five to forty-five.[217] Donaghey was present during the attempt to discharge Mann, presumably lobbying against Mann. The speaker of the house, Allen Hamiter, called attention to Donaghey and others who were, in his judgment, especially obnoxious lobbyists who were "being paid to influence members of the legislature. . . ."[218] Hamiter's vote was decisive in keeping Mann from being fired immediately. He and Donaghey later had some words on the street in Conway where Hamiter had gone to speak at one of the schools. Donaghey pushed Hamiter but did not hit him, and the quarrel must have soon ended since Hamiter spent the night in Donaghey's home at Conway.[219]

Debate on the bill was along predictable lines. The proponents argued that if the appropriation bill were killed, the state capitol would be empty another two years; the opponents contended that the contractors were crooks and that Mann's supervision of the construction work had been poor. HB 489 was defeated by an impressive vote of fifty-five against and thirty-eight for.[220]

To drive the point home even more emphatically after the defeat of the state capitol appropriation, the house passed three concurrent resolutions[221] to discharge Mann immediately without compensation, to require the attorney general to see that Caldwell and Drake lived up to the original contract, and to force Caldwell and Drake to refund to the state the amount of the difference between materials actually used and those specified in the contract. The senate took no action on these three house resolutions, so their legal effect was null and void, but the sentiment expressed was hard to ignore.

After the defeat of the appropriation bill, the *Arkansas Gazette* editorialized on May 13 that the house had delayed "greatly the completion of the capitol in order to whack the present contractors and the architect."[222] Speaker Allen Hamiter offered the opinion that "the new state Capitol may now become the habitat of owls and bats, and I suppose Jeff Davis will be satisfied."[223] The consensus seemed to be that the state capitol was dead in the water.

Still another blow was to come. About $800,000[224] of the original appropriation of $1 million had been spent, and it was assumed that the remaining $200,000 could still be used for construction expenses since the 1903 act provided that the tax of one-half of a mill was to be levied, collected, and appropriated until the capitol was completed. This was thought to be a continuing appropriation, but the attorney general issued an opinion in August of 1907 that the unexpended balance could not be used since appropriations cannot last longer than two years and neither the 1905 nor the 1907 legislatures had renewed the appropriation.[225] The Arkansas Supreme Court sustained the attorney general's opinion but did point out that even though an appropriation could not last longer than two years, the tax levy of one-half of a mill could continue without being renewed every two years.[226] When George Caldwell was asked to comment on this case before the Arkansas Supreme Court, he read the future accurately and said that he was willing to abandon the contract and let someone else complete it as long as the state settled with him on a reasonable basis.[227] Less than six months after Caldwell's remarks, George Donaghey would win the Democratic primary for governor after making the state capitol one of his main issues.

1908–1910

The election of George Donaghey to his first term as governor has been treated at length in chapter 4, but the state capitol was definitely an issue in the 1908 Democratic primary. At various times, three other candidates opposing Donaghey took somewhat different positions on how to complete the capitol. One of the candidates was R. W. McFarlane, a member of the State Capitol Commission. He promised to finish the capitol, as they all did, but was more inclined to keep the status quo and constantly cited the 1907 Joint Committee report as a justification for most of what had been done so far. He withdrew from the race on March 1, 1908.[228]

Another candidate was John H. Hinemon, the former superintendent of public instruction and at the time the President of Henderson College at Arkadelphia, who wanted a speedy conclusion to the capitol project and thought this could best be done by allowing Caldwell and Drake to carry out the contract. William Kirby, the attorney general when the election was held and Donaghey's main opponent in the 1908 primary, took a tougher attitude. He wanted the capitol constructed only by contractors who had not tried to bribe legislators. Donaghey, of course, was the toughest of all and wished to discharge the commissioners, the architect, and the contractors and promised to keep watch on the capitol job "until it had been redeemed from the unscrupulous grafters who are now in charge of it."[229]

Donaghey won the 1908 Democratic primary impressively and his views on the capitol were reflected by the state capitol plank in the platform of the state Democratic party which met in June of 1908. The plank recommended the passage of laws "as will remove all persons and officials connected with or engaged in the construction of the building at once and pass such laws as may be recommended by the 'nominee of our party for governor.'"[230] This powerful vote of confidence was given to Donaghey, according to the platform, because the people had endorsed his views on the state capitol.

Caldwell and Drake must have begun to worry about their future and the state capitol contract at that time, given Donaghey's attitude toward them and the position taken by the state Democratic party. Very little money had been available since April of 1907, $40,000 to $50,000 of weather damage had occurred because of cessation of work, $67,603 had been withheld under the contract until final settlement under a standard clause setting aside 10 percent of every payment until the building was finished, and finally, almost $20,000 in state vouchers for work done had not been paid because no specific appropriation had been made.[231] Payments to Caldwell and Drake had ceased after the attorney general's opinion in August of 1907. All these factors, particularly the almost $90,000 owed to Caldwell and Drake by the state and the uncertain future of their building contract, made settlement with the state on some reasonable basis an attractive alternative.

The position of Caldwell and Drake was further undermined by still another report on the state capitol from Major John Sewall. He was a former army engineer who was in private practice and had been highly recommended by the chief of the Army Corps of Engineers. Donaghey had read one of his articles in a construction trade journal[232] and had written the Chief of Army Engineers in Washington, D.C., about employing him. Sewall came to Little Rock in December of 1907, spent two and one-half days on the job, and reported to Donaghey on December 26, 1907.[233] Donaghey paid Sewall's expenses, which were seventy dollars a day, but chose not to release his report until the 1909 legislative session had begun.

Sewall was highly critical of the work done on the state capitol. Floor strength was dangerously inadequate, fireproofing was so bad that the floors could not stand a serious fire, steel work in the amount of five to six pounds per square foot had been cut from the original plans at a savings to the contractors of $30,000, and interior steel and iron work was no more than 60 percent as strong as it should have been and the floor slabs only about 40 percent as strong as needed. Sewall said it was necessary "to absolutely strip the iron and steel work, from top to bottom. Then strengthen it, so it will carry proper loads, and reconstruct the floor slabs and fireproofing in accordance with the best practice."[234] He estimated that reconstruction could run as high as $175,000.[235] Because Donaghey had hired Sewall, his report was open to a charge of lack of objectivity, and McFarlane responded that Sewall's report was nothing new.[236] Mann said that the $175,000 figure for defective work was absurd.[237]

Prior to the release of the Sewall report, Donaghey gave his 1909 inaugural speech as governor to the Arkansas General Assembly. He recommended a variety of actions to settle the state capitol issue. He asked that the contract with Caldwell and Drake be annulled, that the architect and commissioners be discharged, and a arbitration commission be created to adjudicate claims between the state and Caldwell and Drake.[238] He also suggested that he be authorized to appoint a new State Capitol Commission and an appropriation bill be drawn large enough to finish the work on the capitol.[239]

On February 3, 1909, the Arkansas House of Representatives passed a resolution asking Donaghey to show how Caldwell and Drake had violated the state capitol contract.[240] In response to this resolution,

Donaghey released the Sewall report and accompanying correspondence related to the employment of Sewall to the house of representatives a day after the house resolution had been passed.[241]

Because of the controversy surrounding the Sewall report and the fact that Sewall had been hired and compensated by Donaghey, the House Committee on the State Capitol adopted a resolution[242] to employ two engineers to again investigate the state capitol. Certainly by this time it was the most investigated edifice in the state. The House State Capitol Committee asked the War Department and the Treasury Department for recommendations. Captain Edward Markham was selected from the War Department list and Kort Berle from the Treasury list.[243] They were asked to report on the materials used in the state capitol and the quality of workmanship involved.

In an eighty-four-page report,[244] the two engineers agreed with most of Sewall's criticisms and found that the floors sagged, steel girders were incapable of carrying the floor weight, fireproofing was unsatisfactory, inspection of materials was almost nonexistent, and $200,000 was needed for replacing defective work so that a safety factor of three (three times the load mentioned in the specifications) could be maintained throughout. Mann was taken to task for failing to see that the contract and specifications were followed and the commissioners for exercising poor business judgment. They estimated the cost of completing the state capitol at $1,160,000.

There were some mitigating factors present to encourage Mann and Caldwell and Drake. The two engineers conceded that the $1 million appropriation limitation had caused much trouble.[245] The engineers also felt that the extra payment to Caldwell and Drake of twenty-six thousand dollars to build eight more columns on the west front of the building was justified. More important, they recommended that Mann be retained as the architect despite his poor supervision because of his "well conceived and artistic treatment of [the] Capitol."[246]

The other recommendations were less pleasing to Caldwell and Drake and the commissioners, since one was to replace the commissioners with better qualified people and another was to terminate the contract with Caldwell and Drake with their rights to be adjudicated before a competent body. A structural engineer should be hired to redesign the needed changes and a superintendent of construction employed to remain at the work site constantly.

The report of the two engineers was the sixth report concerning the state capitol, three by architects and three by engineers. There were two by Frank Day, one by Theodore Link, one by Gratz Strickler, one by John Sewall, and one by Markham and Berle. Most of the questions raised in the investigations centered on the two issues of the strength of the floors and the reliability of the iron and steel in the building.

In response to both the Sewall report and the study undertaken by Markham and Berle, Caldwell and Drake deliberately set fire to one of the floors to test the fireproofing.[247] The fire was started on February 8 and left burning to a height of fifteen to eighteen feet for two weeks. The contractors found no significant damage. About a month later,[248] Caldwell and Drake tested the floor of the supreme court room with wet sand piled three feet high for a pressure of 200 pounds per square foot, and no problem was encountered. The State Capitol Commission conducted tests a week later[249] once more on the supreme court room and the state auditor's office and again with wet sand that equaled 300 pounds per square foot. They announced the strength of the floors was sufficient.

On the other hand, the House State Capitol Committee's two engineers tested a committee room on the second floor with a pressure of 100 pounds (committee estimate) per square foot or 130 to 140 pounds per square foot (Caldwell and Drake estimate). The floor sagged between one-half and one inch.[250] Caldwell and Drake complained that the committee-room floor was not yet finished and asked that the tests be stopped because of danger to the 100 convicts who were piling wet sand on the floor. A successful suit was then brought to restrain the House Committee from further tests.[251] The matter was finally compromised by an agreement allowing future tests as long as no property was destroyed and the building was not damaged.[252]

The House State Capitol Committee report to the general assembly on March 24 included the full investigation by the two engineers. In addition to submitting the report of the two engineers to the legislature, the committee recommended a bill (SB 77) that dismissed the present commissioners, terminated the services of the architect, and annulled the contract with Caldwell and Drake. It also created an arbitration commission to settle matters between Caldwell and Drake and the state.[253]

The report of the House State Capitol Committee probably inspired Caldwell and Drake to send a letter to both houses of the general assembly on March 25. They called the report "biased and unfair,"[254] but still offered to finish the building according to the contract within eighteen months for $338,000. The findings of the two engineers and their implicit adoption by the House State Capitol Committee set the stage for legislative action on three important measures to dispose of the state capitol problem. One was SB 394, which appropriated money ($795,000) for additional construction and authorized the governor to appoint another capitol commission. A second senate bill (SB 77) recommended by the House State Capitol Committee discharged the architect and commissioners, canceled the contract with Caldwell and Drake, and set up an arbitration commission to adjudicate the financial claims of Caldwell and Drake. The last bill was a house bill (HB 443) to appropriate a certain sum of money ($175,000) to pay the claims of Caldwell and Drake if the arbitration commission deemed them valid.

As these three bills were drafted, Donaghey met with senators and representatives to ensure that his own views were represented.[255] He even sent a special message to the general assembly on April 26 that urged the passage of a bill to appropriate money to pay Caldwell and Drake in the event the arbitration commission decided that their claims were justified.[256] The $795,000 appropriation bill, the first of the package, passed without great difficulty once a motion to abolish the one-half mill tax for the state capitol failed in the Committee of the Whole on a forty to forty tie vote.[257] The bill, which became Act 238 of 1909, included $175,000 to remove defective work and $330,000 to complete the original Caldwell and Drake contract. It also had a provision allowing the governor to appoint a four-person state capitol[258] commission and another to permit the transfer of unexpended balances from one fund to another.[259]

The second bill (SB 77) discharged the commissioners and the architect, and annulled the contract with Caldwell and Drake. An arbitration commission was created to adjudicate the claims of Caldwell and Drake against the state. The three members of the arbitration commission were named in the bill: the chief justice of the Arkansas Supreme Court and the two sitting federal judges in Arkansas. This bill caused much more controversy, mainly because some senators wanted to protect any of the five existing commissioners who lived in their senatorial districts. The vote in the senate was fourteen to twelve[260] but the margin in the house was not quite as close, forty-six to thirty-eight.[261] This bill, however, failed to contain an appropriation from which arbitration awards could be made.

To fill this gap, an appropriation bill (SB 443) authorizing a maximum of $175,000 for payment of claims was introduced. Donaghey sent a special message to the legislature on April 26 in which he said that Caldwell and Drake had agreed to accept the judgment of the arbitration commission.[262] He later indicated that they had agreed that the specific amount found in the bill would be sufficient. Despite this agreement by Donaghey and the contractors, and a vote of twenty-one to eleven in the senate,[263] the appropriation bill was defeated in the house with only thirty-seven favorable votes to fifty negative ones.[264] The argument that apparently carried the day was that too much had already been paid to Caldwell and Drake, and besides, they owed the state money and not vice versa.[265] This outcome, unfortunately, left the settlement with Caldwell and Drake dangling.

Donaghey tried diligently to salvage what he could, but it was an uphill battle complicated by mistrust on both sides. Attorney General Norwood said that the failure to pass the appropriation bill for the arbitration commission would leave everything in more confusion than before the session convened.[266] He was correct, but Donaghey made enormous efforts to find some way out of the impasse even though there could not have been much love lost between him and Caldwell and Drake.

The problem was this: the Arbitration Commission Act did contain language saying that the commission could fix the amount the state should pay Caldwell and Drake,[267] and another act required the state auditor to issue a warrant once the amount had been decided by the Arbitration Commission, but no precise amount was mentioned in either act. Thus, technically, no appropriation to compensate Caldwell and Drake had been made.

Donaghey still thought Caldwell and Drake could be reimbursed in one of two ways. Assuming that the Arbitration Commission awarded an amount to Caldwell and Drake, they could wait until the next legislative session when a deficiency appropriation could be passed to fund the award. The other possibility was that the State Capitol Commission could issue vouchers to Caldwell and Drake under the authority of existing legislation. These vouchers would be a form of commercial paper, which banks would honor at a small discount and which could be later redeemed by a deficiency appropriation of the next legislature.[268] Caldwell and Drake apparently thought this too risky, and Donaghey's approaches were unsuccessful.

A third attempt seemed on the brink of success before it collapsed.[269] All the partners, Donaghey, Caldwell and Drake, the State Capitol Commissioners, and others agreed that the case would be submitted quickly to the Arbitration Commission, no construction work would take place until an award had been made, and Caldwell and Drake would not insist upon a guarantee that the money be paid to them immediately. This fell apart because the Arbitration Commission said that ninety days would be needed for a decision, and Caldwell and Drake had expected thirty days. The attorney for Caldwell and Drake was emphatic that they wanted an early decision and did not want to wait for testimony and a printed record.[270] Once the thirty-day request was refused, Caldwell left town for good and left everything in the hands of his attorney.[271] Caldwell went to Youngstown, Ohio, where his firm was building a courthouse.

There is still one more piece to this legal puzzle. Caldwell and Drake had been issued about nineteen thousand dollars in vouchers for work performed in the fall of 1907, but could not be paid because the unexpended balances in the state capitol fund could not be used since the legislature had not reappropriated these funds every two years. However, the passage of recent legislation offered some hope. Caldwell and Drake brought a suit against the state for payment of the vouchers and indicated that if the vouchers were paid, they would submit to arbitration and give up possession of the state capitol.[272]

The suit was at first almost friendly in nature since there seemed little doubt that the nineteen thousand dollars was a valid claim. The Pulaski County Circuit Court decided for Caldwell and Drake, but State Auditor John Jobe refused to honor the vouchers until the Arkansas Supreme Court made a final decision. Jobe thought this would not take very long since a transcript could be speedily produced. If the supreme court would agree to hear the case before its summer recess (it was now late June of 1909), the whole matter could be disposed of in ten days.[273] Donaghey agreed with the decision to appeal and said that "all issues dealing with the state capitol should go to the court of last resort."[274] However, the Arkansas Supreme Court did not agree to hear the case before its summer recess and adjourned until September.[275] The final decision of the Arkansas Supreme Court in this case issued in January of 1910 was against Caldwell and Drake.[276]

It would be hard to fault Donaghey who tried very hard for a settlement. Despite the ill will that existed between him and Caldwell and Drake, he made tireless efforts to facilitate a reasonable solution beginning with his effort for legislation to establish a neutral arbitration commission and to designate a specific amount for claims. Once the appropriation bill containing $175,000 for the payment of claims failed to pass, he searched for other creative ways out of the dilemma. During his career Donaghey hurled many accusations against Caldwell and Drake, some with merit and some without, but in attempting to find a just way to compensate them for work performed on the state capitol, he rose above partisanship and personal feelings and performed in a manner worthy of high praise.

During the time that the settlement attempts were being made, Donaghey appointed on June 1 the fourth State Capitol Commission.[277] It would be in existence for eight years, until 1917, and would be the last commission. The fourth commission consisted of the governor; Charles L. Thompson, a Little Rock architect; R. F. Foster, a farmer and businessman from Cleveland County; John I. Moore, a former president of the state senate and a lawyer; and Harmon Remmel, a Little Rock businessman and banker, and more important, the most prominent Republican in the state. Remmel had served as chair of the state Republican party for years and had run three times as a Republican candidate for governor. With the exception of Remmel, whose appointment grated on many die-hard Democrats, the new commission, as Donaghey intended,[278] seemed to hit the right note as a commission not chosen primarily for political reasons. The *Arkansas Gazette* thought that Donaghey had followed his usual policy of appointing practical men from different walks of life and "the personnel of the commission speaks of anything but politics."[279]

At the first meeting of the new commission, Donaghey was elected chair, and an executive committee composed of Donaghey, Thompson, and Remmel was selected.[280] The executive committee was given full power to act for the commission in the event that the commission was not officially meeting or in session. Attorney William Kirby was directed to notify Caldwell and Drake that the commission intended to take possession of the capitol building and begin work.

At the second meeting of the commission on June 25, an offer was extended to Cass Gilbert, a noted architect who had built the Minnesota state capitol and the central public library in St. Louis and was president of the American Institute of Architects.[281] Gilbert inspected the state capitol the next day and accepted the position on June 27.[282] His choice was widely praised, and George Mann, whom he succeeded, wrote and offered his help and stated that his successor "was thoroughly competent."[283] Donaghey called him "the foremost architect in America,"[284] and even allowing for some exaggeration, he "ranked among the top three or four architects in the nation."[285] Gilbert's pay was to be $3,500 for a consultant's fee immediately and 5 percent of the entire cost of the remainder of the work.[286]

Although it was still unclear who legally possessed the state capitol building, Caldwell and Drake or the state of Arkansas through its agency, the State Capitol Commission, Gilbert had two engineers on the job by the middle of July inspecting the building and determining what had to be replaced. Gilbert reported to the commission about a week later that initially the entire interior of the building needed to be replaced, especially the floors where the spans were more than twelve feet apart.[287] He elaborated in a later report that the cast iron columns were split and cracked, the reinforcing rods were fewer than expected and spaced too far apart, the cinder concrete often contained lumps of coal as big as walnuts or hen eggs, and the steel work was about 35 percent below standard requirements for strength.[288] These reports placed Gilbert unequivocally in the same camp as Sewall and the two Washington, D.C., engineers who had also found dangerous structural defects. Caldwell and Drake were outraged and said that tearing out the floors was wanton destruction,[289] but the *Arkansas Gazette* said that "Governor Donaghey stands squarely upon engineering advice and directions."[290]

On July 15, the State Capitol Commission again formally took possession of the state capitol building. About a month earlier, the commission had also officially taken possession and had employed for a short time an engineer and several convicts on the premises. While Caldwell and Drake protested, they did not physically try to prevent this.[291] This new move, however, was more serious, since much of the existing interior was going to be dismantled. Five carpenters and fifteen convicts were to be put to work immediately on the premises.

The commission found that the door to the building had been nailed shut, but they quickly broke it open, and the convicts began work. When the workers returned after lunch, the door had been nailed shut again by the night watchman who was still employed by Caldwell and Drake. The door was broken open for a second time, but after the work force left for the night, the door was nailed shut for a third time.[292] The comic opera overtones of this incident disguised the serious nature of the differences between the two parties. Caldwell and Drake protested vigorously the action of the commission, stating that they were still in legal possession of the building and were willing to carry out the contract.[293] By this time, however, the commission had physical possession of the state capitol building. They posted armed guards, built a fence with a guardhouse every one hundred feet, and required passes for people to enter the capitol.[294] Photographs of the defective work were taken, floors were tested, and the defective work was removed by eighty convicts under the supervision of Gilbert and his engineers.[295] The hope was to have everything cleared and ready by August 1.

On July 20, Caldwell and Drake asked for an injunction in Pulaski County Chancery Court against the state capitol commissioners to restrain them from tearing out any work and to require them to leave the premises. The complaint referred to Donaghey as a "sore-headed competitor" who had sought to ruin them, even to the extent of spending $100,000 to become governor[296] and who had appointed commissioners biased against them.[297] The chancery court granted a temporary restraining order on July 26 in favor of Caldwell and Drake, holding that the portion of the act that terminated the contract with Caldwell and Drake was unconstitutional and that Caldwell and Drake had a right to the possession of the state capitol building.[298]

Notice of the restraining order was served on July 27, but work on the capitol proceeded as usual[299] for several more days. The State Capitol Commission appeared to be ignoring the injunction and apparently had received legal advice that it should do so.[300] Another interesting development that occurred at this same time was the ordering of a company of the state militia to Argenta (North Little Rock) for rifle practice to make up for a bad rifle practice two weeks earlier.[301] They had no orders to come to the state capitol but could quickly have been mobilized for that purpose. It is difficult to determine whether this was just another of the comic opera episodes that so frequently happened while the state capitol was being built, a bluff to show the governor's determination, or more than that. At any rate, they were gone in three days.

Because the work continued in spite of the injunction, the Pulaski County Chancery Court issued contempt citations against Donaghey and the other members of the Commission and ordered them to appear in court on the morning of July 30.[302] Attorneys for Governor Donaghey and the commission argued at the contempt hearing that a governor had immunity from suit and contempt citations while in pursuit of his official duties and that the chancery court had no jurisdiction over the case because the state of Arkansas owned the premises and had merely contracted with Caldwell and Drake to construct a building without giving them any right to possess the premises against agents of the state.[303]

While Donaghey and his fellow commission members were presenting their case in court, the work on the state capitol went on. It stopped August 2 when Donaghey and the commission asked three members of the Arkansas Supreme Court to rule on the case while the supreme court was in summer recess. The contempt citations were suspended along with the construction work until the three judges ruled. The three judges made it clear that they were not sitting as a court but only as individual judges and their decision could, of course, be appealed to the full court. However, there were only five judges on the Arkansas Supreme Court in 1909, and if the three reached the same conclusion, it would be a majority.

The three Arkansas supreme judges decided on August 5 in favor of Donaghey and the other state capitol commissioners. The judges unanimously held that the state had a right to terminate the contract and there was no impairment of the obligations of contract guarantee as long as there were alternate methods, such as the Arbitration Commission, by which the contractors could pursue their claims against the state. They also decided that the contractors had no right to the building.[304]

Caldwell and Drake must have been devastated by this decision. About a week earlier, they had sold their interest in the Southern Construction Company in Little Rock, which owned the Southern Trust Building in the capital city,[305] and on August 7 they decided to shift all their machinery remaining at the state capitol to Omaha, Nebraska, where they had another contract.[306] George Caldwell had already left Little Rock by June. Caldwell and Drake later decided not to appeal the decision[307] to the full court. Some two years later, Caldwell and Drake brought another suit against Donaghey and the State Capitol Commission alleging that they had suffered $250,000 in damages because of the illegal acts of Donaghey and the commission in occupying the state capitol premises. The Arkansas Supreme Court decided the case the same way as the three judges had in 1909 with almost identical reasoning.[308]

With the legal problems solved, work began again on removing the defective construction. By November of 1909, almost all of the inadequate fireproofing had been stripped out and the iron and steel was being strengthened. On December 1, bids were let for the remainder of the contract. The bids asked for projections using both Batesville marble and Bedford stone, and in the two cases where this was done, the additional cost of using Batesville marble ranged from $30,000 in one bid to $45,000 in another.[309] The bids did not include the portion of the building below the basement, the heating and lighting plant, furnishings, and ground terracing and beautification.[310] There were four bidders for the contract, but the first bids were all at least $690,000, when only $550,000 was available, so the builders were asked to revise their estimates accordingly.[311]

This was done by reducing the cost of marble work, ornamental work, and some interior finish.[312] The contract was awarded to William Miller and Sons of Pittsburgh for $535,718.04.[313] They agreed to complete the contracted work by December 1, 1910, with a penalty of $200 per day for each day's delay. They also assumed that Batesville marble would probably not be used due to the high cost.

By the end of 1909, Donaghey was well on his way to having the capitol ready for the 1911 legislative session. The lawsuits were ended, the faulty construction had been taken out, and a brand new architect and construction firm were busily working on the capitol. To dramatize his determination, he announced that he would move his offices to the new capitol early in 1910 or as soon as the roof was built.[314]

1910–1913

Donaghey was distracted from giving his close personal supervision to work on the state capitol by the need to campaign for a second term during January, February, and March of 1910. C. C. Kavanaugh, who had been the sheriff and collector of Pulaski County before he went into private business in 1908,[315] was his opponent. C. C. Kavanaugh was the brother of William M. Kavanaugh, a prominent Little Rock banker and businessman, who had also been the organizer of the Southern Construction Company in 1906, the company in which Caldwell and

Drake had invested and which built the Southern Trust Building in Little Rock.[316]

The state capitol was an issue in the campaign although it was probably no longer of overriding importance. Kavanaugh promised to push the state capitol to a speedy conclusion but was sure that it would cost more than if Caldwell and Drake had done it.[317] He attacked the appointment of Harmon Remmel to the State Capitol Commission, and pledged to dismiss Remmel if elected. Kavanaugh denied that he was supported by Caldwell and Drake. He also charged that Donaghey had brought the state militia to Little Rock to intimidate the court much as Powell Clayton had done during Reconstruction.[318]

Donaghey responded that the capitol issue had now been taken out of politics and the Remmel appointment was one way this had been done. Construction was going so well that the legislature would be able to meet in the new capitol in 1911, and that all this was being accomplished in spite of the opposition of Caldwell and Drake.[319] In the Democratic primary held on March 30, Donaghey was reelected by a massive margin. He carried seventy-three out of seventy-five counties and 69 percent of the popular vote.

While Donaghey was campaigning, operations were proceeding smoothly at the state capitol with the only major problem in 1910 being labor relations. The State Federation of Labor wanted no convicts working on the state capitol and passed a resolution to that effect December 16, 1909,[320] and asked that a committee meet with Donaghey on the matter. It was announced some two months later that the one hundred convicts who had been working at the site would no longer be employed there.[321]

The most serious labor dispute involved the metal workers who walked out on February 3, protesting that a subcontractor was hiring nonunion labor. The walkout was supported by the Central Trades Council, and 175 men quit work.[322] Donaghey was quick to respond in favor of the union, saying that the policy of the State Capitol Commission was that only union members would work on the capitol.[323] The commission met with the union and the Central Trades Council on February 5 and announced that the subcontractor could not resume work unless a satisfactory agreement with the Sheet Metal Workers Union was signed.[324] On February 11, the subcontractor signed an agreement with the Sheet Metal Workers Union to employ only union labor and the sheet metal workers returned to the job.

After this interruption, construction resumed, and the pace quickened. All defective floors and steel work had been replaced by the middle of February.[325] A building inspector was hired to examine the work and to "do away with any controversy between the state and the capitol contractors over materials used in the building or the manner of construction of the building after the building is completed."[326] Donaghey had returned to active supervision after the Democratic primary, and his watchword was "hurry" while he spent "most of his time at the new building and . . . constantly [urged] the contractors on."[327] Four hundred men were at work by the first of June, and prospects for having the legislature meet in the new capitol for the 1911 session looked good,[328] especially since two other fairly minor labor disputes in 1910 had been quickly settled.[329]

Double shifts were initiated in August. The dome of the new capitol was christened in December in a ceremony deliberately kept brief at Donaghey's request.[330] By Christmas of 1910, the main structural work on the building was finished, and the two legislative chambers were ready for occupancy. Payments to William Miller and Sons through December 31 were $438,738 out of the $535,718 appropriated, and Cass Gilbert had been paid $31,463 plus $7,000 for special engineering services.[331] Removal of defective work had cost only $118,000 rather than the $175,000 allocated.

One small cloud appeared on the horizon. There had been no money appropriated for heating and lighting of the new statehouse in the legislation. Donaghey was afraid to rely solely upon the good will of the legislature to pass a deficiency appropriation to pay for heat and light contracted for in advance of the session,[332] so he wrote a letter to each member of the new general assembly, explaining the dilemma and asking whether the situation warranted letting a contract for a temporary heating plant prior to the session in anticipation of an appropriation to cover the costs after the session convened. Legislative response was virtually unanimous[333] in favor. The contract for thirty-eight thousand dollars was let on December 1, 1910. O. C. Ludwig, the secretary of state, once a Donaghey ally but now an enemy, criticized the action of Donaghey saying that the heating plant cost too much and should have been brought before the general assembly.[334]

Secretary of State Ludwig was opposed to any move to the new state capitol, and his opposition turned out to be still another incident in the history of the statehouse that approached burlesque and farce. Ludwig announced that as custodian of the statehouse by law, he could not allow any move to the new capitol until it was fully furnished, lighted, and heated and not an unfinished building "fit for bats to live in."[335] Ludwig refused to allow the transfer of desks and chairs unless there was a formal vote of the legislature to move.[336] Donaghey said that the legislative chambers in the new state capitol would also be ready and waiting on January 9.[337]

The stalemate was finally broken by a caucus of the house and senate in the old state capitol on January 7. There were 101 of the 135 members present—74 members of the house, and 27 members of the senate. A resolution was passed by a vote of 60 to 41 to meet in the new state capitol at noon on January 9.[338] A reporter for the *Arkansas Democrat* analyzed the results and thought that the older members voted no and the newer members voted yes possibly because the older members found the old state capitol to be closer to the other state agencies.[339]

Early in the morning of January 8, the Jones House Furnishing Company went to the old state capitol and carted away five wagonloads of furnishings and deposited them at the new state capitol. Unfortunately for George Donaghey, the first state constitutional officer to move his office was the attorney general, whose office had been in the old state capitol since 1843.[340] Donaghey, of course, was close on his heels. The Little Rock City Council voted on January 10 to change the name of Fifth Street to Capitol Avenue,[341] and the *Arkansas Democrat* editorialized two days later that the new building should be called the "capitol now and not the statehouse anymore."[342]

With this kind of progress on the new state capitol and Donaghey's spectacular reelection margin, the 1911 legislative session should have been very productive for the governor, but such was not the case. In his inaugural address, he asked for three bills pertaining to the state capitol. One was to create a Capitol Arts Commission to decide upon any work of art to be placed on the grounds or in the building.[343] Another was a deficiency appropriation of seventy-five thousand dollars to cover the costs of the heating plant, steps for the main entrance, additional committee rooms, and work below the basement floor line, which was not covered by the contract but had to be done because it was the foundation for everything above it.[344] Donaghey justified the additional work not covered in the original appropriation because of safety and the need to have a properly functioning building for the 1911 session. He also pointed out that some savings had been made. The third bill was a request for an appropriation, no amount specified, to cover items not included in the contract but necessary, such as the unfinished part of the basement floor, terracing around the building, furniture and office fixtures, and a permanent heating and lighting plant.[345]

The bill creating the Capitol Arts Commission (SB 48) was non-controversial, probably because no public funds were involved. It was adopted easily. The members of the commission had final authority on what was to be placed in the capitol building and on the capitol grounds. The governor was automatically a member of the commission. Even after he had left office, Donaghey served on the Capitol Arts Commission for years and was chair when he died.[346]

The seventy-five-thousand-dollar deficiency appropriation (SB 52) to take care of expenses for the temporary heating plant and other items in arrears also passed without much trouble. One damaging amendment, however, had been attached to the deficiency appropriation bill: the seventy-five thousand dollars would come from the state capitol fund instead of general revenues.[347] Since the capitol fund was already depleted, the amendment nullified much of the positive effect of the appropriation.

Donaghey's request for an additional appropriation bill to include the major construction pieces not covered in the contract met with an unexpected defeat because of the opposition of Senator A. W. Covington, a fanatical foe of Donaghey since his indictment for bribery in the capitol scandals. Representative David Bradham of Bradley County, chair of the House State Capitol Committee, introduced an appropriation bill (HB 445) for $672,000, which passed the house by a vote of forty-three to thirty-eight on May 6.[348] In the senate, action was postponed until May 13, which turned out to be adjournment day.[349] Senator Covington killed the bill by a filibuster until the time for adjournment had arrived.[350] Or, in Donaghey's words:

Having passed the House, the complete measure came up in the Senate on the last day of the session for final passage. To the surprise of all except a few of the opposition leaders, it was filibustered to death by a Senator . . . [who] discoursed on the Bible, talked about the superiority of the old blue back spelling book, Webster's dictionary, and anything else that came into his mind. Naturally, I was very much vexed by the opposition of the Senator and his friends, since this group had opposed me during my whole term of office on many other important matters.[351]

Frustrated with what he saw as legislative obstructionism in the regular session of 1911, Donaghey called a special session to deal with important unfinished legislative business. The call consisted of five items, one of which was to make an appropriation to transfer the supreme court and the state treasurer's office to the new capitol.[352] He had toyed with the idea of asking again for the same bill that Covington had talked to death but decided not to[353] in order to keep the session short and reasonably free of politics. He later regretted this decision and felt that it would have been better had he asked the legislature to vote again.

According to Donaghey, there was an urgent need to move the treasurer's office with its vaults so that it could be close to the auditor's office and conserve everyone's time. The bill (HB 25) to move the treasurer's office and the supreme court was noncontroversial and easily passed.

Because of the failure of the $672,000 appropriation bill in the 1911 regular session, the State Capitol Commission found itself in serious financial trouble. It was estimated that less than $200,000 would be raised during the year by the one-half mill tax and no new money could be anticipated. Expenses already obligated included $100,000 for Miller and Sons, $75,000 to pay for the temporary heating plant and work below the basement floor, and other warrants already issued for needed construction and materials.[354] Projections were that only $22,000 would be left in the capitol fund by April of 1912.[355] It was also soon discovered that no specific appropriation had been made to pay for the salaries of the state capitol commissioners or the employees of the commission, and they had to serve without pay until 1913. These ubiquitous delays and mishaps that always plagued the state capitol would be used by Joe T. Robinson in his campaign against Donaghey in 1912.

1913–1917

To the surprise of most of the state and against the advice of many of his advisors, Governor Donaghey decided to run for a third term for governor instead of opposing Jeff Davis in his bid for a second senatorial term. It was a mammoth miscalculation. The reason given for Donaghey's unexpected attempt to gain a third term was to protect the state capitol. He feared that if he did not continue as governor he would lose the ground gained "in the one fixed ambition of my life."[356] His main opponent was Congressman Joe T. Robinson from Lonoke.

The main issues in the 1912 Democratic primary were statewide prohibition and the Turner-Jacobson bill. The state capitol was probably a tertiary issue at best, but it did provoke some exchanges. Robinson said that Donaghey had not finished the capitol in one year as he had promised,[357] but instead had plunged it deeper into politics and that much of the material that had been removed from the capitol was superior to that which replaced it.[358] Donaghey's response was that the state capitol building itself had been completed as promised but it still needed to be furnished and landscaped.[359] Donaghey suffered a humiliating defeat in the 1912 Democratic primary.

Governor Joe T. Robinson in his 1913 inaugural address did not have much to say about the state capitol but did recommend that the work be continued, more furnishings be provided, and a start be made on the improvement of the grounds.[360] Donaghey was more expansive in his farewell address and called for landscaping, finishing the interior, and buying some additional land in front of the building.[361] At the end of his farewell address, Donaghey provided a summary of the most important things accomplished during his administration, and heading the list was the building of the state capitol.[362]

With Donaghey now replaced on the State Capitol Commission by the new governor, events did not look very promising for the state capitol project. However, the old State Capitol Commission appointed by Donaghey in 1909 was to continue in office "until the new state capitol was completed" according to the 1909 legislation. The only change was the substitution of Robinson for Donaghey. This meant that Senator John I. Moore was still a member of the State Capitol Commission, and for once, this was a lucky break for the state capitol.

Senator Moore had been speaker of the Arkansas House of Representatives, president of the Arkansas Senate, and acting governor for four months (from February to May 1907) during the illness of Governor Little. He carried great respect in the legislature, and on February 21, 1913, he introduced still another appropriation bill to bring a final end to the construction of the state capitol.[363] The bill was in two parts. One part consisted of two deficiency appropriations, $32,580 to maintain the building for the next two years, (January 1, 1913 through January 1, 1915) and $34,648 to cover expenses already incurred, such as payment for the state capitol commissioners and their employees, other payments to William Miller and Sons, and payment of gas and electric bills. The main part of the bill was for $432,850 to furnish, beautify, and tidy up any construction loose ends. The total appropriation was in excess of $500,000.

The main portions of the appropriation bill for $432,850 included almost $100,000 for furniture, $40,000 for a heating plant, and another $40,000 for terracing, landscaping, and new marble work.[364] The bill passed the senate by a unanimous vote on February 24 but was amended in the house.[365] The house then passed the amended bill by a vote of sixty-eight to twenty.[366] These house amendments were concurred in by the senate despite Senator Covington's efforts to table the bill,[367] and the final senate vote on passage was twenty-seven to two,[368] with Covington casting one of the two negative votes. Donaghey gave full credit to Senator Moore for pushing it through both houses.[369]

Another turn of events at about this same time also broke favorably for Donaghey. Senator Jeff Davis died on January 2, 1913. Governor Robinson was elected by the Arkansas General Assembly on January 28 to fill Davis's unexpired term.[370] Robinson resigned the governorship on March 10 to become a U.S. senator, and J. M. Futrell, the president of the Arkansas Senate, became acting governor from March until July. The 1909 State Capitol Commission originally appointed by Donaghey was still in office. Charles L. Thompson, the Little Rock architect, had resigned because of time demands,[371] and acting Governor Futrell brought the commission together to ask their advice on a replacement.

The commission unanimously recommended that Donaghey be chosen to fill the vacancy. Governor Futrell made the appointment on July 8, and Donaghey, obviously delighted, said that he was honored to accept because the request came from both the commission and the governor.[372] Donaghey was elected chair of the executive committee and put in charge of construction work at the capitol. This appointment, coming a year after the worst political defeat of his career, touched him deeply as he explained in his book, "I fought and lost; and then won."[373]

Bids for the appropriation items in the 1913 act were advertised in September of 1913. The general construction contract was awarded to

Pelligreen Construction Company of St. Louis and was for $210,900[374] to refinish the interior with marble and to install electrical wiring, elevators, the clock system, and heating apparatus. Additional contracts were let for landscaping ($40,000), building and equipping the outside power plant ($37,779), constructing driveways and walls ($20,383), and painting.[375] Donaghey wanted all the work completed by January 1, 1915, and it was.

The additional money provided in 1913 enabled Cass Gilbert to add eight more offices on the ground floor, line all the corridors with marble, replan the grand stairways with a much heavier use of marble, build an outside heating plant, and change the main entrance door from cast iron to copper bronze.[376] George Washington Hays, elected governor in 1913 and reelected in 1915, described the newly finished statehouse as "one of the most beautiful and substantial capitol buildings to be found anywhere in the United States"[377] and praised the State Capitol Commission, on which he had served since August of 1913, for rendering "efficient and faithful service (myself excepted)."[378]

The life of the State Capitol Commission was extended for another two years[379] until 1917, even though supervision of construction work was no longer needed, so that any outstanding claims and legal suits could be settled. The main claimants were still Caldwell and Drake, who had lost all of their big suits against the state.

There still needed to be some legal adjudication of the claims of Caldwell and Drake against the state and vice versa before the state capitol could be allowed to legally rest in peace. According to Donaghey, Caldwell and Drake agreed to arbitrate under the provisions of legislation that had created a three-person arbitration commission consisting of the two federal judges in the state and the chief justice of the Arkansas Supreme Court.[380] One of the federal judges had died before any proceedings began, and the two remaining judges picked a third judge who was satisfactory to both parties. Pleadings in the case were heard from April of 1916 until January of 1917. The transcript amounted to 685 pages.[381]

Caldwell and Drake claimed $322,329.08 in damages, and the state counter-claimed for $549,927.26.[382] The decision of the arbitration commission on January 18, 1917, was that Caldwell and Drake owed the state $20,837.40. Caldwell and Drake had been allowed claims in the amount of $115,017.20, and the state had been allowed $135,854.66

with the difference of $20,837.40 being owed to the state.[383] Caldwell and Drake's big recovery items were $69,503 for the 10 percent of the contract price that had been retained by the state and $18,000 in unpaid vouchers. The largest claim disallowed was for $75,000 in unearned profits with the commission taking the position that there would have been no profit.[384] The largest recovery for the state was $118,431.10 for the removal and replacement of defective fireproofing and floors and another smaller amount of $11,500 for work on the basement floor.[385]

The amount of $118,431.10 for defective work is the issue around which controversy has centered in trying to make some informed historical judgment between Caldwell and Drake and Donaghey. Was the work really defective and dangerous, or were good work and even better materials torn out to satisfy the ego of someone who became governor, but who was still seeking revenge because he did not receive the original contract to build the capitol? The Arbitration Commission, as well as architects Frank Day and Cass Gilbert and the three engineers from Washington, came down solidly on Donaghey's side. Architects George Mann and Theo Link were of the opposite opinion. Engineer Gratz Strickler probably belongs with Mann and Link.

The commission stated that "the evidence in the case fully sustains the claim of the State that the fireproofing was not done in accordance with the contract and that it was not sufficient to stand the proper tests."[386] The steel was too light, and the reinforcing rods were too far apart as were the beams. While conceding that the expert testimony was not unanimous, the commission concluded that "when the whole of the expert testimony is considered together, it shows very convincingly, we think, that the work was not sufficient and that the capitol building would have been positively dangerous if the floors had not been torn out and replaced."[387]

The *Arkansas Gazette* was pleased "that the State of Arkansas is not indebted to the claimants, Caldwell and Drake, but that Caldwell and Drake are indebted to the state of Arkansas in the sum of $20,837.40."[388] The *Arkansas Gazette* completed this thought one day later in an editorial, the last paragraph of which was addressed to Caldwell and Drake and ended with two words: "Please remit."[389]

Since the state capitol was a state endeavor that dominated political debate in Arkansas for eighteen years, it might be interesting to look at the three main actors in the drama of the state capitol to see how their reputations fared in the process. George Mann was the principal architect of the state capitol, and although not without fault, was probably more sinned against than sinning. Some of the best testimony on behalf of Mann was given by the two engineers who had been hired in 1909 by the House State Capitol Committee to survey the capitol construction. They were highly critical of the work and suggested that the capitol commission and Caldwell and Drake be fired but wanted Mann retained because of his recognized architectural merit and his "well-conceived and artistic"[390] treatment of the capitol.

There is another unexpected contribution of George Mann to the state capitol. The capitol dome was also designed by Mann in an indirect way. Theodore Link, who designed the Mississippi state capitol and its dome, asked Mann's permission to build a dome similar to the one that Mann had submitted in the competition for the Mississippi capitol. Mann consented, and the dome Link constructed in Mississippi served as the model for the Arkansas dome. Donaghey, who did not know that Mann was the original designer, greatly admired it.[391] It is fair to say that the awe and majesty associated with Arkansas's magnificent state capitol building are due in large measure to George Mann.

Mann's reputation, however, is not without blemishes. He was not responsible for the unfair attacks on his 5 percent architect's fee by both Donaghey and Jeff Davis, had nothing to do with the $1 million limitation placed on expenditures by the legislature, and could not have anticipated the vindictive and personal attacks by Jeff Davis and his stubborn opposition to the project itself. On the other hand, he was severely criticized by the 1907 Joint Committee on the State Capitol for failing to call to the attention of the 1903 State Capitol Commission the fact that he had altered the 1899 plans to comply with the $1 million expense limitation.[392] The 1907 Joint Committee also recommended that a superintendent of construction be appointed who would be continuously on the site.[393] This recommendation was to solve two problems for which the committee blamed Mann—poor supervision and too much time away from the construction site. He was also criticized at various times for poor or nonexistent testing of materials such as concrete and steel, and for being too accommodating to Caldwell and Drake when they interpreted the state capitol contract.

Caldwell and Drake, like Mann, were also to some degree victims of circumstance, but they also gave circumstances a push in the wrong direction. They could not have predicted the crisis with the Batesville marble, although Donaghey did, and the delivery delays that added to their costs. Their credibility in the state was ended with the 1905 bribery scandal in which Caldwell and Drake testified that they put up a large sum of money "to protect their interests."[394] This was read by the state legislators and others as confession to bribery. In fact, George Caldwell himself was indicted for bribery but never brought to trial.

From 1905 on, as Caldwell and Drake probably sensed that their days in Arkansas were limited, there was some deterioration in the quality of materials going into the building. This was noted even by those who investigated the capitol and released reports somewhat sympathetic to Caldwell and Drake, such as Theo Link[395] and Gratz Strickler.[396] George Mann, a strong defender of Caldwell and Drake in general, believed that they probably "slighted the work,"[397] but also felt that Donaghey exaggerated this deterioration.

The two major construction issues involved the strength of the floors and the iron and steel in the building. The Arbitration Commission decided unanimously in both cases in favor of the state and Governor Donaghey and against Caldwell and Drake. The commission held that $118,431.10 spent by the state to replace defective construction was an expense that should be reimbursed by Caldwell and Drake. This decision by the Arbitration Commission was also strong support for Donaghey's judgment and actions.

Lastly, what kind of evaluation is due George Donaghey in the building of the state capitol? He focused his ferocious energy on the project and pushed it through despite formidable opposition. He was not always fair in what he did. He attacked Mann unsparingly for his 5 percent architect's fee when he should have known better and pounded Caldwell and Drake relentlessly for many alleged construction deficiencies that the 1907 Joint Committee found to be proper and according to contract. Donaghey also continued to insist that $1 million was sufficient to build the state capitol well beyond the time when it was clear that such a sum was not nearly enough.

On other state capitol issues, Donaghey not only acted responsibly but predicted future events with amazing accuracy. He refused to use Batesville marble, even though it cost him the statehouse contract, because he sensed, quite correctly as it turned out, that problems would arise when a new and untried quarry was used. Donaghey stood steadfast against his former friend and ally, Jeff Davis, on most capitol issues and especially on the most important issue of all—should the capitol be built? Donaghey's most serious charges against Caldwell and Drake that fireproofing was inadequate, floors were not strong enough to carry the recommended pounds per square foot, and iron and steel quality had been slighted were vindicated by most investigations of these accusations.

Possibly Donaghey's greatest service was to restore some integrity to the capitol project when it had been battered by the 1905 scandals. He restored public confidence in two ways. One was to appoint a board of State Capitol Commissioners, including an architect and a financier who was also the leading Republican in the state. This board was generally regarded as highly competent. The other was to select Cass Gilbert, one of America's most distinguished architects, to complete the capitol. George Mann praised Gilbert's selection and said later that "there is no doubt that the present building is a better building than it would have been if my plans had been carried out."[398]

According to Donaghey, the total cost of the state capitol was $2,205,779.42.[399] This beautiful marble building with 286,000 square feet, two legislative chambers with two small domes, and one large dome rising 230 feet above the ground was insured for $300,000,000 in 1990.[400] Dallas Herndon, the first secretary of the Arkansas History Commission, made this statement about Donaghey at the end of the report of the State Capitol Commission (1911–1915):

> No man in Arkansas could have been better fitted for the position he was called to assume than Governor Donaghey, for while any strong, intellectual man might hope to fulfill the duties of governor of the state, Governor Donaghey was a renowned contractor as well, and the desire to give the people of Arkansas a new state capitol that would stand the ravages of time lay next to his heart.

Notes

PREFACE

1. *Arkansas Gazette,* 3 July 1933, p. 1.
2. *The Evening Times* (El Dorado), 3 July 1933, p. 1.
3. There were only three state parks in Arkansas at the time.
4. *El Dorado Daily News,* 4 July 1922, p. 1.
5. *Commissioners' Court of Gregg County, Texas,* 10 May 1897, Folder No. 293-A.
6. George W. Donaghey, *Autobiography of George W. Donaghey* (Benton, Ark.: L. B. White Publishing Company, 1939), 183.
7. *Arkansas Gazette,* 18 December 1912, p. 1.
8. Joe T. Segraves, "Arkansas Politics, 1874–1918" (Ph.D. dissertation, University of Kentucky, 1973), 354.
9. Ibid.
10. James E. Lester, Jr., *The People's College* (Little Rock, Ark.: August House, 1987), 28.
11. Marietta Hyde, ed., *Modern Biography,* 3rd ed. (New York: Harcourt, Brace, and Wold, 1945), XIX.
12. Donaghey, *Autobiography,* 155.
13. George W. Donaghey, *Building a State Capitol* (Little Rock, Ark.: Parke-Harper Company, 1937).
14. George W. Donaghey, *Homespun Philosophy of George W. Donaghey* (Little Rock, Ark.: privately printed, n.d.).
15. Eric Homberger and John Charmley, Eds., *The Troubled Face of Biography* (New York: St. Martin's Press, 1988), XI.
16. Robert Blake, "The Art of Biography," in *The Troubled Face of Biography,* Eric Homberger and John Charmley, Eds. (New York: St Martin's Press, 1988), 93.

ONE The Progressive Movement and the Political Environment of Arkansas

1. John W. Chambers II, *The Tyranny of Change* (New York: St. Martin's Press, 1980), 32.
2. Arthur S. Link and Richard L. McCormick, *Progressivism* (Arlington Heights, Ill.: Harlan Davidson, 1983), 68.
3. James Weinstein, *The Corporate Ideal in the Liberal State* (Boston: Beacon Press, 1968), 112.

4. Ibid., 93.

5. William L. O'Neil, *The Progressive Years* (New York: Dodd Mead, 1975), 88.

6. Norman H. Clark, *Deliver Us from Evil* (New York: Norton and Company, 1976), 4.

7. Link and McCormick, *Progressivism*, 60.

8. George W. Donaghey, *Homespun Philosophy of George W. Donaghey* (Little Rock, Ark.: privately printed, n.d.), 56.

9. C. Vann Woodward, *Origins of the New South 1877–1913* (Baton Rouge, La.: Louisiana State University Press, 1971), 371.

10. Michael D., Moyers "Arkansas Progressivism: The Legislative Record," vol. 1 (Ph.D. diss., University of Arkansas at Fayetteville, 1986), 6.

11. Dewey W. Grantham, *Southern Progressivism* (Knoxville, Tenn.: University of Tennessee Press, 1983), 161.

12. Ibid., 160.

13. George Tindall, *The Emergence of the New South* (Baton Rouge, La.: Louisiana State University Press, 1967), 20.

14. Diane Blair, *Arkansas Politics and Government* (Lincoln, Neb.: University of Nebraska Press, 1988), 12.

15. Calvin R. Ledbetter, Jr., "The Constitutional Convention of 1917–1918," *Arkansas Historical Quarterly* 34 (Spring 1975): 4, 5.

16. Fred Berry and John Novak, *The History of Arkansas* (Little Rock, Ark.: Rose Publishing Company, 1987), 174.

17. Ledbetter, "Constitutional Convention," 29.

18. Ibid., 34.

19. Moyers, "Progressivism," 1:9.

20. Raymond Arsenault, *The Wild Ass of the Ozarks* (Philadelphia: Temple University Press, 1984), 16.

21. Woodward, *Origins*, 386.

22. Richard L. Niswonger, "Arkansas Democratic Politics," (Ph.D. diss., University of Texas at Austin, 1974), 35.

23. Ibid., 69.

24. Ibid.

25. Moyers, "Progressivism," 2:554.

26. Berry and Novak, *History of Arkansas*, 163.

27. Ralph W. Widener, Jr., "Charles Hillman Brough," *Arkansas Historical Quarterly* 34 (Summer 1975): 114.

28. Niswonger, "Arkansas Politics," 372.

29. *Arkansas Gazette*, 15 December 1911, p. 3.

30. Bureau of the Census, *Thirteenth Census of the United States Population, Abstract with Supplement for Arkansas* (Washington, D.C., 1913), p. 65.

31. Niswonger, "Arkansas Politics," 3.

32. *Arkansas Gazette*, 29 January 1912, p. 10.

33. Moyers, "Progressivism," 1:123.

34. Niswonger, "Arkansas Politics," 15.

35. John William Graves, "Negro Disfranchisement in Arkansas," *Arkansas Historical Quarterly* 26 (Autumn, 1967): 211.

36. John L. Ferguson and J. H. Atkinson, *Historic Arkansas* (Little Rock, Ark.: Arkansas History Commission, 1966), 235.

37. Ibid., 244.

38. Niswonger, "Arkansas Politics," 6.

39. Ferguson and Atkinson, *Arkansas*, 243.

40. Niswonger, "Arkansas Politics," 7.

41. Ferguson and Atkinson, *Arkansas*, 277.

42. Blair, *Arkansas Government*, 14.

43. David Y. Thomas, *Arkansas and Its People*, vol. 2 (New York: American Historical Society, 1930), 476.

44. Berry and Novak, *History of Arkansas*, 165.

45. *Arkansas Gazette*, 8 September 1912, p. 18.

46. Ferguson and Atkinson, *Arkansas*, 262.

47. *Arkansas Gazette*, 11 February 1909, p. 1.

48. Niswonger, "Arkansas Politics," 18.

49. Blair, *Arkansas Government*, 38.

50. Ibid., 270.

51. Graves, "Negro Disfranchisement," 209.

52. *Arkansas Gazette*, 7 May 1892 p. 1.

53. Blair, *Arkansas Government*, 35.

54. Niswonger, "Arkansas Politics," 29.

55. Ibid., 197.

56. Grantham, *Southern Progressivism*, 92.

57. Niswonger, "Arkansas Politics," 191.

58. Arsenault, *Wild Ass of the Ozarks*, 223.

59. Niswonger, "Arkansas Politics," 269.

TWO Early Years

1. George W. Donaghey, *Autobiography of George W. Donaghey* (Benton, Ark.: L. B. White Publishing Company, 1939), 8.

2. *Log Cabin Democrat*, 16 December 1937, p. 8.

3. Mrs. Robert Cordell, "Lapile: A Pioneer Community," *Arkansas Historical Quarterly* 6 (Autumn 1947): 280.

4. Donaghey, *Autobiography*, 9.

5. Ibid., 53.

6. Cordell, "Lapile," 278.

7. Donaghey, *Autobiography*, 9.

8. Ibid., 9, 224.

9. Ibid., 45.

10. *Records of Louisiana Confederate Soldiers*, vols. I and II A-6 (Spartanburg, S.C.: Reprint Company, 1984), 648.

11. Donaghey, *Autobiography*, 16.

12. Ibid., 20.

13. Edith Hammond, granddaughter of John Ingram (Betty Donaghey's brother), interview by author, 10 October 1988, Conway, Arkansas.

14. Donaghey, *Autobiography*, 26.

15. *Records of the Tulip School District,* Union County; District No. 43 Record Book.

16. Donaghey, *Autobiography*, 21.

17. Robert McHenry, interview by author, 27 October 1988, Conway, Arkansas.

18. George W. Donaghey, *Homespun Philosophy of George W. Donaghey* (Little Rock, Ark.: privately printed, n.d.), 82.

19. George Donaghey to Edward Donaghey, 30 December 1908, Louvenia Wallace Donaghey Collection, State History Commission, Little Rock, Arkansas.

20. *Arkansas Gazette*, 16 December 1937, p. 6.

21. Donaghey, *Homespun Philosophy*, 339.

22. Donaghey, *Autobiography*, 44.

23. Ibid., 46.

24. Ibid., 49.

25. Ibid., 52.

26. *Faulkner County: Its Land and People* (Conway, Ark.: Faulkner County Historical Society, 1986), 19.

27. Ibid., 430.

28. Robert L. Gatewood, *Faulkner County, Arkansas 1778–1964* (privately printed, 1964), 49.

29. *Faulkner County*, 423.

30. Hubert Lee Minton, "The Evolution of Conway, Arkansas" (Ph.D. diss., University of Chicago, 1939), 24.

31. Robert W. Meriwether, *Hendrix College: The Move from Altus to Conway* (Little Rock, Ark.: Rose Publishing Co., 1976), 36.

32. Donaghey, *Homespun Philosophy*, 333.

33. Donaghey, *Autobiography*, 60.

34. Ibid., 65.

35. Ibid., 67.

36. Rupert Richardson, et.al., *Texas: The Lone Star State*, 3rd ed. (Englewood Cliffs, N.J.: Prentice-Hall, 1970), 261.

37. Donaghey, *Autobiography*, 69, 70.

38. Ibid., 72.

39. Bruce Bullion, Jr., retired chancery court judge and son of Donaghey's chief of staff, interview by author, 16 July 1987, Little Rock, Arkansas.

40. Donaghey, *Autobiography*, 76.

41. Ibid.

42. Frank McMahan could not be located in a "Fugitives from Justice" list for the crime of stabbing, although there was a McMahan wanted for cattle theft in McCulloch County (some distance northwest of Bastrop) in 1878. Donaley E. Brice, reference specialist at the Texas State Library, to Cal Ledbetter, Jr., 27 November 1988, Austin, Texas.

43. Donaghey, *Autobiography*, 77–79.

44.   Ibid., 82.

45.   Worth S. Ray, *Austin Colony Pioneers* (Austin, Tex.: Jenkins Publishing Co., 1970), 328.

46.   *Bastrop Advertiser*, 27 May 1893, p. 1.

47.   Donaghey, *Autobiography*, 84.

48.   Ibid., 87.

49.   Kenneth Kesselus, *Bastrop County before Statehood* (Austin, Tex.: Jenkins Publishing Co., 1986), 273.

50.   Bill Moore, *Bastrop County* (Wichita Falls, Tex.: Nortex Press, 1977), 201.

51.   *The Lone Star State* (Chicago, Ill.: Lewis Publishing Co., 1893), 654.

52.   Donaghey, *Autobiography*, 91.

53.   Donaghey, *Autobiography*, 95.

54.   Ted Worley, "The Population of Conway in 1880," *Faulkner Facts and Fiddlings* 5 (June 1963): 17.

55.   Donaghey, *Autobiography*, 104.

56.   Ibid., 163.

57.   Svend Petersen, "Arkansas State Tuberculosis Sanatorium: The Nation's Largest," *Arkansas Historical Quarterly* 5 (Winter 1946): 312.

58.   Donaghey, *Autobiography*, 106.

59.   Ted Worley, "Notes on the Early History of Conway," *Faulkner Facts and Fiddlings* 5 (December 1963): 8.

60.   Gatewood, *Faulkner County*, 101.

61.   Ibid.

62.   Guy Murphy, executive vice president of the Conway Chamber of Commerce and a noted local historian to whom *Faulkner County: Its Land and People* is dedicated, interview by the author, 29 September 1988, Conway, Arkansas.

63.   Gatewood, *Faulkner County*, 101.

64.   Homer C. Richie, "The Harrods of Happy Hollow," *Faulkner Facts and Fiddlings* 4 (March 1962): 17.

65.   Peggy Jacoway, *First Ladies of Arkansas* (Kingsport, Tenn.: Southern Publishers, 1941), 226.

66.   Donaghey, *Autobiography*, 109.

67.   Ibid., 111.

68.   Ibid., 128.

69.   Jacoway, *First Ladies*, 231.

70.   Donaghey, *Autobiography*, 121.

71.   Harrison Hale, *University of Arkansas 1871–1948* (Fayetteville, Ark.: University of Arkansas Alumni Association, 1948), 43.

72.   Robert Leflar, *The First 100 Years: Centennial History of the University of Arkansas* (Fayetteville, Ark.: University of Arkansas Foundation, 1972), 228.

73.   John H. Reynolds and David Y. Thomas, *History of the University of Arkansas* (Fayetteville, Ark.: University of Arkansas, 1910), 193.

74.   Hale, *University of Arkansas*, 32.

75.   Ibid.

76.   Leflar, *The First 100 Years*, 20.

77. Hale, *University of Arkansas*, 50.

78. Ibid., 44.

79. Donaghey, *Autobiography*, 129.

80. Ibid., 128.

81. Jacoway, *First Ladies*, 225.

82. Edith Hammond, granddaughter of John Ingram and daughter of Lillian Ingram, interview by author, 10 October 1988, Conway, Arkansas.

83. Judge William J. Smith, brother-in-law of Raymond Donaghey, telephone interview by author, 27 September 1989, Little Rock, Arkansas.

84. *Vernon Record*, 12 May 1963.

85. Elizabeth Smith Palmer, sister-in-law of Raymond Donaghey, interview by author, 9 October 1989, Little Rock, Arkansas.

86. *Vernon Record*, 12 May 1963.

87. Elizabeth Smith Palmer interview.

THREE Conway Years

1. George W. Donaghey, *Autobiography of George W. Donaghey* (Benton, Ark.: L. B. White Publishing Company, 1939), 137.

2. Ibid., 141.

3. Ibid., 143.

4. Ibid., 147.

5. Ibid., 141.

6. Allen L. Morton, "The Influence of George Washington Donaghey . . . as seen in Conway," *Faulkner Facts and Fiddlings* 11 (Winter 1969–1970): 80.

7. It was first called the Main Building and later College Hall. It burned in 1928, was partially restored, and was then called the Administration Building. The Administration Building burned in 1982 and was not rebuilt. Bob Meriwether, professor of education, political science, and American history at Hendrix College, interview by author, 29 September 1988, Conway, Arkansas.

8. Morton, "Influence of Donaghey," 81–82.

9. Meriwether interview.

10. Robert L. Gatewood, *Faulkner County, Arkansas 1778–1964* (privately printed, 1964), 93.

11. Ibid.

12. *Arkansas Gazette*, 4 October 1894, p. 1.

13. Ibid., p. 7.

14. Governor James P. Clarke, addressed "To Whom It May Concern," but in G. Donaghey's possession, 16 January 1897, Donaghey Papers (microfilm), UAF.

15. *Arkansas Gazette*, 16 December 1937, p. 6.

16. Donaghey, *Autobiography*, 184.

17. *Arkansas Gazette*, 25 November 1908, p. 2.

18. *Log Cabin Democrat*, 27 January 1989, p. 2.

19. Hubert L. Minton, "The Evolution of Conway, Arkansas" (Ph.D. diss., University of Chicago, 1939), 46.

20.   James Lester, Jr., *Hendrix College: A Centennial History* (Conway, Ark.: Hendrix College Centennial Committee, 1984), 31.

21.   Ibid., 32.

22.   Donaghey, *Autobiography*, 157.

23.   Robert W. Meriwether, *Hendrix College: The Move from Altus to Conway* (Little Rock, Ark.: Rose Publishing Co. 1976), 38.

24.   Donaghey, *Autobiography*, 159.

25.   Ibid., 160.

26.   *Arkansas Gazette*, 20 March 1890, p. 1.

27.   Ibid., 21 March 1890, p. 3.

28.   Lester, *Hendrix College*, 34.

29.   *Arkansas Gazette*, 20 March 1890, p. 1.

30.   Meriwether, *Hendrix College*, 25.

31.   Lester, *Hendrix College*, 34.

32.   *Arkansas Gazette*, 22 March 1890, p. 1.

33.   *Proceedings of the Arkansas State Baptist Convention*, Arkadelphia, Arkansas, 31 October 1891, p. 36.

34.   Minton, "Evolution of Conway," 44.

35.   *Proceedings of the Arkansas State Baptist Convention*, Fort Smith, Arkansas, 4 November 1892, 29.

36.   *Faulkner County: Its Land and People* (Conway, Ark.: Faulkner County Historical Society, 1986), 253.

37.   Donaghey, *Autobiography*, 164.

38.   *Acts of Arkansas* (1907), Act 317, sec. 7. p. 765.

39.   Morton, "Influence of Donaghey," 84.

40.   Speech by George W. Donaghey delivered to the senior class at Arkansas State Teachers College on May 14, 1936, in Conway, University of Central Arkansas, Torreyson Library Archives and Special Collections.

41.   *Log Cabin Democrat*, 20 June 1907, p. 1.

42.   Ibid., 27 June 1907, p. 1.

43.   Ted Worley, *A History of the Arkansas State Teachers College* (Conway, Ark.: privately printed, 1954), 4.

44.   *Faulkner County*, 264.

45.   Nolen Irby to Mrs. G. W. Donaghey, 12 April 1943, Donaghey Papers (original edition), Special Collections Department, University of Arkansas Libraries, Fayetteville, Arkansas—hereinafter cited as Donaghey Papers (original), UAF.

46.   Bureau of the Census, *Abstract of the 13th Census of the United States 1910 with Special Supplement for Arkansas* (Washington, D.C.: Government Printing Office, 1913), 586.

47.   Minton, "Evolution of Conway," 45. Assessed valuation in 1905 was $301,890—see note 20 on p. 45.

48.   *Gregg County Commissioners Court*, folder No. 293-A, 10 May 1892.

49.   June Welch, *The Texas Courthouse* (Dallas, Tex.: G.L.A. Press, 1971), 292.

50.   Donaghey, *Autobiography*, 184.

51.   *Log Cabin Democrat*, 16 December 1937, p. 8.

52.   Donaghey, *Autobiography*, 185.

53. Ibid., 189.

54. Ibid., 194.

55. Dallas Herndon, *Annals of Arkansas*, vol. 1 (Hopkinsville, Ky.: Historical Record Association, 1947), 241.

56. Donaghey, *Autobiography*, 193.

57. *Arkansas Gazette*, 2 October 1904, p. 14.

58. John H. Reynolds and David Y. Thomas, *History of the University of Arkansas* (Fayetteville, Ark.: University of Arkansas, 1910), 161–62.

59. Robert Leflar, *The First 100 Years: Centennial History of the University of Arkansas* (Fayetteville, Ark.: University of Arkansas Foundation, 1972), 393.

60. James Julian, "Prohibition Comes to Conway," *Faulkner Facts and Fiddlings* 11 (Spring 1969): 7.

61. George W. Donaghey, *Homespun Philosophy of George W. Donaghey* (Little Rock, Ark.: privately printed, n.d.), 333.

62. Lester, *Hendrix College*, 38.

63. Julian, "Prohibition," 7.

64. Act 31, *Acts of Arkansas* (1879), 33.

65. Act 74, *Acts of Arkansas* (1881), 140.

66. Julian, "Prohibition," 10.

67. Gatewood, *Faulkner County*, 103.

68. Ibid.

69. Donaghey, *Autobiography*, 156.

70. Ibid.

71. Ted Worley, "The Population of Conway in 1880," *Faulkner Facts and Fiddlings* 5 (June 1963): 3.

72. *Arkansas Gazette*, 14 September 1911, p. 11.

73. Donaghey, *Autobiography*, 156.

74. *Arkansas Gazette*, 14 September 1911, p. 11.

75. "Edward Tabor and his Triennium in Conway," *Log Cabin Democrat* 25 May 1931, p. 4. Reprint of a paper given by Frank Robins as part of the college-day program at the First Methodist Church in Conway.

76. Ibid.; Lester, *Hendrix College*, 38; Minton, "Evolution of Conway," 36; Myrtle Charles, "Early Days at Hendrix College 1887–1910," *Faulkner Facts and Fiddlings* 2 (October 1960): 5.

77. Guy Murphy, executive vice president of the Conway Chamber of Commerce and a noted local historian to whom *Faulkner County: Its Land and People* is dedicated, interview by the author, 29 September 1988, Conway, Arkansas.; Bob Meriwether, professor of education, political science, and American history at Hendrix College, interview by author, 29 September 1988, Conway, Arkansas.

78. Julian, "Prohibition," 11.

79. Ibid.

80. Minton, "Evolution of Conway," 36.

81. Meriwether, *Hendrix College*, 38.

82. Richard M. Pence, grandson of John Pence, interview by author, 10 October 1988, Conway, Arkansas.

83. *Civil Record, Faulkner Circuit Court*, books 4 and 5, pp. 33–38, case 70, R. T. Blackwell et al., ex parte.

84. Julian, "Prohibition," 12–13.

85. *Arkansas Gazette*, 10 August 1888, p. 2.

86. Minton, "Evolution of Conway," 37.

87. "Captain W. W. Martin," *Hendrix College Bulletin* 11 (January 1915): 1.

FOUR The First Term (1909–1910)

1. *Arkansas Gazette*, 15 August 1907, p. 4.

2. *Arkansas Democrat,* 15 September 1907, p. 4.

3. Willard Gatewood, Jr., "John Sebastian Little," in *The Governors of Arkansas*, ed. Timothy P. Donovan and Willard Gatewood, Jr. (Fayetteville, Ark.: University of Arkansas Press, 1981), 128.

4. *Arkansas Gazette*, 7 June 1906, p. 6.

5. Charles Jacobson, *The Life Story of Jeff Davis* (Little Rock, Ark.: Parke-Harper Publishing Co., 1925), 131.

6. *Log Cabin Democrat*, 6 July 1905.

7. Jacobson, *Life of Jeff Davis*, 135–36.

8. Ibid., 136.

9. Raymond Arsenault, *The Wild Ass of the Ozarks* (Philadelphia: Temple University Press, 1984), 233.

10. Ibid.

11. Ibid.

12. Theodore Saloutos, "The Agricultural Wheel in Arkansas," *Arkansas Historical Quarterly*, 2 (June 1943): 140 n. 47.

13. *Arkansas Gazette*, 29 April 1905, p. 1.

14. Arsenault, *Wild Ass of the Ozarks*, 234.

15. *Arkansas Gazette*, 8 August 1906, p. 1.

16. Ibid.

17. William E. Halbrook, "A Review of My Membership in the Farmers' Union," *Arkansas Historical Quarterly* 15 (Autumn 1956): 205.

18. *Log Cabin Democrat*, 8 August 1907, p. 1.

19. Later to become Arkansas State University in Jonesboro, the University of Arkansas at Monticello, Arkansas Tech University at Russellville, and Southern Arkansas University in Magnolia.

20. *Log Cabin Democrat*, 15 August 1907, p. 1.

21. *Arkansas Gazette*, 16 February 1908, p. 10.

22. *Arkansas Democrat*, 5 January 1908, p. 11.

23. Ibid., 2 February 1908, p. 11.

24. Bruce Bullion, Jr., interview by author, 16 July 1987, Little Rock, Arkansas.

25. George W. Donaghey, *Homespun Philosophy of George W. Donaghey* (Little Rock, Ark.: privately printed, 1940), 47.

26. Ibid.

27. G. W. Donaghey to Jo Frauenthal, 2 July 1937, Series 1, item 15, Donaghey Papers (microfilm) UAF.

28. *Arkansas Gazette*, 8 September 1907, p. 4.

29. Ibid.

30. *Arkansas Gazette*, 19 September 1907, p. 2.

31. *Arkansas Democrat*, 12 September 1907, p. 1.

32. *Arkansas Democrat*, 12 September 1907, p. 1; *Log Cabin Democrat* 17 September 1907.

33. *Arkansas Gazette*, 6 October 1907, p. 2.

34. *Log Cabin Democrat*, 10 October 1907.

35. *Arkansas Gazette*, 8 October 1907, p. 12.

36. Ibid., p. 10.

37. Ibid.

38. Ibid.

39. *Arkansas Democrat*, 1 September 1907, p. 5.

40. *Arkansas Gazette*, 12 September 1907, p. 10.

41. Ibid.

42. *Arkansas Democrat*, 22 September 1907, p. 5.

43. Ibid., 10 November 1907, p. 10.

44. Ibid., 23 October 1907, p. 7.

45. *Arkansas Gazette*, 19 February 1908, p. 2.

46. *Arkansas Democrat*, 8 March 1908, p. 2.

47. *Arkansas Gazette*, 20 October 1907, p. 1.

48. Ibid., 23 January 1908, p. 3.

49. Ibid., 19 February 1908, p. 3.

50. Ibid., 29 December 1907, p. 1.

51. Ibid.

52. Ibid.

53. *Arkansas Democrat*, 30 December 1907, p. 2.

54. L. S. Dunaway, *Jeff Davis: His Life and Speeches* (Little Rock, Ark.: Democrat Printing and Lithograph Company, 1913), 125.

55. Ibid., 127.

56. Ibid., 128.

57. Arsenault, *Wild Ass of the Ozarks*, 234.

58. Ibid.

59. Ibid.

60. *Arkansas Gazette*, 19 February 1908, p. 1.

61. *Arkansas Democrat*, 18 February 1908, p. 1.

62. *Arkansas Gazette*, 19 February 1908, p. 1.

63. Arsenault, *Wild Ass of the Ozarks*, 234.

64. *Arkansas Gazette*, 15 February 1908, p. 2.

65. *Arkansas Gazette*, 1 March 1908, p. 1.

66. *Arkansas Democrat*, 1 March 1908, p. 1.

67. *Arkansas Gazette*, 1 March 1908, p. 1.

68. Ibid., 17 March 1908, p. 2.

69. Ibid., 19 March 1908, p. 2.

70. *Arkansas Democrat*, 19 August 1908, p. 1.

71. *Arkansas Democrat*, 8 March 1908, p. 1.

72. George W. Donaghey, *Autobiography of George W. Donaghey* (Benton, Ark.: L. B. White Publishing Company, 1939), 213.

73. *Arkansas Gazette*, 4 March 1910, p. 7.

74. Ibid.

75. *Arkansas Gazette*, 2 January 1908, p. 1.

76. Ibid., 11 March 1908, p. 6.

77. Ibid., 29 March 1908, p. 13.

78. U.S. Bureau of Economic Analysis, *Long Term Economic Growth*, 1860–1970; U.S. Department of Labor, *Monthly Labor Review* (March 1990), 103, 106. On the other hand, the *Arkansas Democrat* in an editorial on August 9, 1909, reported that gubernatorial campaigns had been waged in Texas for twenty-five thousand dollars or less. Texas, of course, was much larger and had a greater population than Arkansas.

79. *Arkansas Gazette*, 25 March 1908, p. 1.

80. *Arkansas Democrat*, 11 April 1908, p. 7.

81. Ibid., 28 March 1908, p. 1.

82. Ibid., 29 March 1908, p. 1.

83. *Arkansas Gazette*, 30 December 1907, p. 1.

84. Defined here as Benton, Carroll, Boone, Madison, Baxter, Fulton, Washington, Madison, Newton, Searcy, Crawford, Franklin, Johnson, Sebastian, Logan, and Scott. See Calvin R. Ledbetter, Jr., et al., *Politics in Arkansas: The Constitutional Experience* (Little Rock, Ark.: Academic Press of Arkansas, 1972), 20.

85. Arsenault, *Wild Ass of the Ozarks*, 235.

86. *Arkansas Gazette*, 29 March 1908, p. 1.

87. Ibid., 30 March 1908, p. 1.

88. *Log Cabin Democrat*, 2 April 1908, p. 4.

89. *Arkansas Democrat*, 27 March 1908, p. 1.

90. *Arkansas Gazette*, 27 March 1908, p. 4.

91. Donaghey, *Autobiography*, 209.

92. Arsenault, *Wild Ass of the Ozarks*, 235.

93. *Arkansas Gazette*, 12 May 1908, p. 1.

94. Donaghey, *Autobiography*, 222.

95. *Arkansas Gazette*, 12 April 1908, p. 1.

96. Ibid., 29 April 1908, p. 10.

97. Ibid., 3 May 1908, p. 3.

98. Ibid.

99. *Arkansas Democrat*, 1 May 1908, p. 6.

100. *Arkansas Gazette*, 26 May 1908, p. 3.

101. *Arkansas Democrat*, 29 May 1908, p. 7.

102. Ibid., 2 June 1908, p. 1.

103. *Arkansas Gazette*, 3 June 1908, p. 1.

104. Ibid.

105. Ibid.

106. *Arkansas Democrat*, 3 June 1908, p. 10.

107. The title of a biography of Jeff Davis by Raymond Arsenault.

108. *Arkansas Gazette*, 4 June 1908, p. 1.

109. Ibid.

110. *Arkansas Democrat*, 3 June 1908, p. 7.

111. *Arkansas Gazette*, 4 June 1908, p. 1.

112. Ibid.

113. Ibid., 4 July 1908, p. 1.

114. Ibid., 3 July 1908, p. 2.

115. Ibid., 4 August 1908, p. 1.

116. Ibid., 29 June 1908, p. 4.

117. Donaghey, *Autobiography*, 215–16.

118. *Log Cabin Democrat*, 20 August 1908, p. 4.

119. Donaghey Scrapbook 1903–1927, Arkansas History Commission, Little Rock, Arkansas.

120. *Arkansas Gazette*, 23 July 1908, p. 2; ibid., 19 August 1908, p. 1.

121. Ibid., 9 August 1908, p. 2.

122. Ibid., 27 August 1908, p. 10.

123. *Arkansas Democrat*, 9 September 1908, p. 2.

124. *Arkansas Gazette*, 29 August 1908, p. 10.

125. *Arkansas Democrat*, 12 August 1908, p. 3.

126. Ibid., 13 September 1908, p. 9.

127. *Arkansas Gazette*, 13 September 1908, p. 1.

128. Ibid.

129. For the sake of consistency, I have used the official returns as reported to the Arkansas House of Representatives from *Journal of the Arkansas House of Representatives* (1907), 30–32; *Journal of the Arkansas House of Representatives* (1909), 42–43.

130. *Arkansas Gazette*, 13 September 1908, p. 1.

131. *Arkansas Democrat*, 8 October 1908, p. 5.

132. Ibid., 6 August 1908, p. 1.

133. Ibid., 6 December 1908, p. 19.

134. Donaghey, *Autobiography*, 217.

135. *Arkansas Democrat*, 27 September 1908, p. 1.

136. Donaghey, *Autobiography*, 218.

137. Ibid., 219.

138. *Arkansas Democrat*, 23 October 1908, p. 5.

139. Bill McCuen, *Historical Report of the Secretary of State* (1986), 201.

140. *Arkansas Gazette*, 22 November 1908, p. 9; ibid., 20 December 1908, p. 1.

141. Bruce Bullion, Jr., retired Chancery Court Judge and son of Donaghey's chief of staff, interview by author, 16 July 1987, Little Rock, Arkansas.

142. Jim Lester, *Hendrix College* (Conway, Ark.: Hendrix College Centennial Committee, 1984), 64.

143. *Arkansas Gazette*, 17 February 1909, p. 1.

144. Ibid., 2 January 1909, p. 1.

145. Donaghey, *Autobiography*, 220.
146. *Arkansas Democrat*, 13 September 1908, p. 9.
147. *Arkansas Gazette*, 4 December 1908, p. 8.
148. *Log Cabin Democrat*, 17 December 1908, p. 1.
149. *Arkansas Democrat*, 5 October 1908, p. 4.
150. *Arkansas Gazette*, 6 January 1909, p. 2.
151. *Arkansas Democrat*, 14 January 1909, p. 4.
152. *Arkansas Gazette*, 11 January 1909, p. 1.
153. George Donaghey to J. N. Heiskell, president of the Gazette Publishing Company, 22 September 1936, J. N. Heiskell Personal Papers, UALR Archives, Little Rock, Arkansas.
154. *Arkansas Gazette*, 15 January 1909, p. 3.
155. *Arkansas Democrat*, 14 January 1909, p. 1.
156. *Journal of the Senate of Arkansas* (1909), 21.
157. *Arkansas Gazette*, 15 January 1909, p. 4.
158. *Arkansas Democrat*, 14 January 1909, p. 4.
159. *Journal of the Arkansas House of Representatives* (1909), 672–73.
160. *Arkansas Gazette*, 3 May 1909, p. 3.
161. *House Journal* (1909), 831–32.
162. *Acts of Arkansas* (1909), Act 207, 607–15.
163. *Arkansas Gazette*, 1 January 1909, p. 4.
164. *Senate Journal* (1909), 52–53.
165. Ibid., 174.
166. *House Journal* (1909), 864.
167. *Arkansas Gazette*, 29 September 1909, p. 1.
168. Ibid., 14 May 1909, p. 7.
169. In the Arkansas House of Representatives by a vote of 67 to 12, *House Journal* (1909), 635; in the Arkansas Senate 28 to 4, *Senate Journal* (1909), 354.
170. *Arkansas Democrat*, 15 April 1909, p. 3.
171. Ibid., 19 April 1909, p. 1.
172. *Journal of the Senate of Arkansas* (1911), 708.
173. *Arkansas Gazette*, 8 April 1909, p. 3.
174. Donaghey, *Autobiography*, 182; Peterson, "State Tuberculosis Sanitorium," 312.
175. *Arkansas Gazette*, 11 April 1909, part II, p. 4.
176. *Arkansas Gazette*, 23 January 1909, p. 1.
177. Ibid.
178. *Senate Journal* (1909), 68.
179. *House Journal* (1909), 233.
180. *Acts of Arkansas* (1909), section 1, 1239.
181. Moyers, Michael D., "Arkansas Progressivism: The Legislative Record," vol. 2 (Ph.D. diss., University of Arkansas at Fayetteville, 1986), 523, 546.
182. *Arkansas Gazette*, 16 April 1909, p. 1.
183. Ibid., 12 May 1909, p. 1.
184. *Arkansas Democrat*, 9 March 1909, p. 7.
185. *Arkansas Gazette*, 6 January 1909, p. 2.

186. *Acts of Arkansas* (1909), Act 176, 541.

187. Ibid., 539.

188. Bruce Bullion, Jr., retired Chancery Court Judge and son of Donaghey's chief of staff, second interview by author, 27 June 1989, Little Rock, Arkansas.

189. Ibid.

190. C. H. Murphy, Jr., son of C. H. Murphy and Bertie Wilson, and chair of the board of Murphy Oil Company, interview by author, 9 July 1987, El Dorado, Arkansas.

191. *Arkansas Gazette*, 2 June 1909, p. 1.

192. Ibid., 14 February 1909, p. 5.

193. Ibid., 1 February 1911, p. 1.

194. Donaghey, *Autobiography*, 174–75.

195. *Arkansas Gazette*, 17 March 1909, p. 12.

196. Donaghey, *Homespun Philosophy*, 161.

197. *Arkansas Democrat*, 14 March 1909, p. 2.

198. *Arkansas Gazette*, 2 June 1907, p. 1.

199. Donaghey, *Homespun Philosophy*, 162.

200. *Arkansas Gazette*, 8 April 1908, p. 5.

201. Ibid., 24 December 1909, p. 1.

202. Ibid., 14 December 1909, p. 14; Ellis, however, was granted a pardon about a year and a half later because he had served his prison time in an exemplary manner and was in poor health (*Arkansas Gazette*, 19 April 1911, p. 5).

203. Donaghey to Heiskell, 22 September 1936, Heiskell Personal Papers, UALR Archives.

204. Ibid.

205. *Senate Journal* (1909), 318.

206. Report of State Auditor John R. Jobe, *Arkansas Gazette* 4 December 1910, p. 9.

207. *Arkansas Gazette*, 18 April 1909, p. 5.

208. *Arkansas Democrat*, 10 June 1909, p. 1.

209. *Arkansas Gazette*, 20 May 1909, p. 1.

210. Ibid., 23 May 1909, p. 15.

211. *Arkansas Democrat*, 28 May 1909, p. 4.

212. *Senate Journal* (1911), 21.

213. Ibid., 22.

214. Donaghey, *Autobiography*, 267.

215. *Arkansas Gazette*, 12 January 1910, p. 12.

216. *Arkansas Democrat*, 10 April 1910, p. 10.

217. William Halbrook, "A Review of My Membership in the Farmers Union," *Arkansas Historical Quarterly* 15 (Autumn 1956): 207.

218. *Arkansas Gazette*, 6 August 1911, p. 3.

219. *Acts of Arkansas* (1909), Act 100, sec. 1, 296–97.

220. *Senate Journal* (1911), 33; *Arkansas Gazette*, 4 September 1911, p. 16.

221. *Arkansas Gazette*, 2 September 1910, p. 1.

222. Ibid., 23 January 1911, p. 1.

223. *Acts of Arkansas* (1909), Act 207, 607–14.

224. *Arkansas Gazette*, 1 June 1909, p. 4.

225. *Arkansas Democrat*, 21 April 1910, p. 5.

226. *Arkansas Gazette*, 16 March 1910, p. 14.

227. Ibid., 3 April 1910, p. 18.

228. Ibid., 7 April 1910, p. 1.

229. *Twenty-First Biennial Report of the Superintendent of Public Instruction of the State of Arkansas* (1909–1910), 7.

230. *Arkansas Gazette*, 25 September 1910, p. 12.

231. *Report of the Superintendent of Public Instruction* (1909–1910), 7.

232. *Arkansas Gazette*, 29 October 1909, p. 1. The dateline is New York, October 28.

233. *Arkansas Democrat*, 9 May 1911, p. 1.

234. *Arkansas Gazette*, 24 March 1910, p. 6.

235. Ibid., 5 October 1910, p. 10.

236. Ibid., 4 May 1910, p. 1.

237. Ibid., 14 October 1909, p. 1.

238. Ibid., 25 October 1909, p. 1.

239. Donaghey, *Autobiography*, 250–51.

240. *Arkansas Gazette*, 28 June 1910, p. 1.

241. Ibid., 25 September 1910, p. 2.

242. Ibid., 11 October 1910, p. 1.

243. *Hot Springs Sentinel-Record*, 10 October 1910, p. 1.

244. *The New York Times*, 11 October 1910, p. 2.

245. Ibid.

246. Donaghey, *Autobiography*, 242.

247. Ibid., 245.

FIVE   The Second Term (1911–1912)

1. George W. Donaghey, *Autobiography of George W. Donaghey* (Benton, Ark.: L. B. White Publishing Company, 1939), 261.

2. *Arkansas Gazette*, 13 August 1909, p. 1.

3. Ibid., 2 December 1909, p. 1.

4. Ibid., 12 December 1909, p. 1.

5. Ibid., 25 July 1909, p. 14.

6. Ibid., 4 June 1908, p. 1.

7. Ibid., 12 December 1909, p. 1.

8. *Arkansas Democrat*, 25 July 1909, p. 4.

9. *Arkansas Gazette*, 12 December 1909, p. 24.

10. Ibid., 4 April 1910, p. 2.; Raymond Arsenault, *Wild Ass of the Ozarks* (Philadelphia:Temple University Press, 1984), 237.

11. *Arkansas Democrat*, 12 December 1909, p. 1.

12. *Arkansas Gazette*, 12 December 1909, p. 1; ibid., 25 January 1910, p. 2.

13. George W. Donaghey, *Building a State Capitol* (Little Rock, Ark.: Parke-Harper Co., 1937), 260.

14. Ibid., 261.

15. Donaghey, *Autobiography*, 263.

16. *Arkansas Gazette*, 20 March 1910, p. 24.

17. Taken from a Donaghey pamphlet entitled "Shall the Ring at Little Rock Elect a Ward Healer," Small Manuscripts Collection, Box VII, No. 11, State History Commission, Little Rock, Arkansas.

18. Ibid.

19. *Arkansas Gazette*, 5 March 1910, p. 1.

20. *Arkansas Democrat*, 27 March 1910, p. 7.

21. *Arkansas Gazette*, 30 March 1910, p. 1; *Arkansas Democrat*, 29 March 1910, p. 3.

22. *Arkansas Gazette*, 30 March 1910, p. 1.

23. *Arkansas Democrat*, 11 April 1908, p. 7.

24. *Arkansas Gazette*, 7 June 1910, p. 10.

25. Ibid.

26. Ibid., 4 April 1910, p. 2; Ibid., 15 September 1910, p. 10.

27. Ibid., 30 April 1910, p. 5.

28. Ibid.

29. Ibid., 3 May 1910, p. 10.

30. *Arkansas Democrat*, 16 April 1910, p. 4.

31. Ibid., 17 April 1910, p. 3.

32. John Ferguson, state historian, interview by author, 26 June 1989, Little Rock, Arkansas.

33. *Arkansas Gazette*, 31 March 1910, p. 4.

34. Ibid., 20 April 1910, p. 10.

35. Ibid., 2 June 1910, p. 6.

36. *Arkansas Democrat*, 8 June 1910, p. 2.

37. *Arkansas Gazette*, 8 June 1910, p. 1.

38. *Arkansas Democrat*, 8 June 1910, p. 2.

39. *Arkansas Gazette*, 9 June 1910, p. 9.

40. Ibid.

41. Ibid., 9 June 1910, p. 1.

42. *Arkansas Gazette*, 10 April 1910, p. 1.

43. *Arkansas Democrat*, 8 June 1910, p. 3.

44. *Arkansas Gazette*, 11 June 1910, p. 1.

45. Ibid., p. 10.

46. Ibid., p. 1.

47. *Arkansas Democrat*, 31 August 1910, p. 2.

48. *Arkansas Gazette*, 24 September 1910, p. 3.

49. Ibid., 10 June 1910, p. 3.

50. *Arkansas Democrat*, 11 September 1910, p. 4.

51. *Arkansas Gazette*, 10 June 1910, p. 3.

52. Ibid., 21 August 1910, p. 1.

53. Ibid., 16 August 1910, p. 4.

54. Donaghey, *Autobiography*, 229.

55. *Arkansas Gazette*, 24 August 1910, p. 3.

56. Ibid., 28 August 1910, p. 8.

57. *Arkansas Democrat*, 28 August 1910, p. 1.

58. *Arkansas Gazette,* 7 September 1910, p. 1.
59. Ibid., 8 September 1910, p. 1.
60. Ibid., 7 September 1910, p. 1.
61. *Arkansas Democrat,* 10 September 1910, p. 1.
62. *Arkansas Gazette,* 11 September 1910, p. 1.
63. Ibid.
64. *Arkansas Gazette,* 11 September 1910, p. 1.
65. *Biennial Report of the Secretary of State* (1909–10–11–12), 399.
66. Ibid., 391. The total vote for governor was 150, 578.
67. Donaghey, *Autobiography,* 229.
68. *Hodges v. Dawdy,* 104 Ark. 583 (1912).
69. *State ex rel Little Rock v. Donaghey,* 106 Ark. 56 (1912).
70. *Arkansas Democrat,* 2 August 1910, p. 2.
71. *Arkansas Gazette,* 14 August 1910, p. 11.
72. *Arkansas Democrat,* 4 August 1910, p. 1.
73. 111,478 to 101,612.
74. *Arkansas Gazette,* 8 January 1911, p. 1.
75. Ibid., 4 December 1910, p. 9.
76. Ibid., 8 January 1911, p. 1.
77. Ibid., 9 January 1911, p. 1.
78. *Arkansas Democrat,* 9 May 1910, p. 1.
79. *Journal of the Arkansas House of Representatives* (1911), 40.
80. Ibid.
81. Michael D. Moyers, "Arkansas Progressivism: The Legislative Record," vol. 1 (Ph.D. dissertation, University of Arkansas at Fayetteville, 1986), 211.
82. *House Journal* (1911), 52.
83. *Arkansas Democrat,* 9 May 1911, p. 1.
84. *Twenty-First Biennial Report of the Superintendent of Public Instruction* (1909–1910), 18.
85. *House Journal* (1911), 686, 688.
86. Ibid., 569.
87. *Journal of the Senate of Arkansas* (1911), 361.
88. *House Journal* (1911), 1025.
89. *Arkansas Gazette,* 13 May 1911, p. 3.
90. *Senate Journal* (1911), 309–10.
91. Ibid.
92. *Arkansas Gazette,* 2 June 1911, p. 3.
93. *Senate Journal* (1911), 728; *House Journal* (1911), Extraordinary Session, 60–61.
94. *Arkansas Gazette,* 6 June 1911, p. 3.
95. Ibid. See also *Ark. Const.* (1874), Art. VI, sec. 15, 16.
96. Ibid., 7 June 1911, p. 3.
97. Ibid.
98. Donaghey, *Autobiography,* 257.
99. *Senate Journal* (1911), 49–50.
100. Ibid., 51.

101.   *House Journal* (1911), 104.

102.   *Arkansas Gazette,* 14 June 1911, p. 5.

103.   *Senate Journal* (1911), 120–22.

104.   Ibid., 706.

105.   *Arkansas Gazette,* 2 June 1911, p. 1.

106.   *Arkansas Democrat,* 2 June 1911, p. 6.

107.   *Arkansas Gazette,* 14 May 1911, p. 3.

108.   *Arkansas Democrat,* 10 May 1911, p. 1.

109.   *Arkansas Gazette,* 3 June 1911, p. 4.

110.   Ibid., 4 May 1911, p. 3.

111.   Ibid., 7 May 1911, p. 8.

112.   Ibid., 14 May 1911, p. 1.

113.   *Senate Journal* (1911), 705-08.

114.   *Arkansas Gazette,* 22 May 1911, p. 3.

115.   *Senate Journal* (1911), 704; *House Journal* (1911), Extraordinary Session, 2.

116.   *Arkansas Gazette,* 23 May 1911, p. 14.

117.   *Senate Journal* (1911), 705.

118.   *Arkansas Gazette,* 3 June 1911, p. 2.

119.   *Arkansas Gazette,* 4 June 1911, p. 13.

120.   Ibid., 2 June 1911, p. 1.

121.   *Arkansas Democrat,* 30 May 1911, p. 4.

122.   *Senate Journal* (1911), 712–13.

123.   Ibid., 718.

124.   *House Journal* (1911), Extraordinary Session, 79–80.

125.   Ibid., 81–82.

126.   *Senate Journal* (1911), 725.

127.   *Acts of Arkansas* (1911), Act 1, 495–581.

128.   *Arkansas Democrat,* 19 August 1911, p. 1.

129.   Ibid., 12 March 1912, p. 4.

130.   "My Campaign for a Third Term," p. 5, a ten-page memorandum written by Donaghey, Louvenia Wallace Collection, Container 2, folder labeled "Reminiscences," State History Commission, Little Rock, Arkansas.

131.   *Arkansas Gazette,* 11 June 1911, p. 3.

132.   Ibid., 10 June 1911, p. 3.

133.   Ibid.

134.   *Senate Journal* (1911), 24.

135.   *Arkansas Gazette,* 9 July 1911, p. 5.

136.   Ibid., 28 April 1912, p. 4.

137.   *Arkansas Democrat,* 31 July 1911, p. 3; *Arkansas Democrat,* 12 August 1911, p. 1.

138.   *Arkansas Gazette,* 18 August 1912, p. 9.

139.   *Arkansas Democrat,* 17 October 1911, p. 2.

140.   *Arkansas Gazette,* 25 August 1911, p. 1.

141.   *Arkansas Democrat,* 27 July 1911, p. 2.

142.   *Arkansas Gazette,* 9 January 1912, p. 6.

143.   Ibid., 4 January 1912, p. 5.

144.   Ibid., 2 July 1912, p. 11.

145.   *Arkansas Democrat*, 9 October 1911, p. 1.

146.   *Arkansas Gazette*, 31 October 1911, p. 1.

147.   Bruce Bullion, Jr.,retired Chancery Court Judge and son of Bruce Bullion, interview by author, 16 July 1987, Little Rock, Arkansas.

148.   *Arkansas Gazette*, 8 December 1912, p. 1.

149.   Ibid., 2 January 1912, p. 3.

150.   Ibid., 28 August 1911, p. 4.

151.   Ibid., 21 April 1912, p. 9.

152.   *Arkansas Democrat*, 5 September 1912, p. 1.

153.   *Arkansas Gazette*, 20 June 1912, p. 5.

154.   *Twenty-Second Biennial Report of the Superintendent of Public Instruction of the State of Arkansas* (1911–12), 8.

155.   *Arkansas Gazette*, 4 December 1910, p. 9.

156.   Ibid., 5 December 1912, p. 1.

157.   *Arkansas Democrat*, 29 July 1911, p. 3.

158.   *Arkansas Gazette*, 22 November 1912, p. 8.

159.   *Arkansas Democrat*, 6 January 1913, p. 3.

160.   Ibid., 13 November 1911, p. 12.

161.   *Arkansas Gazette*, 23 June 1912, p. 5.

162.   Ibid., 8 August 1912, p. 1.

163.   Donaghey, *Autobiography*, 256.

164.   *Arkansas Gazette*, 7 August 1912, p. 2.

165.   George W. Donaghey, *Homespun Philosophy of George W. Donaghey* (Little Rock, Ark.: privately printed, 1940), 110.

166.   Ibid.

167.   Ibid., 112.

168.   Donaghey, *Autobiography*, 257.

169.   Norwood—*Arkansas Gazette*, 4 May 1910, p. 3, and Robinson—*Arkansas Gazette*, 15 September 1910, p. 10.

SIX   Third Term Defeat and Vindication (1912–1913)

1.   George W. Donaghey, *Building a State Capitol* (Little Rock, Ark.: Parke-Harper Co., 1937), 288.

2.   Nevin Neal, "A Biography of Joseph T. Robinson," (Ph.D. diss., University of Oklahoma, 1958), 93.

3.   Charles Jacobson to Joe T. Robinson, no date or place given but a response letter from Robinson indicates early September of 1911, Robinson Papers, Special Collections, University of Arkansas Libraries, Fayetteville, Arkansas.

4.   George W. Donaghey, *Autobiography of George W. Donaghey* (Benton, Ark.: L. B. White Publishing Company, 1939), 272.

5.   Donaghey, *Building*, 289.

6.   "My Campaign for a Third Term," 4, Louvenia Wallace Collection, Container 2, folder labeled "Reminiscences," State History Commission, Little Rock, Arkansas.

7.   Joe T. Robinson to E. C. Horner, 7 December 1911, Robinson Papers.

8.   *Arkansas Gazette*, 2 June 1910, p. 1.

9.   Neal, "Biography of Robinson," 10.

10. Ibid.

11. *Arkansas Gazette*, 15 September 1910, p. 10.

12. Donaghey, *Autobiography*, 276.

13. Calvin R. Ledbetter, Jr., "Joe T. Robinson and the Presidential Campaign of 1928," *Arkansas Historical Quarterly* 45 (Summer 1986): 98.

14. Ibid.

15. *Arkansas Gazette*, 4 May 1910, p. 3.

16. *Arkansas Democrat*, 29 June 1911, p. 3.

17. *Arkansas Gazette*, 5 July 1911, p. 2.

18. *Arkansas Democrat*, 21 October 1911, p. 1.

19. Stuart Towns, "Joseph T. Robinson and Arkansas Politics: 1912–1913," *Arkansas Historical Quarterly* 24 (Winter 1965): 298.

20. Donaghey, *Autobiography*, 273, 275.

21. *Arkansas Gazette*, 16 September 1911, p. 2.

22. Ibid., 22 October 1911, p. 1.

23. Ibid.

24. Ibid.

25. Ibid.

26. *Arkansas Gazette*, 5 November 1911, p. 13.

27. *Arkansas Democrat*, 31 October 1911, p. 1.

28. *Arkansas Gazette*, 19 October 1911, p. 2.

29. *Arkansas Gazette*, 6 November 1911, p. 2; *Arkansas Democrat* 6 March 1912, p. 12.

30. Donaghey, *Autobiography*, 278.

31. *Arkansas Gazette*, 30 December 1911, p. 3: *Arkansas Democrat*, 11 January 1912, p. 7.

32. Hal Norwood to Joe T. Robinson, 4 November 1911, Robinson Papers.

33. *Arkansas Democrat*, 5 June 1912, p. 1.

34. *Arkansas Gazette*, 11 January 1912, p. 14.

35. Ibid., 14 January 1912, p. 1.

36. Ibid.

37. Ibid.

38. Ibid., 15 January 1912, p. 6.

39. Hal Norwood to Joe T. Robinson, 18 January 1912, Robinson Papers.

40. Senator James P. Clarke to Joe T. Robinson, 3 February 1912, Robinson Papers.

41. Joe T. Robinson to Thal Brasher, 6 December 1911, Robinson Papers.

42. Neal, "Biography of Robinson," 99.

43. *Arkansas Gazette*, 28 January 1912, p. 8.

44. "My Campaign for a Third Term," 7.

45. Donaghey, *Autobiography*, 277; *Arkansas Gazette*, 22 January 1912, p. 1.

46. *Arkansas Gazette*, 3 March 1912, p. 3.

47. Ibid.

48. *Arkansas Gazette*, 8 March 1912, p. 16.
49. Ibid.; ibid., 11 March 1912, p. 1.
50. *Arkansas Democrat*, 18 March 1912, p. 4.
51. Ibid., 22 March 1912, p. 5.
52. *Arkansas Gazette*, 24 March 1912, p. 29.
53. Ibid., 26 March 1912, p. 1.
54. Ibid., 27 March 1912, p. 1.
55. *Arkansas Democrat*, 5 June 1912, p. 5.
56. *Arkansas Gazette*, 5 June 1912, p. 14.
57. Ibid., 29 March 1912, p. 1.
58. Ibid., 30 March 1912, p. 1.
59. Fletcher Chenault to Joe T. Robinson, 15 September 1911, Robinson Papers.
60. *Log Cabin Democrat*, 1 April 1912, p. 1.
61. *Arkansas Democrat*, 1 April 1912, p. 12.
62. John A. Thompson, "Gentleman Editor: Mr. Heiskell of the *Gazette*—The Early Years: 1902–1922," (M.A. thesis, University of Arkansas at Little Rock, 1983), 69.
63. George W. Donaghey, *Homespun Philosophy of George W. Donaghey* (Little Rock, Ark., privately printed, 1940), 52.
64. *Arkansas Gazette*, 29 March 1912, p. 4.
65. Ibid.
66. Neal, "Biography of Robinson," 99.
67. *Arkansas Gazette*, 21 April 1912, p. 5.
68. Ibid., 23 August 1912, p. 1.
69. *Arkansas Gazette*, 26 April 1912, p. 5.
70. Forty-six advertisements in the *Arkansas Gazette* and forty-five in the *Arkansas Democrat* while Robinson had thirty-two and thirty respectively.
71. *Arkansas Gazette*, 6 June 1912, p. 10.
72. Ibid.
73. Ibid.
74. *Arkansas Democrat*, 6 June 1912, p. 1.
75. *Arkansas Gazette*, 7 June 1912, p. 3.
76. *Arkansas Democrat*, 6 June 1912, p. 6.
77. *Arkansas Gazette*, 4 August 1912, p. 19.
78. Ibid., 12 April 1912, p. 6.
79. Ibid., 6 March 1912, p. 1.
80. Donaghey, *Autobiography*, 279.
81. *Arkansas Democrat*, 5 July 1912, p. 14.
82. *Arkansas Gazette*, 2 April 1912, p. 4.
83. Ibid., 26 August 1912, p. 3.
84. Ibid., 28 August 1912, p. 2.
85. Ibid.
86. Ibid., 3 July 1912, p. 1. Donaghey once commented to the Negro Baptist State Convention in 1910 that they "didn't vote much. This, perhaps, is best" (*Arkansas Gazette*, 26 November 1910, p. 10).
87. Ibid., 3 August 1912, p. 1.

88. *Arkansas Democrat*, 31 August 1912, p. 1.

89. *Arkansas Gazette*, 11 February 1912, p. 1.

90. Ibid., 8 September 1912, p. 1.

91. Ibid.

92. *Arkansas Democrat*, 9 September 1912, p. 1.

93. *Biennial Report of the Secretary of State* (1909–10–11–12), 408–11.

94. *Arkansas Democrat*, 12 September 1912, p. 1. My figures do not quite agree with those quoted in this article, but even so, there was an amazing switch from dry to wet.

95. *Acts of Arkansas* (1913), Act 59, 180.

96. *Secretary of State's Report* (1909–10–11–12), 408–11.

97. *Arkansas Gazette*, 4 August 1912, p. 19.

98. *Secretary of State's Report* (1909–10–11–12), 408–11.

99. Joe T. Seagraves, "Arkansas Politics, 1874–1918," (Ph.d. diss., University of Kentucky, 1973), 346.

100. David Y. Thomas, "Direct Legislation in Arkansas," *Political Science Quarterly* 29 (March 1914): 99. An additional reason was that it had not been submitted as one of the first three constitutional amendments in 1912, and the Arkansas Supreme Court had ruled that despite initiative and referendum, there was still a limitation of three constitutional amendments at any one election. *State ex rel. Little Rock v Donaghey*, 106 Ark. 56 (1912).

101. Donaghey, *Autobiography*, 255.

102. *Arkansas Gazette*, 30 August 1912, p. 1.

103. Ibid., 7 September 1912, p. 1.

104. *Arkansas Gazette*, 2 January 1912, p. 1.; ibid., 21 March 1912, p. 1.

105. Ibid.

106. Donaghey, *Autobiography*, 284.

107. *Journal of the Senate of Arkansas* (1913), 24.

108. *Arkansas Gazette*, 7 December 1912, p. 1.

109. Jane Zimmerman, "The Convict Lease System in Arkansas and the Fight for Abolition," *Arkansas Historical Quarterly* 8 (Autumn 1949): 183.

110. "The Governors Conference," *Survey* 29 (December 12, 1912): 347.

111. *Arkansas Gazette*, 19 December 1912, p. 1.

112. Thomas L. Baxley, "Prison Reforms During the Donaghey Administration," *Arkansas Historical Quarterly* 22 (Spring-Winter 1963): 81.

113. Donaghey, *Autobiography*, 285.

114. Ibid., 286.

115. Ibid., 288–89.

116. *Arkansas Gazette*, 18 December 1912, p. 1.

117. Donaghey, *Autobiography*, 290.

118. *Senate Journal* (1913), 26.

119. *Arkansas Gazette*, 17 December 1912, p. 1.

120. Ibid., 18 December 1912, p. 1.

121. Ibid., 17 December 1912, p. 12.

122. Ibid., 1 January 1913, p. 1.

123. Neal, "Biography of Robinson," 113.

124.   *Arkansas Democrat*, 19 December 1912, p. 1.

125.   Ibid., 18 December 1912, p. 1.

126.   Ibid., 17 December 1912, p. 4.

127.   Ibid., 18 December 1912, p. 6.

128.   Baxley, "Prison Reforms," 83.

129.   *Arkansas Gazette*, 1 January 1913, p. 9.

130.   Ibid., 21 December 1912, p. 6.

131.   Ibid., 5 January 1913, p. 22.

132.   Zimmerman, "Convict Lease System," 184.

133.   Ibid., 183.

134.   Donaghey Collection, Donaghey Scrapbook, 1903, Arkansas History Commission, Little Rock, Arkansas.

135.   *New York Times*, 19 January 1913, magazine sec., p. 11.

136.   Donaghey Collection, Donaghey Scrapbook, 1912.

137.   Donaghey Collection, Donaghey Scrapbooks, 1903 and 1912.

138.   Donaghey, *Autobiography*, 295.

139.   *Arkansas Democrat*, 3 January 1913, p. 3.

140.   *Arkansas Gazette*, 5 January 1913, p. 1.

141.   Ibid.

142.   *Arkansas Democrat*, 7 January 1913, p. 10.

143.   *Historical Report of the Secretary of State* (1986), 300.

144.   *Arkansas Democrat*, 6 January 1913, p. 3.

145.   *Arkansas Gazette*, 7 January 1913, p. 1.

146.   Donaghey, *Building*, 299.

147.   Thompson, "Mr. Heiskell of the *Gazette*," 69.

148.   *Senate Journal* (1913), 94.

149.   Donaghey, *Building*, 315.

150.   *Senate Journal* (1913), 17.

151.   Ibid., 19.

152.   Ibid., 22.

153.   Ibid., 35.

154.   Ibid.

155.   Ibid., 28.

156.   Ibid.

157.   Ibid., 27.

158.   Ibid.

159.   Ibid., 36–37.

160.   *Arkansas Democrat*, 17 January 1913, p. 6.

161.   Ibid.

162.   *Arkansas Gazette*, 29 March 1912, p. 4.

163.   Ibid., 17 January 1913, p. 1.

164.   "New Conditions Seen in Politics," source unknown, Donaghey Scrapbook.

165.   The defeat of Turner-Jacobson in 1912 only involved methods of tax assessment. The State Tax Commission was still intact.

166.   *Acts of Arkansas* (1913), Act 59, sec. 6, 182.

SEVEN A Model Ex-Governor (1913–1937)

1. *Arkansas Democrat,* 9 June 1938, p. 1.
2. *Polk's City Directory of Little Rock (1926),* 87.
3. *Arkansas Democrat,* 11 March 1923, p. 4.
4. *Arkansas Gazette,* 11 March 1923, p. 18.
5. UALR Archives and Special Collections, A-86, Box 12, file 18.
6. Ibid., A-86, Box 12, file 19.
7. *Polk's City Directory of Little Rock (1929),* 390.
8. Ibid. (1926), 396.
9. *Arkansas Democrat,* 15 December 1937, p. 2.
10. *Arkansas Gazette,* 2 April 1926, p. 1.
11. Ibid.
12. *Arkansas Democrat,* 1 April 1926, p. 1.
13. George W. Donaghey, *Autobiography of George W. Donaghey* (Benton, Ark.: L. B. White Publishing Company, 1939), 304.
14. Charles Eichenbaum, lawyer and tenant in the Donaghey Building in 1928, interview by author, 29 June 1989, Little Rock, Arkansas..
15. Donaghey, *Autobiography,* 297.
16. UALR Archives and Special Collections, A-86, Box 12, file 3.
17. Donaghey, *Autobiography,* 297.
18. Ibid., 305.
19. George W. Donaghey, *Homespun Philosophy of George W. Donaghey* (Little Rock, Ark., privately printed, 1940), 378.
20. UALR Archives, A-86, Box 13, file 4.
21. George W. Donaghey to Mrs. Ona Breed, 28 June 1937, Donaghey Papers (Microfilm), UAF, Series 1, item 13.
22. Donaghey, *Autobiography,* 313.
23. Donaghey, *Homespun Philosophy,* 378.
24. *Arkansas Gazette,* 13 March 1912, p. 1.
25. James E. Lester, Jr., *Hendrix College: A Centennial History* (Conway, Ark.: Hendrix College Centennial Committee, 1984), 64.
26. Donaghey Papers (Microfilm), UAF, Series 2, item 80.
27. Katie Rice, church historian, First Methodist Church, Little Rock, Arkansas.
28. Donaghey Collection, Donaghey Scrapbook, 1903, Arkansas History Commission, Little Rock, Arkansas.
29. James E. Lester, Jr., *The People's College* (Little Rock, Ark.: August House, 1987), 28.
30. Donaghey Papers (Microfilm), UAF, Series 3, item 92.
31. Ibid.
32. *Arkansas Democrat,* 15 December 1937, p. 2.
33. Ibid., 14 March 1923, p. 1.
34. Ibid., 18 May 1924, magazine section, p. 1.
35. *Arkansas Gazette,* 15 March 1923, p. 1.
36. *Arkansas Democrat,* 14 March 1923, p. 1.

37.   Ibid., 18 May 1924, magazine section, p. 1.

38.   *Arkansas Gazette*, 22 May 1924, p. 1.

39.   Ibid. The cost of the Main Street Bridge was $1,044,000 and the Broadway Bridge $971,000.

40.   Admiral E. W. Kittelle to George Donaghey, 28 May 1924, Donaghey Scrapbook, 1903.

41.   Masonic Lodge records can be found in the Albert Pike Memorial Temple in Little Rock.

42.   Donaghey, *Autobiography*, 112–14.

43.   Ibid., 309.

44.   Ibid., 219.

45.   Ibid.

46.   Ibid., 309.

47.   *Arkansas Democrat*, 7 July 1929, p. 3.

48.   Lester, *People's College*, 22.

49.   Donaghey, *Homespun Philosophy*, 266.

50.   UALR Archives, A-86, Box 4, file 1.

51.   Louvenia W. Donaghey Collection, Container 1, Arkansas History Commission, Little Rock, Arkansas.

52.   *Arkansas Democrat*, 7 July 1929, p. 3.

53.   Louvenia W. Donaghey Collection, Container 1. Actually, Donaghey did not found LRJC, but his money guaranteed its existence.

54.   *Arkansas Democrat*, 10 October 1937, p. 1.

55.   *Arkansas Gazette*, 10 October 1937, p. 5.

56.   Dr. Alfred Kahn, retired physician and son of Alfred Kahn, one of the first trustees of the Donaghey Foundation, interview by author, 10 July 1989, Little Rock, Arkansas.

57.   Lester, *People's College*, 28; Phillip Anderson, lawyer and member of the Donaghey Foundation since 1976, interview by author, 7 July 1989, Little Rock, Arkansas.

58.   UALR Archives, Board of Trustees meetings of 23 January 1930, and 2 July 1930, A-86, Box 4, file 1; *Arkansas Gazette*, 16 December 1937, p. 6.

59.   Lester, *People's College*, 109 (for 1954–55); Grainger Williams, retired insurance executive and former member of the Little Rock University Board, interview by author, 18 July 1989, Little Rock, Arkansas. The budget in 1956–1957 was $400,000 with $82,000 from Donaghey.

60.   Lester, *People's College*, 128.

61.   Donaghey Papers (Microfilm), UAF, Series 3, item 10.

62.   Ibid., *Little Rock Junior College Chatter*, 23 March 1939.

63.   Lester, *People's College*, 135.

64.   UALR Archives, A-86, Box 4, folders 8–11.

65.   UALR Development Office.

66.   Anderson interview.

67.   *College Chatter*, 18 February 1941, Donaghey Papers (Microfilm), UAF, Series 3, item 92.

68. Lester, *People's College*, 169.

69. *Arkansas Democrat*, 10 October 1937, p. 1.

70. *Conway Log Cabin*, 16 December 1937, p. 1.

71. *Arkansas Gazette*, 15 December 1937, p. 1.

72. *Arkansas Democrat*, 14 December 1937, p. 1.

73. Ibid., 16 December 1937, p. 1.

74. *Arkansas Gazette*, 17 December 1937, p. 27.

75. Ibid.

76. Donaghey Papers (Microfilm), UAF, Series 3, item 8.

77. *Arkansas Gazette*, 17 December 1937, p. 27.

78. Anne McMath, *First Ladies of Arkansas* (Little Rock, Ark.: August House, 1989), 128.

79. *Arkansas Gazette*, 16 December 1937, p. 6.

80. Ibid.

81. Ibid.

82. Ibid.

83. Earl Hodges to Mrs. George Donaghey, 26 December 1937, Louvenia W. Donaghey Collection, Container 4.

84. Louvenia W. Donaghey Collection, Container 4.

85. Jo Frauenthal to Mrs. George Donaghey, 30 April 1940, Louvenia W. Donaghey Collection, Container 4.

86. Bruce Bullion to George Donaghey, 2 July 1936, Donaghey Papers (Microfilm), UAF, Series 3, item 92.

87. *Arkansas Gazette*, 16 December 1937, p. 4.

88. *McGehee Times*, 16 December 1937.

89. *Arkansas Democrat*, 15 December 1937, p. 8.

90. Ibid., 16 December 1937, p. 18.

91. Donaghey Papers (Microfilm), UAF, Series 3, item 65.

92. Ibid.

93. Ibid.

94. *Arkansas Gazette*, 3 July 1933, p. 1.

95. Donaghey Papers (Microfilm), UAF, Series 3, item 65.

96. T. W. Kirkwood, manager of the Donaghey Building, to C. B. Clark, 14 March 1941, Donaghey Papers (Microfilm), UAF, Series 4, item 30. Kirkwood conveyed Mrs. Donaghey's concerns to C. B. Clark who lived in Strong, about eight miles from the park.

97. George W. Donaghey to John W. Murphy, who lived in Strong, 20 July 1937, Donaghey Papers (Microfilm), UAF, Series 1, item 22.

98. Donaghey Papers (Microfilm), UAF, Series 3, item 92.

99. *Arkansas Gazette*, 16 May 1938, p. 2.

100. *El Dorado Evening Times*, 16 May 1938, p. 2.

101. Annette Pagan, mayor of Strong, telephone interview by author, 30 November 1989.

102. Donaghey, *Autobiography*, 96. See picture of Donaghey at age twenty-one following p.

103.   Donaghey Papers (Microfilm), UAF, Series 3, item 65.

104.   Donaghey, *Autobiography*, 109.

105.   Eichenbaum interview.

106.   *Polk County Democrat*, 13 November 1913, p. 2.

107.   Ibid.; *Memphis Commercial Appeal*, 8 November 1913, p. 9, and Dr. Alfred Kahn, retired physician, interview by author, 10 July 1989, Little Rock, Arkansas.

108.   Donaghey, *Homespun Philosophy*, 403.

109.   Donaghey Papers (Microfilm), UAF, Series 3, item 65.

110.   C. H. Murphy, Jr., son of Donaghey's secretary, Bertie Wilson, and Chairman of the Board of Murphy Oil Company, interview by author, 9 July 1987, El Dorado, Arkansas.

111.   Donaghey, *Homespun Philosophy*, 393.

CONCLUSION

1.   *Arkansas Gazette*, 1 October 1989, Sec. C, p. 1.

2.   *Arkansas Gazette*, 1 January 1991, p. 9B. The six universities involved are Arkansas State University (Jonesboro), Arkansas Tech University (Russellville), Southern Arkansas University (Magnolia), University of Central Arkansas (Conway), University of Arkansas at Monticello, and the University of Arkansas at Little Rock.

3.   Timothy J. Kennedy, "Initiated Constitutional Amendments in Arkansas: Strolling Through the Mine Field," *University of Arkansas at Little Rock Law Journal* 9 (1986–87): 5. In addition, two more constitutional amendments were initiated in 1988.

4.   Joe T. Segraves, "Arkansas Politics, 1874–1914," (Ph.D. diss., University of Kentucky, 1973), 354.

5.   *Arkansas Democrat*, 4 August 1910, p. 1.

6.   *Arkansas Gazette*, 17 December 1909, p. 2.

APPENDIX

1.   Raymond Arsenault, *The Wild Ass of the Ozarks* (Philadelphia: Temple University Press, 1984) 73.

2.   *Journal of the Senate of Arkansas* (1899), 28.

3.   Ibid.

4.   *Acts of Arkansas* (1899), 382.

5.   *Senate Journal* (1899), 10.

6.   *Journal of the House of Representatives of Arkansas* (1899), 90.

7.   Ibid.

8.   *Senate Journal* (1899), 89

9.   *Arkansas Democrat*, 23 February 1899, p. 1.

10.   *Senate Journal* (1899), 176.

11.   Ibid., 177.

12.   Ibid., 188.

13.   *Arkansas Democrat*, 21 March 1899, p. 2.

14.   *Arkansas Gazette*, 24 March 1899, p. 4.

15. *Senate Journal* (1899), 278; *Arkansas Democrat*, 19 April 1899, p. 4.

16. George W. Donaghey, *Building a State Capitol* (Little Rock, Ark.: Parke-Harper Company, 1937), 12.

17. *Arkansas Democrat*, 11 May 1899, p. 7.

18. Ibid., 11 January 1899, p. 4.

19. John A. Treon, "Politics and Concrete: The Building of the Arkansas State Capitol, 1899–1917," *Arkansas Historical Quarterly* 31 (Spring 1972): 103.

20. *Arkansas Democrat*, 15 May 1899, p. 1.

21. Donaghey, *Building*, 21.

22. Ibid., 15.

23. Ibid., 23.

24. *Arkansas Democrat*, 17 May 1899, p. 4.

25. Treon, "Politics and Concrete," 102.

26. *Arkansas Democrat*, 1 April 1962.

27. Donaghey, *Building*, 25.

28. *Arkansas Gazette*, 18 October 1899, p. 8.

29. Donaghey, *Building*, 32.

30. Ibid., 46.

31. *Arkansas Gazette*, 27 November 1900, p. 4.

32. *First Biennial Report of the Arkansas Capitol Commission* (1901), p. 11.

33. *Arkansas Democrat*, 14 November 1900, p. 1.

34. Donaghey, *Building*, 47.

35. *Arkansas Gazette*, 16 April 1899, p. 3.

36. Arsenault, *Wild Ass of the Ozarks*, 75.

37. *State v. Sloan*, 66 Ark. 579 (1899).

38. *Arkansas Democrat*, 4 July 1899, p. 1.

39. Arsenault, *Wild Ass of the Ozarks*, 79.

40. *Arkansas Gazette*, 22 November 1900, p. 8.

41. Ibid., 28 November 1900, p. 1.

42. *House Journal* (1901), 185.

43. Ibid., 186.

44. Ibid., 177–78, 181.

45. Ibid., 176.

46. Donaghey, *Building*, 74.

47. Ibid., 65.

48. *Senate Journal* (1901), 240.

49. *Arkansas Gazette*, 13 February 1901, p. 8.

50. *Senate Journal* (1901), 241.

51. Ibid.

52. Donaghey, *Building*, 81.

53. Ibid., 78.

54. Donaghey, *Building*, 83.

55. Arsenault, *Wild Ass of the Ozarks*, 120.

56. *House Journal* (1901), 37.

57. *Senate Journal* (1901), 26.

58. Ibid., 27.
59. Arsenault, *Wild Ass of the Ozarks*, 121.
60. *Senate Journal* (1901), 27.
61. Ibid., 242.
62. Ibid., 94.
63. *Arkansas Democrat*, 14 February 1901, p. 8.
64. *House Journal* (1901), 561.
65. *Arkansas Gazette*, 30 April 1901, p. 4.
66. *Acts of Arkansas* (1901), Act 132, sec. 10, 221.
67. *Senate Journal*, (1901), 332.
68. Donaghey, *Building*, 82.
69. Ibid., 88.
70. Arsenault, *Wild Ass of the Ozarks*, 135. The other two members of the commission were W. N. Norton of Forrest City and J. E. Martin of Conway.
71. Donaghey, *Building*, 89.
72. *Arkansas Democrat*, 11 July 1901, p. 3.
73. *Arkansas Gazette*, 10 September 1901, p. 6.
74. Ibid., p. 8.
75. Arsenault, *Wild Ass of the Ozarks*, 136.
76. *Arkansas Gazette*, 10 September 1901, p. 6.
77. Treon, "Politics and Concrete," 146–47.
78. Donaghey, *Building*, 91.
79. *Arkansas Democrat*, 8 November 1901, p. 7.
80. Ibid., 9 November 1901, p. 1.
81. *Arkansas Gazette*, 13 November 1901, p. 3.
82. Ibid.
83. Treon, "Politics and Concrete," 108.
84. *Arkansas Democrat*, 18 December 1901, p. 4.
85. Ibid., p. 5.
86. *Arkansas Gazette*, 14 November 1901, p. 4.
87. Ibid., 29 January 1902, pp. 1, 2.
88. *Arkansas Gazette*, 25 July 1902, p. 1.
89. Ibid., 8 April 1902, p. 3.
90. Ibid.
91. C. Fred Williams, "James Philip Eagle," in *The Governors of Arkansas*, ed. Timothy P. Donovan and Willard B. Gatewood, Jr. (Fayetteville, Ark.: University of Arkansas Press, 1981), 90.
92. Arsenault, *Wild Ass of the Ozarks*, 158.
93. *Arkansas Gazette*, 20 April 1902, p. 1.
94. *Arkansas Democrat*, 20 October 1902, p. 4.
95. Donaghey, *Building*, 95.
96. Ibid., 98.
97. Treon, "Politics and Concrete," 109.
98. *Arkansas Democrat*, 24 October 1902, p. 5.
99. *Arkansas Gazette*, 17 February 1903, p. 4.

100. *Arkansas Democrat*, 24 October 1902, p. 4.

101. Donaghey, *Building*, 99; *Arkansas Gazette*, 8 May 1907, p. 8.

102. *Senate Journal* (1903), 38.

103. Ibid., 101.

104. Ibid., 102.

105. *Arkansas Democrat*, 11 February 1903, p. 4.

106. *House Journal* (1903), 280.

107. Ibid., 427.

108. *Arkansas Gazette*, 26 March 1903, p. 3.

109. *Senate Journal* (1903), 279.

110. *House Journal* (1903), 580–87.

111. Ibid., 587.

112. *Arkansas Gazette*, 16 April 1903, p. 1.

113. *Senate Journal* (1903), 303.

114. *Arkansas Democrat*, 17 April 1903, p. 1.

115. Ibid., p. 6.

116. Ibid., 19 April 1903, p. 4.

117. *House Journal* (1903), 624–38. The commissioners elected were R. W. McFarlane of Sebastian County, J. M. McCaleb of Sharp County, W. B. Alexander of Pine Bluff, Dr. J. M. Flenniken of Camden, and Z. T. Matthews of Jonesboro.

118. Donaghey, *Building*, 101.

119. Ibid., p. 4.

120. *Cox v. State*, 72 Ark. 94 (1904).

121. Ibid., 72 Ark 100 (1904).

122. *Acts of Arkansas* (1903), Act 146, sec. 8. 256.

123. *Arkansas Gazette*, 29 April 1903, p. 4.

124. *Report of the Commission for the Building of the State Capitol,* 1906 p. 26. There is also a payment of $250 to Donaghey listed on 16 July 1903, for his work as foreman (*House Journal* [1905], 458).

125. Donaghey, *Building*, 112.

126. Ibid., 106.

127. *Capitol Commission Report*, 1906, p. 26.

128. *Arkansas Gazette*, 13 August 1903, p. 8.

129. Ibid., 14 August 1903, p. 1.

130. Ibid.

131. *Capitol Commission Report*, 1906, p. 31.

132. Treon, "Politics and Concrete," 135.

133. *Arkansas Gazette*, 14 August 1903, p. 1.

134. Donaghey, *Building*, 147.

135. *Arkansas Gazette*, 8 March 1904, p. 8.

136. Ibid., 26 May 1904, p. 2.

137. *Arkansas Democrat*, 13 September 1904, p. 3.

138. *Arkansas Gazette*, 30 August 1904, p. 6.

139. Treon, "Politics and Concrete," 112.

140. *Arkansas Gazette*, 22 January 1905, p. 2.

141. *House Journal* (1905), 46.
142. Ibid., 47.
143. Ibid., 45–46.
144. *Arkansas Gazette*, 16 February 1905, p. 3.
145. Ibid., *Senate Journal* (1905), 131.
146. *Arkansas Gazette*, 16 February 1905, p. 4.
147. *Senate Journal* (1905), 412.
148. Ibid., 409.
149. *House Journal* (1905), 425–26.
150. Ibid., 428.
151. *Senate Journal* (1905), 410–11.
152. Donaghey, *Building*, 133–36.
153. *Arkansas Gazette*, 11 April 1907, p. 6.
154. *Senate Journal* (1905), 336.
155. *Arkansas Gazette*, 18 April 1905, p. 8.
156. Donaghey, *Building*, 149.
157. *Senate Journal* (1905), 404–06
158. *House Journal* (1905), 718.
159. Ibid., 738.
160. *Arkansas Democrat*, 29 April 1905, p. 3.
161. *Arkansas Gazette*, 30 April 1905, p. 13.
162. Ibid.
163. Ibid., 12 May 1905, p. 4.
164. *Arkansas Democrat*, 2 June 1905, p. 1.
165. *Arkansas Gazette,* 18 April 1905, p. 8
166. Ibid., 1 June 1905, p. 1.
167. Ibid., 30 June 1905, p. 1.
168. Ibid., 29 June 1905, p. 6.
169. Ibid.
170. Ibid., 5 July 1905, p. 1.
171. *Arkansas Democrat*, 25 July 1905, p. 1.
172. *Butt v. State*, 81 Ark. 179 (1907).
173. Ibid., 182.
174. Ibid., 183.
175. *Arkansas Democrat*, 18 November 1907, p. 10.
176. Ibid., 9 May 1910, p. 1.
177. *Arkansas Gazette*, 15 October 1905, p. 9.
178. Treon, "Politics and Concrete," 114.
179. Donaghey, *Building*, 158–59.
180. Ibid., 160.
181. *Arkansas Gazette*, 16 June 1906, p. 4.
182. Ibid., 8 August 1906, p. 9.
183. *Arkansas Democrat*, 30 June 1906, p. 1.
184. *Arkansas Gazette*, 29 June 1906, p. 6.
185. Ibid.

186. *Arkansas Gazette*, 8 August 1906, p. 2.
187. *Arkansas Democrat*, 8 August 1906, p. 1.
188. *Arkansas Gazette*, 8 August, 1906, p. 2; *Arkansas Democrat*, 8 August 1906, p. 5.
189. *Arkansas Gazette*, 9 August 1906, p. 2.
190. *Arkansas Democrat*, 9 August 1906, p. 8.
191. *House Journal* (1907), 851, 853.
192. Ibid., 906.
193. Ibid.
194. Ibid., 821
195. *Capitol Comission Report*, (1906), 75.
196. *House Journal* (1907), 46.
197. Ibid., 45.
198. *Senate Journal* (1907), 67.
199. Ibid.
200. *Arkansas Gazette*, 2 February 1907, p. 3.
201. *Arkansas Democrat*, 25 January 1907, p. 3.
202. Ibid., 8 February 1907, p. 1.
203. *House Journal* (1907), 768.
204. Ibid.
205. *Arkansas Gazette*, 22 February 1907, p. 8.
206. *House Journal* (1907), 864–93.
207. Ibid., 875.
208. Ibid., 770.
209. Ibid., 775.
210. Ibid., 776.
211. Ibid., 944–50.
212. Ibid., 948, 950.
213. *Arkansas Democrat*, 4 May 1907, p. 4.
214. *Arkansas Gazette*, 8 May 1907, p. 8.
215. *Arkansas Gazette*, 4 May 1907, p. 3.
216. *House Journal* (1907), 961.
217. Ibid., 992.
218. *Arkansas Gazette*, 14 May 1907, p. 3.
219. Ibid., 18 May 1907, p. 2.
220. *House Journal* (1907), 1014–15.
221. HCR 21, 22, 23.
222. *Arkansas Gazette*, 13 May 1907, p. 4.
223. *Arkansas Democrat*, 13 May 1907, p. 3.
224. *House Journal* (1907), 776.
225. *Arkansas Gazette*, 18 August 1907, p. 1.
226. *Moore v. Alexander*, 85 Ark 171 (1908).
227. *Arkansas Gazette*, 6 October 1907, p. 1.
228. *Arkansas Democrat*, 1 March 1908, p. 1.
229. *Arkansas Gazette*, 8 October 1907, p. 10.
230. Ibid., 4 June 1908, p. 1.

231. *Jobe v. Caldwell*, 99 Ark. 20 (1911).
232. Donaghey, *Building*, 189.
233. *Arkansas Gazette*, 5 February 1908, p. 1.
234. *House Journal* (1909), 196.
235. Ibid.
236. *Arkansas Gazette*, 6 February 1909, p. 1.
237. Ibid., 9 February 1909, p. 1.
238. *Senate Journal* (1909), 46.
239. Ibid., 47.
240. *House Journal* (1909), 180.
241. Ibid., 185.
242. Ibid., 285
243. *Arkansas Gazette*, 2 March 1909, p. 1.
244. *House Journal* (1909), 474–508.
245. *Arkansas Democrat*, 24 March 1909, p. 1.
246. *House Journal* (1909), 483.
247. *Arkansas Gazette*, 23 February 1909, p. 1.
248. Ibid., 11 March 1909, p. 6.
249. Ibid., 18 March 1909, p. 10.
250. *Arkansas Democrat*, 5 March 1909, p. 2.
251. Ibid., 6 March 1909, p. 1.
252. *Arkansas Gazette*, 7 March 1909, p. 1.
253. *Acts of Arkansas* (1909), Act 143, 432.
254. *Arkansas Gazette*, 26 March 1909, p. 8.
255. Ibid., 22 January 1909, p. 10; ibid., 18 March 1909, p. 3; ibid., 20 March 1909, p. 10; ibid., 11 April 1909, p. 9.
256. *Senate Journal* (1909), 322.
257. *Arkansas Gazette*, 5 May 1909, p. 3.
258. *Acts of Arkansas* (1909), Act 238, sec. 1, 727.
259. Ibid., sec. 9, 732.
260. *Senate Journal* (1909), 199.
261. *House Journal* (1909), 608.
262. *Senate Journal* (1909), 322.
263. Ibid., 356.
264. *House Journal* (1909), 888.
265. *Arkansas Gazette* 12 May 1909, p. 3.
266. Ibid., 10.
267. *Acts of Arkansas* (1909), Act 143, sec. 2, 433.
268. *Arkansas Democrat*, 6 June 1909, p. 1.
269. *Arkansas Gazette*, 17 June 1909, p. 1.
270. *Arkansas Democrat*, 17 June 1909, p. 3.
271. *Arkansas Gazette*, 17 June 1909, p. 1.
272. Ibid., 22 June 1909, p. 9.
273. Ibid., 25 June 1909, p. 1.
274. Ibid.

275. *Arkansas Gazette*, 13 July 1909, p. 1.

276. *Caldwell v. Jobe*, 93 Ark. 503 (1910).

277. *Arkansas Gazette*, 2 June 1909, p. 1.

278. Donaghey, *Building*, 227.

279. *Arkansas Gazette*, 2 June 1909, p. 1.

280. Ibid., 13 June 1909, p. 1.

281. Ibid., 25 June 1909, p. 6.

282. Ibid., 27 June 1909, p. 11.

283. Ibid., 7 July 1909, p. 2.

284. Donaghey, *Building*, 237.

285. John A. Treon, "Politics and Concrete: The Building of the Arkansas State Capitol, 1899–1917," *Arkansas Historical Quarterly* 31 (Spring 1972): 127.

286. *Arkansas Gazette*, 22 August 1909. p. 1.

287. Ibid., 22 July 1909, p. 9.

288. Ibid., 9 October 1909, p. 1.

289. *Arkansas Democrat*, 22 July 1909, p. 6.

290. *Arkansas Gazette*, 23 July 1909, p. 4.

291. *Arkansas Democrat*, 14 June 1909, p. 1.

292. *Arkansas Gazette*, 16 July 1909, p. 1.

293. Ibid., 18 July 1909, p. 1.

294. *Arkansas Democrat*, 22 July 1909, p. 5.

295. *Arkansas Gazette*, 22 July 1909, p. 1.

296. Ibid., 21 July 1909, p. 1.

297. *Arkansas Democrat*, 21 July 1909, p. 9.

298. *Arkansas Gazette*, 27 July 1909, p. 1.

299. *Arkansas Democrat*, 27 July 1909, p. 1.

300. *Arkansas Gazette*, 7 August 1909, p. 1.

301. *Arkansas Democrat*, 28 July 1909, p. 1.

302. *Arkansas Gazette*, 30 July 1909, p. 1.

303. Ibid., 31 July 1909, p. 1.

304. *Arkansas Democrat*, 5 August 1909, p. 1.

305. *Arkansas Gazette*, 25 July 1909, p. 14.

306. Ibid., 7 August 1909, p. 4.

307. *Arkansas Democrat*, 5 February 1910, p. 1.

308. *Caldwell v. Donaghey*, 108 Ark. 60 (1913).

309. *Arkansas Gazette*, 2 December 1909, p. 12.

310. *Arkansas Democrat*, 8 December 1909, p. 7.

311. *Arkansas Gazette*, 7 December 1909, p. 10.

312. Ibid., 8 December 1909, p. 1.

313. Ibid.

314. Ibid., 10 December 1909, p. 5.

315. *Arkansas Gazette*, 12 December 1909, p. 1.

316. Ibid., 1 December 1907, p. 12. See also note 305 for the sale of Caldwell and Drake's interest in the Southern Construction Company.

317. Ibid., 9 January 1910, p. 1.

318. Ibid., 2 January 1910, p. 11.
319. Ibid., 20 February 1910, p. 23.
320. *Arkansas Democrat*, 16 December 1909. p. 1.
321. *Arkansas Gazette*, 12 February 1910, p. 3.
322. Ibid., 3 February 1910, p. 1.
323. *Arkansas Democrat*, 4 February 1910, p. 1.
324. *Arkansas Gazette*, 6 February 1910, p. 13.
325. Ibid., 12 February 1910, p. 3.
326. Ibid., 5 May 1910, p. 10.
327. Ibid., 29 May 1910 p. 17.
328. *Arkansas Democrat*, 9 June 1910, p. 2.
329. *Arkansas Gazette*, 3 June 1910, p. 1; *Arkansas Democrat*, 7 July 1910, p. 1.
330. Ibid., 11 December 1910, p. 12.
331. Ibid., 19 February 1911, p. 3.
332. Donaghey, *Building*, 265.
333. Ibid., 268.
334. *Arkansas Gazette*, 4 December 1910, p. 8.
335. *Arkansas Democrat*, 3 December 1910, p. 1.
336. *Arkansas Gazette*, 9 December 1910, p. 5.
337. Ibid., 7 January 1911, p. 8.
338. Ibid., 8 January 1911, p. 1.
339. *Arkansas Democrat*, 7 January 1911, p. 11.
340. Ibid., 9 January 1911, p. 7.
341. *Arkansas Gazette*, 10 January 1911, p. 5.
342. *Arkansas Democrat*, 12 January 1911, p. 4.
343. *Senate Journal* (1911), 40.
344. *Senate Journal* (1911), 39.
345. Ibid., 40.
346. Certificate of appointment by Governor J. M. Futrell, 5 November 1936, Series 3, item 28, Donaghey Papers (Microfilm) UAF.
347. *Senate Journal* (1911), 128.
348. *House Journal* (1911), 1025.
349. *Senate Journal* (1911), 445.
350. *Arkansas Gazette*, 13 May 1911, p. 3.
351. Donaghey, *Building*, 282–83.
352. *Senate Journal* (1911), 705.
353. Donaghey, *Building*, 283.
354. *Arkansas Democrat*, 12 July 1911, p. 1.
355. *Arkansas Gazette*, 17 April 1912, p. 5.
356. Donaghey, *Building*, 289.
357. *Arkansas Gazette*, 12 January 1912. p. 9.
358. Ibid., 9 January 1912, p. 3.
359. Ibid., 22 October 1911, p. 1.
360. *Senate Journal* (1913), 51.
361. Ibid., 36.

362. Ibid.

363. *Senate Journal* (1913), 226.

364. Donaghey, *Building*, 307–08.

365. *House Journal* (1913), 865.

366. Ibid.

367. *Arkansas Gazette*, 12 March 1913, p. 3.

368. *Senate Journal* (1913), 357.

369. Donaghey, *Building*, 312.

370. Calvin R. Ledbetter, Jr., "Joe T. Robinson and the Presidential Campaign of 1928," *Arkansas Historical Quarterly* 45 (Summer 1986): 99.

371. *Arkansas Gazette*, 9 July 1913, p. 1.

372. *Arkansas Democrat*, 9 July 1913, p. 8.

373. Donaghey, *Building*, 312.

374. *Arkansas Gazette*, 12 October 1913, p. 6.

375. *Arkansas Gazette*, 30 September 1914, p. 8; ibid., 6 March 1914, p. 8; Donaghey, *Building*, 334.

376. Donaghey, *Building*, 325–30.

377. *Senate Journal* (1915), 21.

378. Ibid.

379. Donaghey, *Building*, 341.

380. Ibid.

381. Ibid., 343.

382. *Arkansas Gazette*, 19 January 1917, p. 10.

383. "In the Matter of the Adjustment of the Controversy between the State of Arkansas and Caldwell and Drake," Container 1, p. 45, Louvenia W. Donaghey Collection, State History Commission, Little Rock, Arkansas. Subsequently cited as "Arbitration Report."

384. "Arbitration Report," 19–21.

385. *Arkansas Gazette*, 19 January 1917, p. 10.

386. "Arbitration Report," 37.

387. Ibid., 39.

388. *Arkansas Gazette*, 19 January 1917, p. 10.

389. Ibid., 20 January 1917, p. 6.

390. *House Journal* (1909), 484.

391. Treon, "Politics and Concrete," 128, 138.

392. *House Journal* (1907), 774.

393. Ibid., 776.

394. *Arkansas Gazette*, 30 June 1905, p. 6.

395. *House Journal* (1907), 906.

396. Ibid., 948.

397. Treon, "Politics and Concrete," 147.

398. Ibid.

399. Donaghey, *Building*, 351–53.

400. *Arkansas Gazette*, 1 October 1989, Sec. C, p. 1.

Selected Bibliography

Primary source material on Donaghey is limited, but his three books, *Autobiography of George W. Donaghey* (Benton, Arkansas: L. B. White Publishing Co., 1939), *Building a State Capitol* (Little Rock, Arkansas: Parke-Harper Co., 1937), *Homespun Philosophy* (n.p., n.d. [but probably 1939 or 1940]), are invaluable, especially his autobiography, which is a relatively straightforward account of his life with very few factual errors or incorrect dates. *Building a State Capitol* is a little technical but understandable and includes political incidents as well as construction details. *Homespun Philosophy* is a compilation of articles that Donaghey wrote for the *Donaghey News,* an in-house publication for tenants of the Donaghey, Waldron, and Wallace buildings. It is uneven in quality but does offer his views on more than 150 issues of his day.

Donaghey's papers are housed at the University of Arkansas, Fayetteville, in the Special Collections Department. The Special Collections Department at the University of Arkansas also contains the Joe T. Robinson papers and the Charles H. Brough, Hal Norwood, and Harmon Remmel collections, all of which have some relevance to Donaghey. Much material about Conway, Donaghey's home town, the establishment of Conway's three institutions of higher education, and Donaghey's role in all three can be found at the Archives and Special Collections, Torreyson Library, University of Central Arkansas. Details of his thirty-year connection with Hendrix College are available at the Hendrix Archives, located in the O. C. Bailey Library on campus. The George W. Donaghey Foundation minutes and financial reports along with records of the Chickasaw Land Company are at the Archives and Special Collections, Ottenheimer Library, University of Arkansas at Little Rock. The Arkansas History Commission in Little Rock contains the Louvenia Wallace Donaghey Collection and two scrapbooks kept by Donaghey himself—one devoted mainly to public reaction to the pardoning of 360 convicts in 1912 and the other a chronology of important events in his political career.

Primary Source Material

Newspapers

Arkansas Gazette. 1880–1940.
Arkansas Democrat. 1880–1940.
Log Cabin Democrat (Conway). 1898–1937.

Public Documents

Acts of Arkansas 1879–1915.
Arkansas, *Biennial Report, Auditor of State*, 1907–1908, 1909–1910, 1911–1912.
Arkansas, *Biennial Report, Secretary of State*, 1899–1920.
Arkansas, *Biennial Report of the Superintendent of Public Instruction*, 1909–1910, 1911–1912.
Arkansas, *Journal of the House of Representatives of Arkansas*, 1899–1915.
Arkansas, *Journal of the Senate of Arkansas*, 1899–1915.
Bryant, Winston. *Historical Report of the Secretary of State.* 3 vols. Little Rock, Arkansas: Secretary of State's Office, 1978.
McCuen, Bill. *Historical Report of the Secretary of State.* Little Rock, Arkansas: Secretary of State's Office, 1986.
Minutes of the Gregg County Commissioners Court, Gregg County, Texas, 10 May 1892.

Legal Documents

Report of the Commission to Settle the Controversy between the State of Arkansas and Caldwell and Drake, 1917.
R. T. Blackwell et al., ex Parte. Civil Record, Faulkner Circuit Court, Case No. 70 (1888).
Butt v. State, 81 Ark. 173 (1907).
Caldwell v. Jobe, 93 Ark. 503 (1910).
Caldwell v. Donaghey, 108 Ark. 60 (1913).

Donaghey v. Donaghey, Insanity hearing, County Court of Faulkner County, (1896).
Hodges v. Dawdy, 104 Ark. 583 (1912).
Jobe v. Caldwell, 99 Ark. 20 (1911).
Moore v. Alexander, 85 Ark. 171 (1908).
State ex rel Little Rock v. Donaghey, 106 Ark. 56 (1912).

Reports and Proceedings

Proceedings of the 1891 and 1892 Arkansas Baptist State Conventions, Ouachita Baptist University Archives.
Report of the Joint Committee on State Capitol, May 3, 1907.
Reports of the State Capitol Commissions. 1901, 1903–04, 1906, 1911, 1911–1915.

Interviews

(Unless otherwise indicated, all interviews were personal interviews conducted by the author.)

Anderson, Phillip, lawyer and member of the Donaghey Foundation since 1976, 7 July 1989, Little Rock, Arkansas.
Bullion, Bruce, Jr., retired chancery judge and son of Bruce Bullion, Donaghey's chief of staff, 16 July 1987, Little Rock, Arkansas.
———, 2nd interview, 27 June 1989, Little Rock, Arkansas.
Brewczynski, Genevieve, retired secretary who did some office work for Donaghey, 3 July 1989, Little Rock, Arkansas. Telephone interview.
Dillard, Tom, director of the Archives and Special Collections at the University of Central Arkansas, 29 September 1988, Conway, Arkansas.
Eichenbaum, Charles, lawyer and tenant in the Donaghey Building in 1928, 29 June 1989, Little Rock, Arkansas.
Ferguson, John, state historian, 26 June 1989, Little Rock, Arkansas.
Hammond, Edith, granddaughter of John Ingram, Donaghey's uncle, 10 October 1988, Conway, Arkansas.
Hartje, George, lawyer, 10 October 1988, Conway, Arkansas.
Heigel, Ted, retired, 27 October 1988, Conway, Arkansas.
Kahn, Dr. Alfred, retired physician, 10 July 1989, Little Rock, Arkansas.

Kesselus, Kenneth, Rector of the Calvary Episcopal Church, Bastrop, Texas, 18 November 1988, Bastrop, Texas.

Kuyendall, Iva, retired, 20 January 1989, Conway, Arkansas. Telephone interview.

Lisenby, Foy, professor of history at the University of Central Arkansas, 10 October 1988, Conway, Arkansas.

McHenry, Robert, retired, 27 October 1988, Conway, Arkansas.

Meriwether, Bob, professor of education, political science and American history at Hendrix College, 29 September 1988, Conway, Arkansas.

Moore, Waddy, professor of history at the University of Central Arkansas, 6 October 1988, Conway, Arkansas.

Murphy, C. H., Jr., chairman of the board of Murphy Oil Company, 9 July 1987, El Dorado, Arkansas.

Murphy, Guy, executive vice-president of the Conway Chamber of Commerce, 29 September 1988, Conway, Arkansas.

Ott, Robert, owner of the Ott Insurance Company, 29 September 1988, Conway, Arkansas.

Pagan, Annette, mayor of Strong, Arkansas, 30 November 1989, Strong, Arkansas. Telephone interview.

Palmer, Mrs. Elizabeth Smith, sister-in-law of Raymond Donaghey, 9 October 1989, Little Rock, Arkansas.

Pence, Richard Martin, grandson of John Pence, 10 October 1988, Conway, Arkansas.

Remmel, Paul, retired and ninety-eight years old at the time of the interview, nephew of Harmon Remmel, who lived in that household for thirty-five years beginning at age five, 3 July 1989, Little Rock, Arkansas.

Robins, Frank E., III, publisher of the *Log Cabin Democrat,* 20 January 1989, Conway, Arkansas.

Ross, Margaret, retired *Gazette* staff historian, 23 June 1989, Little Rock, Arkansas.

Smith, Judge William, brother-in-law of Raymond Donaghey, 27 September 1989, Little Rock, Arkansas. Telephone interview.

Ward, John, executive vice-president for Public Affairs, University of Central Arkansas, 6 October 1988, Conway, Arkansas.

Williams, Grainger, retired insurance executive and former member of the UALR board, 18 July 1989, Little Rock, Arkansas.

Secondary Source Material

Books

Arbuthnot, Mary Hill, and Dorothy Broderick. *Time for Biography.* Glenview, Illinois: Scott, Foreman, and Co., 1969.

Arsenault, Raymond. *The Wild Ass of the Ozarks.* Philadelphia: Temple University Press, 1984.

Baker, Russell P. *Township Atlas of Arkansas.* Hot Springs, Arkansas: Arkansas Genealogical Society, 1984.

Barber, James David. *The Presidential Character.* 2d ed. Englewood Cliffs, N.J.: Prentice-Hall, 1977.

Berry, Fred, and John Novak. *The History of Arkansas.* Little Rock, Ark.: Rose Publishing Co., 1987.

Blair, Diane. *Arkansas Politics and Government.* Lincoln, Nebraska: University of Nebraska Press, 1988.

Chambers, John Whiteclay II. *The Tyranny of Change.* New York: St. Martin's Press, 1980.

Clark, Norman H. *Deliver Us from Evil.* New York: Norton and Company, 1976.

Donaghey, George W. *Autobiography of George W. Donaghey.* Benton, Arkansas: L. B. White Publishing Co., 1939.

―――. *Building a State Capitol.* Little Rock, Arkansas: Parke-Harper Co., 1937.

―――. *Homespun Philosophy of George W. Donaghey.* N.p., n.d.

Donovan, Timothy P., and Willard Gatewood, Jr., eds. *The Governors of Arkansas.* Fayetteville, Arkansas: University of Arkansas Press, 1981.

Dunaway, L. C. *What a Preacher Saw.* Little Rock, Arkansas: Parke-Harper Co., 1925.

DuVall, Leland, ed. *Arkansas: Colony and State.* Little Rock, Arkansas: Rose Publishing Co., 1973.

Faulkner County: Its Land and People. Conway, Arkansas: Faulkner County Historical Society, 1986.

Ferguson, John L., and J. H. Atkinson. *Historic Arkansas.* Little Rock, Arkansas: Arkansas History Commission, 1966.

Frantz, Joe. *Texas.* New York: W. W. Norton and Co., 1976.

Gatewood, Robert L. *Faulkner County, Arkansas: 1778–1964.* Conway, Arkansas: Faulkner Press, 1964.

Gittinger, Ray. *The Formation of the State of Oklahoma.* Norman, Oklahoma: University of Oklahoma Press, 1939.

Gould, Lewis L. *Progressives and Prohibitionists.* Austin: University of Texas Press, 1973.

———. *The Progressive Era.* Syracuse, N. Y.: Syracuse University Press, 1974.

Grantham, Dewey W. *Southern Progressivism.* Knoxville, Tennessee: University of Tennessee Press, 1983.

Hale, Harrison. *University of Arkansas 1871–1948.* Fayetteville, Arkansas: University of Arkansas Alumni Association, 1948.

Hay, Samuel P. *Conservation and the Gospel of Efficiency.* New York: Atheneum, 1969.

Hinshaw, Jerry. *Call the Roll.* Little Rock, Arkansas: Rose Publishing Co., 1985.

Homberger, Eric, and John Charmley. *The Troubled Face of Biography.* New York: St. Martin's Press, 1988.

Hyde, Marietta, ed. *Modern Biography.* 3rd ed. New York: Harcourt, Brace, and World, 1945.

Jacobson, Charles. *The Life Story of Jeff Davis.* Little Rock, Arkansas: Parke-Harper Publishing Co., 1925.

Jacoway, Peggy. *First Ladies of Arkansas.* Kingsport, Tennessee: Southern Publishers, 1941.

Kesselus, Kenneth. *Bastrop County before Statehood.* Austin: Jenkins Publishing Co., 1986.

Key, V. O. *Southern Politics.* New York: Albert A. Knopf, 1949.

Kirby, Jack Temple. *Darkness at the Dawning.* New York: J. P. Lippincott, 1972.

Leflar, Robert. *The First 100 Years: Centennial History of the University of Arkansas.* Fayetteville, Arkansas: University of Arkansas Foundation, 1972.

Lester, James E., Jr. *Hendrix College: A Centennial History.* Conway, Arkansas: Hendrix College Centennial Committee, 1984.

———. *The People's College.* Little Rock, Arkansas: August House, 1987.

Link, Arthur S., and Richard L. McCormick. *Progressivism.* Arlington Heights, Illinois: Harlan Davidson, 1983.

McMath, Anne. *First Ladies of Arkansas.* Little Rock, Arkansas: August House, 1989.

McReynolds, Edwin C. *Oklahoma*. Norman, Oklahoma: University of Oklahoma Press, 1954.

Meriwether, Robert W. *Hendrix College: The Move from Altus to Conway*. Little Rock, Arkansas: Rose Publishing Co., 1976.

Molitor, F. A., and E. J. Beard. *Manual for Resident Engineers*. New York: John Wiley and Sons, 1912.

Niswonger, Richard L. *Arkansas Democratic Politics, 1896–1920*. Fayetteville, Arkansas: University of Arkansas Press, 1990.

O'Neil, William L. *The Progressive Years*. New York: Dodd Mead, 1975.

Reynolds, John Hugh and David Y. Thomas. *History of the University of Arkansas*. Fayetteville, Arkansas: University of Arkansas, 1910.

Richardson, Rupert, Ernest Wallace, and Adrian Anderson. *Texas: The Lone Star State*. 3d ed. Englewood Cliffs, N.J.: Prentice-Hall, 1970.

Riggs, Bess. *A Brief History of the Education of the Deaf in the State of Arkansas*. Little Rock, Arkansas: Arkansas School for the Deaf, 1934.

Sinclair, Andrew. *Prohibition*. Boston: Little, Brown, and Co., 1962.

Stephenson, Wendell Holmes, and E. Merton Coulter, eds. *A History of the South*. Vol. X, *The Emergence of the New South* by George Tindall. Baton Rouge: Louisiana State University Press, 1967.

———. Vol. IX, *Origins of the New South* by C. Vann Woodard. Baton Rouge: Louisiana State University Press, 1971.

Stroud, Hubert, and Gerald Hanson. *Arkansas Geography*. Little Rock, Arkansas: Rose Publishing Co., 1981.

Thomas, David Y. *Arkansas and Its People*. 4 vols. New York: American Historical Society, 1930.

Timberlake, John. *Prohibition and the Progressive Movement: 1900–1920*. Cambridge: Harvard University Press, 1963.

Tucker, David M. *Arkansas: A People and Their Reputation*. Memphis: Memphis State University Press, 1985.

Weinstein, James. *The Corporate Ideal in the Liberal State*. Boston: Beacon Press, 1968.

Williams, Harry Lee. *Behind the Scene in Arkansas Politics*. Jonesboro, Arkansas: Privately printed, 1931.

Work Projects Administration. *Arkansas: A Guide to the State*. New York: Hastings House, 1941.

Worley, Ted. *A History of the Arkansas State Teachers College*. N.p., privately printed, 1954.

Dissertations and Theses

Arsenault, Raymond. "From Populism to Progressivism in Selected Southern States: A Statistical Reinterpretation." Senior thesis, Princeton University, 1969.

Minton, Hubert Lee. "The Evolution of Conway, Arkansas." Ph.D. diss., University of Chicago, 1939.

Moyers, Michael D. "Arkansas Progressivism: The Legislative Record." 2 vols. Ph.D. diss., University of Arkansas at Fayetteville, 1986.

Neal, Nevin. "A Biography of Joseph T. Robinson." Ph.D. diss., University of Oklahoma, 1958.

Rimmer, Martha. "Charles E. Taylor and his Administration, 1911–1919, Progressivism in Little Rock." M.A. thesis, University of Arkansas at Fayetteville, 1977.

Segraves, Joe Tolbert. "Arkansas Politics, 1874–1918." Ph.D. diss., University of Kentucky, 1973.

Thompson, John A. "Gentleman Editor: Mr. Heiskell of the *Gazette*—the Early Years: 1902–1922." M.A. thesis, University of Arkansas at Little Rock, 1983.

Articles and Periodicals

Baxley, Thomas. "Prison Reforms During the Donaghey Administration." *Arkansas Historical Quarterly.* 22 (Spring 1963): 76–84.

Besom, Bob. "Harmon L. Remmel and the Arkansas Anthracite Coal Company, 1905–1923." *Arkansas Historical Quarterly* 47 (Autumn 1988): 273–87.

Buchanan, Bruce. "Private Lives and Public Careers." *Political Science and Politics.* 21 (Spring 1988): 250–56.

"A Businesslike Governor." *The World's Work*, December 1908. 10965–10966.

Charles, Myrtle. "Early Days at Hendrix College 1887–1910." *Faulkner Facts and Fiddlings* 2 (October 1960): 5–24.

Clark, Sam. "Green Grove Lodge, No. 107." *Faulkner Facts and Fiddlings* 11 (April 1960): 12–16.

Cook, Charles Orson. "The Glory of the Old South and the Greatness of the New. Reform and the Divided Mind of Charles Hillman

Brough." *Arkansas Historical Quarterly* 34 (Autumn 1975): 227–41.

Cordell, Mrs. Robert. "Lapile: A Pioneer Community." *Arkansas Historical Quarterly* 6 (Autumn 1947): 275–85.

Crawford, Charles W. "From Classroom to State Capitol." *Arkansas Historical Quarterly* 21 (Autumn 1962): 213–20.

Donaghey, George W. "Why I Could Not Pardon the Contract System." *Survey,* 21 December 1912, 22–30.

Eno, Clara B. "Old and New State Capitols of Arkansas." *Arkansas Historical Quarterly* 4 (Autumn 1945): 241–49.

Falconer, William. "Our Liquor Licensing System." *Publications of the Arkansas Historical Association* 3 (1911): 325–31.

Farmer, Rod. "Direct Democracy in Arkansas, 1910–1918." *Arkansas Historical Quarterly* 40 (Summer 1981): 99–118.

Gatewood, Willard. "Theodore Roosevelt in Arkansas, 1901–1912." *Arkansas Historical Quarterly* 32 (Spring 1973): 3–24.

"The Governors Conference." *Survey,* 21 December 1912, 347–48.

"A Governor, 360 Convicts, and the Lease System." *Survey,* 28 December 1912, 383–84.

Grantham, Dewey W. "The Contours of Southern Progressivism." *American Historical Review* 86 (October 1981): 1035–59.

Graves, John William. "Negro Disfranchisement in Arkansas." *Arkansas Historical Quarterly* 26 (Autumn 1967): 199–225.

Grushow, Ira. "Biography and Literature." *Southern Humanities Review* 14 (Spring 1980): 156–60.

Halbrook, William. "A Review of My Membership in the Farmers Union." *Arkansas Historical Quarterly* 15 (Autumn 1956): 202–08.

Julian, James P. "Prohibition Comes to Conway." *Faulkner Facts and Fiddlings* 11 (Spring 1969): 7–13.

Kennedy, Timothy J. "Initiated Constitutional Amendments in Arkansas: Strolling Through the Mine Field." *University of Arkansas at Little Rock Law Journal* 9 (1986–87): 1–62.

Ledbetter, Calvin R., Jr. "The Constitutional Convention of 1917–1918." *Arkansas Historical Quarterly* 34 (Spring 1975): 3–40.

———. "Joe T. Robinson and the Presidential Campaign of 1928." *Arkansas Historical Quarterly* 45 (Summer 1986): 95–125.

Link, Arthur. "The Progressive Movement in the South, 1870–1914." *North Carolina Historical Review* 23 (January–October 1946): 172–95.

Lynch, Bill. "Captain William W. Martin." *Arkansas Historical Quarterly* 11 (Spring 1952): 41–55.

Mitchell, Constance. "Conway—Now and Then." *Faulkner Facts and Fiddlings* 4 (December 1962): 3–13.

Morton, Allen Leon. "The Influence of George Washington Donaghey . . . as seen in Conway." *Faulkner Facts and Fiddlings* 11 (Winter 1969–70): 79–85.

Mulhollan, Paige. "The Issues in the Davis-Berry Senatorial Campaign in 1906." *Arkansas Historical Quarterly* 20 (Spring 1961): 118–25.

Niswonger, Richard L. "William F. Kirby, Arkansas's Maverick Senator." *Arkansas Historical Quarterly* 37 (Autumn 1978): 252–63.

Richie, Homer C. "The Harrods of Sleepy Hollow." *Faulkner Facts and Fiddlings* 4 (March 1962): 3–20.

Robinson, Joe T. "Suffrage in Arkansas." *Publications of the Arkansas Historical Association* 3 (1911): 167–74.

Russell, Marvin F. "The Rise of a Republican Leader." *Arkansas Historical Quarterly* 36 (Autumn 1977): 234–57.

Saloutos, Theodore. "The Agricultural Wheel in Arkansas." *Arkansas Historical Quarterly* 2 (June 1943): 127–40.

Sanders, Jill. "The City Officials of Conway, 1875–1890." *Faulkner Facts and Fiddlings* 13 (Fall 1971): 75–86.

Taylor, Elizabeth. "The Woman Suffrage Movement in Arkansas." *Arkansas Historical Quarterly* 15 (Spring 1956): 17–52.

Thomas, David Y. "Direct Legislation in Arkansas." *Political Science Quarterly* 29 (March 1914): 84–110.

———. "The Initiative and Referendum in Arkansas Comes of Age." *American Political Science Review* 27 (February 1933): 66–75.

Thrall, David Y. "James E. Harkrider . . . and Early Days in Conway." *Faulkner Facts and Fiddlings* 6 (Summer 1964): 37–41.

Towns, Stuart. "Joseph T. Robinson and Arkansas Politics: 1912–1913." *Arkansas Historical Quarterly* 24 (Winter 1965): 291–307.

Treon, John A. "Politics and Concrete: The Building of the Arkansas State Capitol, 1899–1917." *Arkansas Historical Quarterly* 31 (Summer 1972): 99–149.

Widener, Ralph W., Jr. "Charles Hillman Brough." *Arkansas Historical Quarterly* 34 (Summer 1975): 99–121.

Worley, Ted. "The Population of Conway in 1880." *Faulkner Facts and*

Fiddlings 5 (June 1963): 3–36.

———. "Notes on the Early History of Conway." *Faulkner Facts and Fiddlings* 5 (December 1963): 3–12.

Zimmerman, Jane. "The Convict Lease System in Arkansas and the Fight for Abolition." *Arkansas Historical Quarterly* 8 (Autumn 1949): 171–88.

Index